Settled Out of Court

SETTLED OUT OF COURT
The Social Process
of Insurance Claims Adjustment

H. LAURENCE ROSS
University of New Mexico

ALDINE PUBLISHING COMPANY/New York

First published 1970 by
Aldine Publishing Company
200 Saw Mill River Rd.
Hawthorne, N.Y. 10532

10 9 8 7 6 5 4 3 2

ISBN: 0-202-30286-3 cloth;
        0-202-30296-2 paper
Library of Congress Number: 80-68523

Printed in the United States of America

In Memory Of
John C. Phillips

Foreword

A few years ago Bayless Manning, former Dean of the Stanford Law School, made the following observations:

> With their emphasis on classical legal analysis and doctrine, our schools do a consistently poor job of communicating to law students a sense of institutional environmental context. I mean this as a sweeping, almost universal statement....They study to be lawyers, but have almost no sense at all of the way in which law firms operate, how the practicing profession is organized or what lawyers do in their professional lives. Law students read snippets of thousands of statutes, but typically know almost nothing about legislatures, how they work or why. They study property, but learn almost nothing about real estate.
>
> Admittedly, the details of institutional context can only be acquired by personal experience, but a great deal can be conveyed by reading and by expository presentation. Yet law students do not read outside their casebooks and are typically

given no hint by their teachers as to what they might profitably read if they were moved to do so. A pernicious side effect of the socratic technique has been that, in faculty circles, low social status is attached to lecture materials or other expository presentation that would provide the student with a sense of institutional context for the "legal" problems he is supposed to master.

Of course, law school cannot teach law students how all major institutional contexts work. But that is no excuse for the present tendency to abjure responsibility for offering *any* sense of institutional context and thus providing the student with a real compensation as to what is going on behind the paper opinions, statutes and regulations with which law school inundates him.(Manning, 1976)[1]

On behalf of my fellow law teachers, I hereby plead guilty for all of us.

Perhaps especially do torts teachers need to obey Dean Manning's injunction. First year law students spend almost all their time on appellate tort cases—on tort doctrine and legal precedent. But in addition to tort doctrine, the world of tort law has a darker side, the intensely pragmatic world of tort practice—a side which will often twist and even wildly distort scholarly tort rules and doctrines amidst bargaining between lawyers and insurance adjusters. Almost fifty years ago the then Dean of the Harvard Law School, James Landis, in reviewing the Columbia Study's exposure of the world of tort settlement versus tort doctrine, said it all when he said that "Taught law is not tort law."

For some time, however, we torts teachers have had available a book that brilliantly exposes the *real* tort law that we might well have recommended that law students "might profitably read" in order to get a thorough "sense of institutional environmental context" as to the settlement of tort claims. And that book—now revised in an edition directed to the law school student—is H. Laurence Ross's *Settled Out Of Court*.

Not only will law students get a rich sense of the world of tort law as it is currently practiced, but they will come away with a far better basis on which to judge the bitter struggle going on between the advocates of no-fault reform and those who defend fault-based liability. My own prejudice is that we will all of us (except, let it be quickly admitted, personal injury lawyers) be better off under no-fault than under traditional tort liability. But such is Professor Ross's scholarship and insight that he by no means slights the problems that even a no-fault scheme will at least on occasion present to frustrated claimants. No-fault insurance will still leave us to the often not-so-tender mercies of insurance companies, which frustration Professor Ross captures as well as he does that of the tort liability system. Even so, as Professor Ross's work suggests, both the theory and experience under no-fault indicate that an insurance mechanism is superior to that of lawyers' fault-finding. Given all the inevitable problems that will always plague insurance—problems Professor Ross effectively lays bare—it rather clearly makes sense to eliminate, where possible, the most glaring and intractable difficulties of insurance by having claims (1) based on the simple occurence of an accident instead of a finding of fault; (2) payable for clear, identifiable losses, as opposed to amorphous, litigable items like pain and suffering; and (3) payable by one's own insurance company, as opposed to a stranger's.

In short, the thrust of Professor Ross' work seems to suggest that while no-fault insurance is by no means a panacea, after an accident most of us end up being treated much better under insurance rules by insurance companies than under legal rules by lawyers.

But regardless of one's view of fault-based versus no-fault insurance, all of us — professors, students, lawyers, insurance personnel, consumer advocates, and consumers — will be much the wiser concerning the institutional context of settling insurance claims because of Professor Ross's splendid book — now thankfully more widely available through this revised edition.

Jeffrey O'Connell
Professor of Law
University of Illinois

Preface

Settled Out Of Court is a classic of the law and behavioral sciences field, and I welcome the publication of a new edition. Ross makes what would seem a simple point—problems dealt with by people acting within bureaucracies will be solved in ways which serve the interests of those people as they go about their day-to-day work, and these interests are not necessarily the same as those of the organization. While this idea may seem obvious, it is, nonetheless, regularly overlooked by those concerned with law. Scholars, journalists and reformers often write as if the impact of law on behavior were direct and easy to predict. Ross emphasizes that the impact of law on behavior is problematic and often but one of many social and institutional influences.

Undoubtedly, this new edition of Settled Out of Court will be read with profit by those interested in sociology. However, I think law students and legal scholars should read it too. Law schools are just beginning to offer seminars and elective courses on the process of dispute resolution, and academic lawyers are just beginning to take account of the reality that trials and appeals stand only at the margin of complex processes which suppress some disputes and affect the resolution of others in ways not contemplated by law books. Lawyers play many roles in these processes. Sometimes they guard the legal system and their own self-interest by turning away potential clients; at other times they change a client's grievance into something that can be settled by a gesture of apology and the payment of money; less frequently, they translate the clients' complicated history into a cause of action which will be tried and perhaps become the subject of an appeal. Only a few of these laywers' roles involve legal research, filing complaints based on real legal analysis or advocacy before judges and jurors. The picture painted by Ross in this book is at least as relevant to real practice skills as is, say, an understanding of the many meanings of the *Palsgraf* case or *Hadley v. Baxendale.*

Courses in restitution, and occasionally contracts, often devote time to techniques for overturning insurance releases—for obvious reasons, insurance releases are a staple in teaching such things as misrepresentation, duress, mistake, and interpretation against the party who drafted a document. An understanding of the system described by Ross would help students understand the contradictions between the ideas of individualism and choice which rationalize free contract and the reality in many situations where a release is under attack. Most students lack experience, and what is offered in appellate opinions as "the facts" typically is, at best, unenlightening if not actually misleading.

I do not think that Ross's book should be confined to the late afternoon ghetto of odd seminars and courses for law professors and students with eccentric tastes. I would like to see it up front in the prime time of the first-year curriculum. Today's torts and contracts teachers so invade each other's turf that both could draw on it. To a large extent, the conventional first year of law school is a morality play inculcating traditional normative ideas of individual fault and choice without regard to questions of structure. Moreover, students are offered a model of how the legal system operates, and, by implication, how it should operate. "Facts" are established by an "adversary" process, the elements of which are seldom examined critically, and decisions are reached by the "application" of legal norms. Of course, by the last half of the twentieth century, at least some lessons of legal realism have become the conventional wisdom of the law schools. Most law professors acknowledge that judges seek to carry out some purpose by the rules they adopt and the way in which they apply them. However, few teachers ask whether these goals are likely to be attained in light of social systems such as Ross describes here. Both reformers and law teachers have been quick to see the solution of particular social problems as calling for the creation of new causes of action, but they seldom have thought seriously about how these causes of action might be implemented in a world where there are high cost barriers to litigation and where some social actors have major advantages in the adversary process.

Certainly, these traditional pictures have important functions. Students, and to some extent the public, may see lawyers as those who make order out of chaos by applying reason to discover normatively correct solutions to human problems. And most students would rather imagine themselves arguing great causes before a bench of Holmes, Cardozo and Hand than dealing with one of Ross's insurance adjusters. The conventional first year pushes away the nasty reality of bargaining in situations where the lawyer's own interest often is different than that of the client. In fact, while the actual practice of law often resembles the work of the mental health professions, many students believe that their professional efforts will be based on considerations of reason rather than of emotion. Perhaps the profession gains status by its conventional image, and perhaps lawyers are allowed to play vital roles because of the public misperception of what is it that they do. Indeed, perhaps better people come to law school than would apply if a more empirically accurate view were commonly held.

However, the distortions involved in the conventional view have real costs. On one hand, they may breed a cynical response from students when they discover the realities of practice, and today they often make this discovery early in their law school career when they participate in clinical programs. It is far too easy to leap to the conclusion that the kind of thinking that goes on in law school classrooms is only some kind of ivory tower exercise which is irrelevant to the real work of lawyers. On the other hand, it is easy to compartmentalize one's thought and rely on law school theories to rationalize a position even when one's experience in practice should teach otherwise. The conventional picture often makes evaluation of the present legal system and proposed reforms difficult if not impossible. For example, one can demonstrate that torts rules are stated in a form which would produce efficient results if these rules had a direct impact on behavior; that is, they seem aimed at minimizing the sum of accident and accident prevention costs. If one were only interested in the symbolic nature of law, this might be enough. If, however, one is interested in the likely impact of these rules on behavior, Ross's picture of the process of dealing with automobile accidents should make us wonder whether costs are being imposed where an efficiency analysis would tell us they should be placed.

Elaine [Walster] Hatfield and I suggested that the process described by Ross has another cost likely to be overlooked in a conventional analysis. American social norms indicate that one who has caused harm should accept responsibility and compensate the victim. The tort system looks as if it allows a jury to impose blame and a court to demand compensation. Ross's story points out that the real system tends to induce people to deny responsibility while passing their problem on to an insurance adjuster whose tactics often will leave the victim with a token settlement and a real sense of injury. Indeed, the insured risks losing insurance coverage if s/he accepts responsibility at the scene of an accident and tries to see that the victim is compensated fully. One cannot open up this kind of analysis without a picture of adjusters and the realities of settling claims which so often violates the sense of justice held by non-lawyers.

Of course, assigning *Settled Out of Court* will add to the student's reading burden, and an instructor will have to find a way to connect its story with the study of doctrine. Most of my students in the dispute-resolution-process seminar have found the book easy to read, and they have been quick to make the connections. It may be that, perhaps paradoxically, one makes the reading burden in law school lighter by assigning more material. It may be easier to understand doctrine when one can see what the fight is all about than when it is viewed as a kind of logical puzzle. It may be easier to cope with demands that the present system and proposed reforms be evaluated when one understands the present system in operation and the likely impact of reforms when they collide with that system. Perhaps there are other ways to paint the empirical picture, but, it seems to me, assigning *Settled Out of Court* is a good one.

Stewart Macaulay
Professor of Law
University of Wisconsin
Madison

ACKNOWLEDGEMENTS

The research reported here was made possible by the generous support and cooperation of several organizations. I am deeply grateful to the Insurance Company of North America, which, I have been authorized to reveal, is the Acme Insurance Company of this book. INA provided the funds to release me in part from teaching for two years so that I could accomplish the research, and its executives and adjusters freely gave unlimited time and counsel to make my work possible. I appreciate their support and cooperation as well as their trust and confidence.

I am also grateful for additional financial support to the Walter E. Meyer Research Institute of Law, the New York University Faculty of Arts and Sciences Research Fund, and to the Russell Sage Foundation, which provided a Residency in 1963-64 at the Center for the Study of Law and Society at the University of California, Berkeley, where this work originated. The University of Denver provided research assistance and released me from some teaching duties to prepare the manuscript of the book.

I am indebted to the managements and adjusters of "Great Plains" and "Mid-West" insurance companies, and to the many attorneys who donated their time to this research. Joseph Halpern, Darryl Kaneko and Fran Bernat enhanced this book by their statistical and editorial advice.

This book is above all indebted to the many colleagues whose advice and ideas have blended my own thoughts. Although it is both difficult and impolitic to name the most influential, I would not like this book to appear without being sure the following names occurred somewhere: Howard S. Becker, Erving Goffman, Stewart Macaulay, Sheldon Messinger, Philippe Nonet, Jeffrey O'Connell, Thomas C. Schelling, Jerome H. Skolnick, Erwin O. Smigel, Carl M. Stevens, Anselm Strauss, and Robert B. Yegge.

Contents

Settled Out of Court

1. Introduction

THIS IS A book about law, though it seldom mentions courtrooms, judges, pleadings and motions, or even juries and verdicts. This book is concerned with the law in action, with the legal system as it operates for the ordinary citizen on a day-to-day basis. The principal institution of the law in action is not trial; it is settlement out of court.

A fact that may seem as strange to the first-year law student as to the layman is that most of a citizen's rights and duties, though based in law, are determined without reference to any court by a set of personnel quite different from those to be found in a courtroom. Although all rights properly called legal could be asserted and adjudicated in a court, on the whole it is the smallest percentage that in fact are thus determined. One reason we fail to realize this is that we overlook the legal relationships involved in many of our ordinary social transactions. For instance, all our purchases, including that of a drugstore Coke, are embedded in the context of a commercial law that bristles with explicit and implicit rights and duties on the part of buyer and seller, the breach of which creates a claim for one or the other party. The regulations applicable to the conduct of business are so numerous and pervasive that their violation is virtually a way of life to the ordinary businessman. To drive without breaching the ubiquitous standards of the law of negligence is virtually impossible, and the same law attaches to every roller skate on a sidewalk, every grape seed in the aisle of a supermarket, and every Oriental carpet on a polished floor. That legal rights and duties are involved in these everyday transactions and occurrences is virtually never recognized except when something unexpected disrupts routine.

Not only is the existence of ordinary legal relationships generally unrecognized by the layman; even when the unexpected happens, and the legal basis of a relationship is bared, the formal machinery of the law is seldom involved. It could not, indeed, become so involved without a revolutionary increase in the scale of such machinery. In the criminal law, for instance, it is estimated that only one-seventh of all felony prosecutions in the United States end in jury trials. For the State of California, 99 per cent of traffic violations, 95 per cent of other misdemeanors, and 76 per cent of felonies are disposed of before trial.[1] If every defendant were to have a formal trial, the number of courts, juries, judges, and related personnel would have to be increased extravagantly, and the resultant cost would be a social burden of remarkable proportions. Likewise in the civil law: even in New York City, a remarkably litigation-conscious jurisdiction, 98 per cent of bodily injury negligence claims are terminated without adjudication by a court.[2]

Where are these other decisions made? Who, other than judges and juries, determines the legal rights of the vast majority of citizens? In answer to these questions, a large and diverse array

1. Harry Kalven, Jr., and Hans Zeisel, *The American Jury* (Little, Brown, 1966), pp. 18–19, footnote 12.
2. Marc A. Franklin, Robert H. Chanin, and Irving Mark, "Accidents, Money and the Law: A Study of the Economics of Personal Injury Litigation," in Walter E. Meyer Research Institute of Law (ed.), *Dollars, Delay and the Automobile Victim: Studies in Reparation for Highway Injuries and Related Court Problems* (Bobbs-Merrill Company, 1968), pp. 39–40.

of personnel and forums could be cited. Perhaps the first to occur to the lawyer would be administrative tribunals, which resemble courts in many aspects, but which tend to operate less formally, with a different and less adversary procedure, more lenient rules of evidence, and more specialized decision-makers. The number of commissions, agencies, and panels making legally relevant decisions almost certainly exceeds the number of courts and is an important factor in determining legal rights. According to Kenneth Culp Davis, in the year ending in June, 1963, there were 7,095 trials in the United States District Courts. In that same year, over 17,000 cases were closed by agency decision on merits after hearing and preliminary decision, an additional 17,000 were closed by agency final decision on merits without preliminary decision, and a further 16,000 were closed by preliminary decision alone. However, even these formal administrative decisions, like the decisions of courts, formed only a small proportion of the total number of cases filed and disposed of. The Securities and Exchanges Commission, for example, had only 175 formal cases in the year ending June 30, 1963, but passed upon 1,157 registration statements and issued 30,000 advisory letters concerning the laws it administers. The Federal Communication Commission had only 226 formal cases but licensed over 735,000 transmitters. The Immigration Service had less than 14,000 formal cases but granted or denied almost 700,000 applications.[3]

Formal decision-making procedures, be they applied by courts or administrative agencies, are thus shown to be quantitatively unimportant in the working out of legal rights and duties. To be sure, formal decisions are qualitatively important, for they set standards which informal decisions are expected to follow. However, informal decisions are responsive to other considerations as well, and they cannot be understood as mechanical applications of the formal rules. As Glendon Schubert says:

> The proper subject of study is not "law" in the classical sense of verbal statements purporting to rationalize the

3. Kenneth Culp Davis, *Administrative Law: Cases—Text—Problems* (West Publishing Co., 1965), p. 4.

content of constitutional and statutory documents, or appellate court opinions. Inquiry [ought to focus] on what human beings, cast in socially defined roles in certain characteristic types of decision-making sequences which traditionally have been identified as "legal," do in their interactions and transactions with each other." [4]

To understand the legal system and the nature of rights and duties, it is not sufficient to know the formal rules; one must know the law in action. The same principle holds for reasonable criticism and proposals for reforming the law. In the words of the now well-known "Michigan study" of automobile accident victims:

The impressive fact remains that a substantial majority of "serious" cases, and the great mass of all cases, were terminated without court intervention. . . . If the handling of the great mass of injury claims is to be improved, it is the adjustment process rather than the judicial process which will have to be changed. [5]

The perspective described here has been applied in some notable studies of the criminal law. [6] I believe that the present study represents the first effort to apply it to the law of negligence.

I have said that this is a book about law. It is also a book about sociology, the science that studies man and his institutions, of which the law is a part. In this book I wish to stress the sociological insight that rules are in part a function of the apparatus that applies them. It follows that the term "law" may have at least three distinct meanings, corresponding to three modes of application:

First, law can be understood as those rules that are enunciated

---

4. Glendon Schubert, "Behavioral Jurisprudence," *Law and Society Review* 2:407, 1968, pp. 408–409.

5. Alfred F. Conard, James N. Morgan, Robert W. Pratt, Jr., Charles F. Voltz, and Robert L. Bombaugh, *Automobile Accident Costs and Payments: Studies in the Economics of Injury Reparation* (University of Michigan Press, 1964), pp. 3–4.

6. See, for instance, Jerome Skolnick, *Justice Without Trial* (John Wiley, 1966) and Donald J. Newman, *Conviction: The Determination of Guilt or Innocence Without Trial* (Little, Brown, 1966).

by legislators and by appellate judges. These are the rules that appear in print, in newspapers and law books, and that are learned by rote, plus or minus some comprehension, by law students. This understanding is certainly that of most of my fellow students from law school days, and I dare say of many of my teachers as well.

Second, law can be understood as those rules that arise in the course of applying the first-level laws in the situation of a trial court. Many students of jurisprudence have taken this position, most notably (and with considerable overstatement) Jerome Frank.[7] This law of the lower court, particularly the law of the jury, is based on the law of the higher court, but with important and meaningful differences. The differences are not merely a function of the jury's lack of expertise, as Frank at times seemed to imply. The differences have now been documented in some detail by the Jury Project of the University of Chicago, and have been shown to have a distinct logic of their own.[8]

The literature of jurisprudence has less often been concerned with a third meaning of law, which concerns those rules that arise in the course of applying the formal rules in private negotiated settlements. Holmes' revolutionary thought, that law is what the courts will do, did not go far enough. Quantitatively speaking, even trial courts are trivial mechanisms for determining legal relationships. The rules of the third level, the law in action, are not completely independent of the first and second levels, but, being further removed from the appellate courts in time, space, procedure, and personnel, they are more subject to distortions, modifications, and even negations of the formal rules than are the rules of the second level.

Students of trial court law have found it to be bent from the formal law in the direction of a sense of fairness brought to bear by the judge or jury in the individual case. The departure from formal law may be greater in cases decided by a jury, but it occurs as well in disputes decided by a judge. Where the

---

7. Jerome J. Frank, *Courts on Trial* (Princeton University Press, 1949); also *Law and the Modern Mind* (Doubleday Anchor, 1963).

8. See Kalven and Zeisel, *op. cit.*; also Harry Kalven, Jr., "The Dignity of the Civil Jury," *Ohio State Law Journal* 19:158, 1958.

unqualified formal rule strikes the decision-maker as unjust, his application of the rule bends it in the direction of his idea of justice, whether by distorting the facts of the situation so that the rule appears to give good results, or by overriding the rule and hiding behind a screen of rationalization or the silence of the jury room.[9]

Law in action, as exemplified by the situation at hand—the adjustment of claims by representatives of insurance companies —involves additional sources of distortion of formal rules, virtually ignored by the students of courtroom law. These are the formally irrelevant situational pressures on the negotiators. The key role in this situation is that of the adjuster, who is typically a low-level employee of a large formal organization. (Sociologists customarily speak of such large, rule-oriented organizations as "bureaucracies," following Max Weber; the term as used here in the technical sense is not pejorative.[10]) In addition to his personal views of justice and equity, the adjuster brings to his work the pressures he feels in his role as an employee. Both intended and deliberate company policies on the one hand and unintended and "accidental" pressures on the other affect the adjuster's performance and modify the outcomes of his negotiation of legal claims.

An important consequence of this fact is that the law as it is experienced by the average man exercising his legal rights out of court is a different institution from the law obtaining in the courtroom, just as that in turn differs from the law of the casebooks and of the appellate courts. This book will explore these differences in the particular matter of the law of negligence in automobile accidents. It will further attempt to explain the source of the differences in terms of the attitudes and opinions of the parties to negotiation, the social pressures on these parties, and the advantages and disadvantages conferred upon the parties by the peculiar institution of negotiation. An additional goal of this book, based upon the foregoing analyses, will

9. See note 8 above; also Bernard Botein, *Trial Judge* (Simon and Schuster, 1952).

10. See H. H. Gerth and C. Wright Mills, *From Max Weber: Essays in Sociology* (Oxford University Press, 1958), pp. 196–244.

be to evaluate the law of negligence both in terms of its relationship to the standards of formal law and in terms of how well it fills the needs that it could in fact fill in an automobile-based society. I write this book with the knowledge that its particular topic is of great practical importance today, and with and, to my way of thinking, a shallow conception of negligence the belief that much of the current debate is based on a formal law. Many critics of the current system, I believe, write in ignorance of the fact that the law in action is much broader and more benevolent than they assume from a reading of the formal law. On the other hand, many proponents of the status quo strike me as being just as ignorant of the differences between formal law and law in action as are the critics, and their defenses seem more reasonable when applied to a law that once—or never—was, than to the system as it now in fact works from day to day. I hope that the description and explanation of the law in action contained in this volume will add clarity to the currently heated discussion of the virtues and defects of the negligence law, and that it will add a realistic dimension to the proposals made for its modification or replacement by a different system.

Method

The study was undertaken with the generous support and cooperation of three major American insurance companies. The bulk of the research was done in cooperation with a large and well-known company which will here be called Acme. Acme is a very old, established stock (as opposed to mutual) insurance company which writes all lines of insurance. Although it is not primarily concentrated in the automobile field, it has a considerable business in this line. Acme is representative of such familiar companies as the Travelers Insurance Company, Aetna Casualty and Surety Company, and the Hartford Accident and Indemnity Company. The findings developed in interviews and observations at Acme were verified by repeating the work with two very large "mass-market" insurance companies, here called Mid-West and Great Plains. Both of these companies are quite prominent in the automobile insurance field, and seek continued expansion in this line. These companies sell directly to the public, rather than through independent insurance agents, and partly in consequence their rates are somewhat lower than Acme's. A significant part of automobile insurance today is being handled by companies like these, such as Allstate Insurance Company, Government Employees Insurance Company, and Farmers Insurance Group.

I began my work by interviewing adjusters and their supervisors. The interviews were lengthy, lasting as long as two hours, and covered the following topics: the informant's past career and future plans, his feelings about his work, his manner of going about such things as investigation and evaluation of claims, the techniques of negotiation with claimants and their lawyers, his treatment of the problems posed by uncertain liability, and his opinions of the negligence law and proposed changes. Other topics were covered as they arose, and no set pattern of questions was routinely followed. The interviews were recorded on a tape recorder and were transcribed. In this book, excerpts from the interviews are presented as illustrative materials, but during the research they also served as sources of hypotheses which were further tested in additional interviews and in the statistical analysis reported in Chapter 5. A total of 67 adjusters were interviewed, in six different locations. All men who worked in the Long Island, New York and Harrisburg, Pennsylvania offices of Acme were interviewed. At Mid-West and Great Plains, the comparison was between employees in the central Pennsylvania and the Philadelphia area offices. Thus, for each company, approximately half the interviews were done in a metropolitan region and half in a rural and small-city region. It was expected that variations in the work of the adjuster might appear in the regions studied, as the areas differed considerably in the average value of claims (and consequently the price of insurance), the proportion of claims represented by attorneys, the reputed honesty and "claims consciousness" of typical claimants, the fees charged by physicians, and other factors. This expectation was confirmed in the interviews, the regional differences surpassing the differences observed between companies. The interviews were supplemented by observations of the

adjusters at work. In both offices of Acme, and in the Philadelphia office of Mid-West, several adjusters agreed to my com-
panionship as they made their rounds of work. My general procedure was to accompany a man on whatever tasks he happened
to have scheduled for the day. I took notes on what I saw, and
discussed them with the adjuster as we drove in the company
car from appointment to appointment. I spent about 30 days
traveling in this manner.

The observations yielded a good many examples of investigative techniques and negotiations with unrepresented claimants,
but not too many cases of negotiation with attorneys. As a supplementary measure, a group of twelve law students in a seminar
on negotiation at the University of Denver each attended five
such negotiation sessions and provided me with their field notes
and a taped transcript of at least one negotiation. These materials have added to the data on negotiation in Chapter 4.

I also interviewed 17 attorneys for plaintiffs, mainly in Harrisburg, but also in New York City, repeating many of the questions on evaluation and negotiation that I asked the adjusters.
In both areas a random sample of attorneys' names was drawn
from closed Acme files. Nearly all the attorneys whose names
were drawn in Harrisburg agreed to be interviewed, but cooperation in New York was very poor, perhaps because the
metropolitan attorneys felt they had something to hide.[11] Because of the poor cooperation, no claim of representativeness
can be made concerning the interviews with metropolitan attorneys. However, the attorney interviews were intended mainly
to corroborate the interviews with the adjusters, and I do not
feel that the small numbers and the non-random character of
the attorney sample affect the validity of the conclusions presented in this book.

The ideas suggested by the interviews and observations with
adjusters and attorneys were put to a statistical test with the

11. Compare the description of the metropolitan bar in Jerome E. Carlin,
Lawyers' Ethics: A Survey of the New York City Bar (Russell Sage Foun-
dation, 1966) with Joel F. Handler's study of a small-city bar in *The
Lawyer and His Community: The Practicing Bar in a Middle-Sized City*
(University of Wisconsin Press, 1967).

help of an analysis of 2,216 files on bodily injury claims closed
by the Acme Insurance Company in March and April of 1962.
The sample was a national one, drawn from files that had been
closed for five years and were slated for destruction. The files,
coded and processed on a computer, form the substance of the
numerical data reported in Chapter 5 and of various other places
throughout the book. I wish to stress that the ideas presented
in Chapter 5 arose in the interviews and observations, and not
in the data processing. The computer analysis constituted a test
of previously formulated hypotheses, based on the national experience of one large and presumably not unrepresentative
insurance company.

I was able to make an extensive search of the meager published literature pertaining to the adjustment of insurance claims
using the excellent library of the Insurance Society of New
York. In addition, all three of the cooperating companies provided reports of special studies undertaken by their own staffs.
These materials have been particularly helpful in Chapters 2
and 6. Chapter 6 also benefited from a three-week visit to the
offices of the study of insurance being undertaken by the United
States Department of Transportation in Washington, D.C.

More detailed descriptions of various aspects of the research
method will be found at various places in this book, particularly
in Chapter 5 where the procedures used in the statistical analysis
are given closer scrutiny. Here, I wish merely to clarify the
foundation of the findings reported in this book in the wide
variety of techniques applied to the problem. This variety com-
pensates to some degree for the inherent weakness of each technique. In particular, the limitations of possible lack of representativeness found in the interviews are balanced by the broad
scope of the national sample on which the statistical investigation was based. The inherent shallowness involved in dealing
with files and the great gaps in data caused by the incomplete-
ness of many of the files are balanced by the depth and detail
available in the interviews. Possible concealment and misstate-
ments in the interviews receive partial compensation from the
large numbers of interviews conducted, many of them with
men with whom a high degree of rapport had been established,

as well as representation of both sides of the negotiation table in the interviews and observations.

Automobiles, Accidents, and the Formal Law

This book is specifically concerned with the law of negligence as applied to injuries incurred in automobile accidents. The importance of this law in the lives of Americans can be appreciated with a bit of reflection on the automobile and traffic accidents.

The automobile is essentially a twentieth-century phenomenon. The first gasoline-powered car appeared in the workshop of the Duryea brothers in Springfield, Massachusetts, in 1893. In 1900 there were a mere 8,000 automobiles in the United States, and these were properly regarded as rich men's toys. However, within the first two decades of this century the combination of greatly lowered prices and improved roads had made the automobile more available and more useful. By 1920, there were 9 million motor vehicles in the United States, and by 1950, almost 50 million. In 50 years the automobile had become a virtual necessity and an omnipresent feature of American life.[12]

As of 1966, there were 78 million passenger cars in the United States—more than half the automobiles in the world! Four of every five American families owned at least one car; one seventh of all persons employed were in the vehicle transportation business; and one fourth of all retail sales were automotive.[13] American society had profoundly changed, and the automobile was an integral part of that change. As the population flowed from the countryside to the cities, these urban centers changed from densely populated, highly centralized agglomerations into sprawling profusions of single-family houses, set in gardens, covering and incorporating much of the countryside. Industry and commerce were greatly freed from the magnetic pull of

12. Edward C. Fisher, *Vehicle Traffic Law* (Northwestern University Traffic Institute, 1961), especially Chapter 1, pp. 1–13.
13. Automobile Manufacturers Association, *Automobile Facts and Figures,* 1967 edition; see also H. Laurence Ross, "Social Problems of the Automobile," *Annals of the Society of Chartered Property and Casualty Underwriters* 21:227, 1968.

the city center. The ties of residence to work and leisure were lengthened and lost their common direction. Urban political boundaries lost their functional meaning, and miles of streets and acres of pre-twentieth-century edifices became obsolete. The automobile brought a new kind of freedom to American society, and it was eagerly accepted.

The automobile also brought new kinds of problems in the wake of its transformation of society. The old central cities strangled in traffic congestion, and the facilities remaining there declared their existence to be threatened. Both central cities and the suburbs experienced unprecedented problems of air pollution and lacked the political means to coordinate their preventive efforts. Racial and class ghettoes were now politically as well as spatially segregated, and the poor were in large measure left to rely on their own resources.

Perhaps the most significant problem created by the automobile was traffic accidents, which rapidly increased with the growing automobile population (though safer vehicles and highways steadily reduced the death rate per mile traveled.) In the mid-1960's, 40,000 fatal accidents were being experienced each year. For every 100 million vehicle-miles, there were 5.5 deaths. Over one million nonfatal injuries, and $12 million in property damage were being experienced annually.[14]

The nature of traffic accidents is still far from well understood. What does seem clear, given the state of knowledge at the moment, is that accidents are a product of a system composed of vehicles, roads, and drivers, and that no component can be singled out for responsibility. In the words of the most recent survey of the field:

> The concept of "cause" has little operational significance in the study of accidents. Traffic accidents are most meaningfully viewed as failures of the system rather than as failures of any single component. To a larger extent than usually appreciated, several factors simultaneously contribute to most accidents; changes made in any of these could have prevented the accident or at least moderated

14. National Safety Council, *Traffic Accident Facts*, 1966 edition.

it. Statements of the form that "80 percent of accidents are *caused* by the driver" represent a simplistic view of the situation and are not supported by the technical literature that we have reviewed. It is not presently possible to identify factors whose removal or control will reduce the accident rate by a specified amount.[15]

Although the science of traffic safety is unwilling to place responsibility on any single component of the system, the law—both civil and criminal—has made a choice. It blames the driver. An important assumption of the tort law—which governs the remuneration of the injured accident victim through the means studied in this research—is that an accident represents harm done by one person to another through carelessness.[16]

The fundamental concept in the law relevant to accidents is negligence, which may be defined as an omission or commission of an act that is unreasonable as judged by the standard of the ordinarily prudent person under the circumstances prevailing and that creates a risk of harm to others. Negligence is a question of fact, and its formal determination involves careful consideration of the particular circumstances of a given accident, and of what an ordinarily prudent person would do. In other words, the decision as to whether there has been negligence involves a highly individualized and specific investigation and decision process.

In traffic cases, a common rule is that obeying traffic laws is expected of the ordinarily prudent person, and that proof of violation of a traffic law leads to the presumption of negligence. However, the formal law of negligence is not thereby necessarily

15. Arthur D. Little, Inc., *The State of the Art of Traffic Safety: A Critical Review and Analysis of the Technical Information on Factors Affecting Traffic Safety*, report for the Automobile Manufacturers Association, June, 1966, p. 31.

16. A complete exposition of the formal law will be found in legal textbooks such as William L. Prosser, *Torts* (Foundation Press, 1964). A digest of tort rules particularly relevant to liability insurance appears in James H. Donaldson, *Casualty, Claim Practice* (Richard D. Irwin, 1964). See also *Restatement, Second, Torts*, Sections 282, 463. Although the tort law is modified by no-fault statutes in many states, it still provides the basic rules relevant to serious injuries in most jurisdictions.

reduced to simpler proportions. Many traffic laws involve very complex questions of fact: for example, what constitutes "following too closely," or speed "reasonable and proper" under the circumstances? Moreover, the presumption of negligence involved in violating a traffic law is rebuttable by showing that an ordinarily prudent man in specific circumstances might not have obeyed the rule. Again, the standard of the reasonably prudent man can be invoked to show negligence in the absence of a violation of a traffic law.

An important defense to a claim based upon negligence is that of contributory negligence. The contributory negligence doctrine holds that even though the defendant was negligent, the plaintiff is entitled to no recovery if he also was negligent, and if his negligence contributed to the accident in some degree. Even if the plaintiff's negligence was considerably less than that of the defendant, he recovers nothing at all. The most common form of contributory negligence, as judged from recountings of the events of accidents, would appear to be the failure to look around and see the approaching danger.[17] In increasing numbers of states, the doctrine of contributory negligence is being replaced by that of comparative negligence, whereby the plaintiff's recovery is merely reduced, rather than eliminated, by his negligence. However, the rule of contributory negligence governed in all the jurisdictions studied at the time of this research.

The formal law of negligence is further complicated by a wide variety of other doctrines: "last clear chance," guest statutes, family-suit statutes, infant rules, etc. Since it is the purpose of this section merely to sketch the formal law, explanation of these doctrines will be omitted, although they may be important in individual cases.

A person who is injured because of the negligence of another is entitled to damages, or money payments compensating him for his loss. Ordinary damages are not imposed, like fines, to punish the negligent party, but are based upon the loss experienced by the plaintiff. Part of the loss, termed special damages,

nds to the out-of-pocket expenses that are a consequence

: *Selected Reports from Case Studies of Traffic Accidents* (North-
niversity Traffic Institute, 1960).

of the injury. These may be both past and estimated future expenses. Typical are doctor and hospital bills and lost wages. The plaintiff is also entitled to recovery for his general damages, which are somewhat more abstract: pain and suffering, inconvenience, and disfigurement. Like the determination of negligence, the determination of damages also involves a highly individualized decision, related to such questions as how much the plaintiff actually suffered or how unattractive he has become as a result of the injuries, and posing the difficult problem of translating the answers to these questions into dollar figures.

The claims under consideration in this research all involved insured defendants. Since approximately nine in ten drivers today are covered by automobile liability policies, this is by far the most common situation. Therefore, in order fully to understand the formal aspects of the law, it is necessary to examine briefly the common liability insurance relationship.

Insurance is protection in the event of misfortune, and this is the function of automobile liability policies, like all insurance policies. However, the protection offered by a liability policy is given not to the injured party, but to the person against whom the injured party might claim on the grounds of negligence. Thus, if Driver A runs into Pedestrian B, the protection of liability insurance applies to A and not to B. B is protected only to the extent that his compensation is necessary in order to protect A from B's legal claim for negligence. (Most liability policies form part of a package that may also contain a small medical payments policy which directly protects B for his medical expenses only; we are not here concerned with this type of protection.)

The usual liability policy protects the negligent person or "tortfeasor" by promising to pay any amount (up to a specified maximum) for which the insured may be held legally liable, and by promising to defend (and investigate) any claims that may be brought against him on these grounds. The liability insurance policy also gives the insurer the right to negotiate an informal settlement, whereby the injured party signs a release of liability for the insured—thus extinguishing his right to prosecute the claim in court—in return for a payment.

In sum, the formal law provides that one who can prove injuries at the hands of a negligent person may recover his losses under the various categories of damages. This formal right can be pursued in court. Most automobile injury claims, however, are decided in private negotiation between the injured or their lawyers and insurance company adjusters. The balance of this book describes the law of negligence in action and the working out of claims on a routine, day-to-day basis.

Overview

I believe that an understanding of the law in action can best proceed from an analysis of the personalities of and pressures upon the personnel who administer the law. The key figure in the settlement of automobile bodily injury claims is the adjuster, for as the front-line representative of the insurance company he occupies the most powerful role in settlement. I shall begin with an analysis of this key role.

The recruiting procedures used by insurance companies, and the nature of the work experience that awaits the recruit, secure a group of basically conservative men as adjusters or claims men. Adjusters' political, economic, and social values are generally conservative, and their attitudes towards the insurance company's obligations to third parties are specifically conservative. Moreover, many claims men relish their adversary role, particularly vis-à-vis the plaintiff's attorneys. Consequently, adjusters generally approach a new claim with the hope of denying it or of making as low a payment as possible in settlement.

Modifying this negative set is the fact that many claims men feel a degree of ethical restraint in adjusting claims. In accord with contemporary ideas concerning the social responsibilities of business, adjusters feel constrained to admit liability when they cannot honestly deny it, and to refrain from pushing a bargain below the minimum "going rate," which translates as the repayment of out-of-pocket losses or special damages. The relative helplessness of the unsophisticated and unrepresented claimant is acknowledged by adjusters, and they declare themselves unwilling to exploit their advantage to the extent that might be possible.

More important than attitudes and values, I believe, in determining the actions of an adjuster, are the pressures he experiences from others—from the bureaucracy through the medium of his supervisors, from the claimant and the claimant's attorney, and occasionally from other parties. The principal pressure on the adjuster from his supervisor is to close cases promptly. There is, of course, pressure to close them cheaply, but it is not in practice as insistent and is easier to resist by depicting troublesome cases as worthy cases. Adjusters quickly learn that claims are extinguished most easily by paying them. Unclosed files form visible accumulations and generate complaints to managers and supervisors, whereas closed files trouble no one. Thus, there is strong pressure originating within the company to offer payment whenever a claims man is faced with a firm demand from a claimant.

The claimant and his attorney are also a source of pressure on the adjuster. Although they are of course expected to be adversary, they can facilitate the adjuster's work, for example by providing documents that will support the claim in the scrutiny of a supervisor, and cooperating in medical examinations, in return for consideration from the adjuster. The attorney in particular, since he may have repeated dealings with the same adjuster or at least the same company, may be in a position to demand consideration over and above what the claim might merit on the basis of formal law.

The insured might be expected to be an interested party to the claim against him. His behavior is alleged to be faulty, and he thus has a personal and reputational stake in opposing the claim. In many companies, his insurance premium will be increased in the event of a paid claim, and in large claims there arises the possibility of a judgment in excess of the policy limits, in which case the insured would have to pay out of his own pocket. Despite these facts, the insured is seldom capable of exercising pressure in a routine claim because he has no effective sanctions that he can apply to the adjuster.

Balancing these pressures against the adjuster's attitudes and values, the net result appears to be a preference for denying claims, but a realistic willingness to pay them in the face of a determined presentation, despite the explicit contrary wishes of higher management. This model is confirmed by the fact that the large majority of all claims presented to the insurance company are indeed paid.

Evaluation and investigation of claims consist mainly in discovering violations of the traffic law and collecting medical bills. Although the formal tort law is concerned with issues of duty and lack of care, of reasonableness, foreseeability, and such matters, these questions seldom arise in the routine settlement process. Instead, concern focuses on vehicle speed and position, on what was seen and what was done. The fine weighing of evidence concerning negligence envisaged by the formal law does not in fact take place. The heart of the negligence issue in the routine claim concerns whether one or both parties violated a traffic law, and the resolution of this issue is generally in terms of very mechanical considerations, such as who was to the rear or to the left, whether a light was red or amber, etc. The ostensible purpose of traffic law is to foster safe and efficient transportation, not to decide the matter of negligence, but its role in the latter process is virtually definitive. Similarly, medical bills have no necessary relationship to such matters as the amount of pain and inconvenience experienced because of an injury, but in the routine case the value of the entire claim is a rough function of the bills accumulated.

The vast bulk of automobile bodily injury claims are settled through negotiation, which has the advantage of avoiding the costs associated with more formal procedures such as trial. In the routine claim, such matters as the costs of intensive investigation and attorneys' fees loom very large compared with the amount purportedly at stake. Other things being equal, it is rational for the insurance company to pay any amount short of expected processing costs on any bona fide claim, and it is rational for the claimant to discount his expectations of recovery at trial by an amount equal to his expected costs. These facts encourage negotiated settlement by creating a range of potential agreements in the great majority of cases. For example, if both parties estimate their costs in taking a claim to court to be $1000, there can be no claim for less than $2000 for which there is not a zone of potential agreement, or points at which both parties, if rational, would prefer settlement to trial. A consequence of this situation is that claimants can routinely obtain money in return for their good faith and persistence alone, while in large cases the companies probably routinely profit from discounts that reflect a similar bargaining advantage.

The negotiated settlement, which employs different tactics, uses different skills and facilities, and produces different results from litigation, strongly affects the law in action. The working out of legal rights on a day-to-day basis is indeed based upon the formal law: payment does follow liability and damages, at least as these are interpreted by the insurance company. However, the law in action does not follow the formal law to the limits. Some important differences can be noted:

First, the law in action is simplified. Liability is understood in mechanical terms rather than those of morality which are embodied in the formal law. The tort law is not a fault system, but is rather a traffic code system. The criterion of proper driving is not that of the reasonably prudent man, but that of the rigid adherent to petty regulations. Moreover, if the tort law in action is not based on fault, neither is it the individualistic enterprise that its proponents and defenders intend. The settlement process seldom concerns the experiences of the claimant in terms of pain, suffering, and inconvenience. The gathering of medical bills, rather than the recounting of distress, is the substance of claims evaluation.

Second, the law in action is distorted from the formal law in certain understandable directions. This distortion is seen, for instance, in the fact that most claims—even those of apparently doubtful formal liability—receive some payment. The law in action is more generous than many critics believe, not because the bureaucracy is charitable, but because it negotiates. On the other hand, the law in action is often arbitrary and capricious in terms of the formal law. It rewards disproportionately those claimants who are most sophisticated and best represented, rather than (as the critics would have it) those who are most needy, and in addition to those whose cases are most in accord with the rule (as the formal law would have it).

How well does the tort law in action fit the needs of traffic accident victims? On the whole, the knowledge I have acquired in the course of this study inclines me to the side of the critics who maintain that it is inadequate as the principal source of reparation for these victims. I find the following arguments persuasive:

First, the formal purposes and proclaimed functions of the tort law are largely irrelevant to the compensation of accident victims. The underlying law is one of rights and wrongs, whereas the problem as generally conceived today is one of needs. In the underlying law, the role of insurance is to protect the negligent driver, whereas it is the victim who needs the protection. The disjunction between law and the insurance system, on the one hand, and the needs of the victims, on the other, is not inherent in these institutions. Law is a versatile social instrument that can be altered to achieve a wide range of goals, and insurance is a competent tool for handling any situation in which a risk can be evaluated.

Second, the law in action, although it partly bridges the gap through its generosity, introduces additional distinctions among claimants corresponding to sophistication rather than need, which render the entire enterprise even less rational as a solution to the problems of the accident victim.

It is hard for me to accept the argument that the existing system of law and insurance deserves retention because it rewards the innocent and punishes the guilty, or because it tailors the result to individual circumstances. The present system is individualistic mainly in theory; in practice it is categorical and mechanical, as any system must be if it is to handle masses of cases in an efficient manner. Concerning guilt and innocence, the common meaning of these terms would have to be virtually abandoned in order to apply them to what is in practice termed fault today. In my opinion, the determination of liability is best regarded as an expensive and time-consuming game, the outcome of which is very largely as irrelevant to the question of virtue as it is to the question of need.

I believe it is proper for social scientists to offer suggestions for the resolution of social problems based upon a careful investigation of the problems. My understanding of the needs generated by automobile accidents, coupled with what I have learned concerning how the present system works, leads me to endorse the suggestion that the problems of accident victims could be significantly ameliorated by relegating the issue of fault to the criminal law, and substituting for the present tort law a system of insurance payable in the event of accident regardless of fault. I would retain what I believe to be the major virtue of the present system, which is that it provides a fund to which all drivers contribute and from which victims of driving may draw. I would accept the fact that even a highly individualistic law, when required to handle masses of cases, becomes categorical, and thus would support the institution of a reparations system that was admittedly categorical. I understand that a system of insurance affording coverage to all accident victims could be supported from the proceeds of eliminating abstract general damages and foregoing the dubious benefits of the enormously costly game of determining liability.

The changes I support are embodied in the series of compensation-type reforms originating with the Columbia proposal of 1932 and taking modern form as "no-fault" insurance.

2. Adjusters and Others

WHEN CARS CRASH and people are injured, the basis is laid for claims on the grounds of negligence. Since about nine in ten drivers in the United States are insured,[1] the responsibility for handling claims very largely rests with insurance companies, generally with specialized employees—termed adjusters or claims men—whose job combines investigation, evaluation, and negotiation of claims.

The claims of which I speak are formally grounded in law. They are assertions of legal rights. However, in the majority of such claims, neither the claimant nor the defendant (realistically, the insurance company) has recourse to legal professionals. Most claims are processed and terminated between the adjuster and the unrepresented claimant.[2] Lawyers, when they appear in

1. This estimate was furnished in a private communication from the Insurance Information Institute, which reports that exact figures are not available.
2. In the Acme files, about seven in ten claims were found to be closed without representation.

the picture, are likely to appear first on the side of the claimant. The insurance company will usually assign legal professionals to a claim only in the event of suit, but even in these circumstances the adjuster remains the company's principal investigator, evaluator, and negotiator. Not until trial does the role of the defense attorney come to exceed that of the adjuster in importance.

The adjuster is, then, the key man in the handling of most automobile injury claims. His attitudes and values and the pressures that he feels in the course of doing his job constitute important factors in determining the negotiated settlements which are his routine work product. These attitudes, values, and pressures are matters that enter, along with the formal law, into determining the legal rights of claimants as expressed in their recoveries. They help to create the difference between the formal law and the law in action.

This chapter is primarily concerned with describing claims men as I came to know them in the course of my research. It will explore the background, selection, and training of adjusters, and describe their attitudes and opinions. The problems and pressures derived from supervisors, colleagues, insureds, and other people met in the course of daily rounds will be analyzed. In summary, a picture will be sketched of how these factors affect the adjusters' approach to claims, and thus influence the outcomes of claims on a day-to-day basis.

The conclusions presented here are limited by the nature of the data, and I would like to stress the limitations before presenting the conclusions. First, these data have been gathered concerning only adjusters who are directly employed by insurance companies. The "house adjuster" is used by many large insurance companies in populated territories, and probably the majority of adjusters are thus employed. However, large numbers of claims men, rather than working for insurance companies, are employed by two varieties of firms that do nothing but adjust claims. These are adjustment "bureaus," cooperatively owned by several insurance companies, which handle claims for their members, and independent adjusting firms, some consisting only of a single adjuster, which handle claims on a fee basis for any company.[3] Independent adjusters are used by some smaller insurance companies to handle all their claims, and by many of the larger companies when their regular staff requires temporary supplementation, or when claims arise in an isolated area or in a part of the country in which a company writes little business. (Unlike a fire claim, an automobile claim can arise far from the company's underwriting territory.)

Bureau adjusters ought to be very similar to house adjusters, since the bureaus are in effect claims departments for several companies. Independent adjusters, on the other hand, may operate under rather different supervisory strains. For example, an open file in the company claims department means additional chores for a limited staff and, as will be seen later, there is strong pressure on head adjusters to close files and thus to settle claims. To the independent, on the other hand, additional investigation and negotiation duties may represent a higher fee as well as possibly a lower settlement, which may please the client company, and there may be less pressure to settle claims expeditiously.[4]

The house adjuster and the independent are also differentiated by the fact that the former has a certain amount of opportunity to climb the organizational ladder into the higher management of a large corporation. Corporate rules may therefore be more important for him than for the independent, whose opportunity lies more in the direction of gathering the contacts and experience needed to start his own small firm. This opportunity, while perhaps less exalted, seems realizable at an earlier career stage than the comparable opportunity for a house adjuster, thus suggesting possible personality differences among men choosing between these alternative employments.

Another possible limitation of the generalizations to be pre-

---

3. See Robert I. Mehr and Emerson Cammack, *Principles of Insurance* (Richard D. Irwin, 1961), pp. 798–799.

4. Paradoxically, in some cases the independent may experience an even more insistent pressure to settle, as when a small claim begins to accumulate hourly fees that loom large in relation to the amount demanded in settlement. In this situation, the independent may have to continue handling the case at a reduced charge or even without compensation in order to retain his insurance company client.

sented derives from the fact that data for the study were provided mainly by three companies which, although all quite important, together write only a small fraction of the total automobile insurance in the country. Furthermore, the companies were all large, reputable, and financially sound. I think it is reasonable to assume that in the absence of contrary evidence the findings based on these three companies—which differ considerably in ownership, manner of selling insurance, underwriting and rating practices, and general "style"—may adequately represent the situation among the general run of well-known insurance companies.[5] There may, however, be important differences between companies such as these and the smaller companies that write insurance in a limited region, or companies that specialize in high-risk business such as insuring youthful and elderly drivers or metropolitan taxicabs.

With these limitations in mind, let me turn to the research findings.

The Career of the Adjuster

From the standpoint of prestige and income, the occupational position of the adjuster can be described as lower white-collar, comparable to such positions as bank teller, bookkeeper, retail salesman, and many other jobs in the insurance field. These occupations require some degree of general education but have few specific requirements; they pay modestly, on the same level as skilled manual work; and they require moderate but not extraordinary levels of intelligence and judgment. These are the routine jobs of the great bureaucracies, private and governmental, that characterize modern society. Employment in these occupations is growing rapidly, and has profoundly changed the social class and political structure of our society. It may surprise the general reader that the sociology of occupations has paid very little attention to lower white-collar jobs, focusing

5. Similarity of claims-handling policies among major insurance companies is the principal thesis of Jerry S. Rosenbloom, *Automobile Liability Claims : Insurance Company Philosophies and Practices* (Richard D. Irwin, 1968).

instead on the professions and, to a lesser degree, on business and traditional labor. These concerns reflect the sociologist's abiding interest in the extremes, the top and bottom of society, to the relative exclusion of the middle.[6] Although the following discussion suffers from a lack of comparative materials, perhaps it will help to stimulate future parallel studies in this heartland of contemporary occupations.

Some information of the background of adjusters was obtained from a questionnaire distributed to a number of Acme employees through a company newspaper with a circulation that is limited but not precisely known. It received responses from 242 claims men and supervisors, 82 technical and safety employees, and 64 managers and executives. Since, as with most mail questionnaires, the response seemed to be far from complete, the tabulations must be taken as suggestive rather than conclusive concerning the similarities and differences among these groups.

All three groups of Acme employees came from an impressive variety of backgrounds. They came from large cities, small cities and suburbs, and small town and rural areas in approximately equal numbers. Again, approximately equal numbers in all three groups came from white-collar and blue-collar backgrounds. Occupational "inheritance" was quite rare: only 6.7 per cent of the claims men came from families with fathers engaged in any phase of the insurance industry.

Nearly all the employees responding to the questionnaire had attended college—a finding expected because of Acme's hiring preferences—but the colleges were not the elite ones, and the claims men had been poor performers in college. Averages of "A" or "B" were claimed by 21 per cent of the claims men, 43 per cent claimed "C" and 37 per cent admitted to mostly "D" grades. In contrast, 70 per cent of the executives claimed "A" and "B" averages, and none admitted to "D." [7] Five of six claims

6. A major exception is the polemical and now dated book by C. Wright Mills, *White Collar: The American Middle Classes* (Oxford University Press, 1953).

7. The superior grades reported by the executives may reflect the influence of present status on the recollection of past performance. For example, in an unpublished study of the Colorado bar by G. M. Sykes, about 70 per cent of the respondents claimed to have been in the top 50 per cent of their law school classes.

men had completed college, and 22 per cent of them attended law school. (A full 59 per cent of the executives attended law school.) The interviews of adjusters indicate that the law schools attended by claims men were typically of the local and proprietary type, and that many of the men had difficulty in obtaining admission to the bar. Although claims men at Acme were above average in intelligence—Personnel Department tests show them to have a median IQ of 116—they were academically marginal, having obtained mediocre grades from non-elite educational institutions.

Entry into claims work was virtually always casual and unplanned. Rarely did a claims man have claims or insurance in mind as a career, even as recently as his college days. Serious plans for work in insurance developed for more than half the men only upon actually being offered an insurance job.[8] Large numbers of men had seriously considered careers in law (60 per cent) and in teaching (44 per cent), and many had been in these fields before taking their present jobs.

Adjustment is a very visible job—many people come into contact with adjusters—and its recruitment practices are relatively open. Commonly, entry into the field took place after discharge from the Army. The future adjuster, being uncommitted to a specific career, found himself in claims work because it was the first opportunity that occured to him, often through a newspaper advertisement. In some cases, specific albeit casual interest in insurance had been generated by knowing someone in claims work, or by favorable experience with an adjuster in the course of making a claim. The following is a routine example:

> When I graduated from college I bumped into a former classmate in a drugstore and he kind of got me interested in it. He explained it—he didn't explain the adverse conditions—and it kind of fascinated me: company car, expense account, the type of job where if you do your work you're on your own, you set your own hours, no clock to punch; and this is the type of work I wanted to do. In any event,

8. This finding is not unusual. According to Miller and Form, "Accident is the deciding factor in determining the occupation of a majority of workers." Quoted in Robert Hoppock, *Occupational Information* (McGraw-Hill, 1957), p. 93.

as I was explaining about the recession period it was hard to get a job, so I applied, answering the ads through and through, and this was mostly in the sales field, in which I guess I had six or seven interviews. After the test they determined I wasn't a qualified salesman. I often wonder how these tests proved I was not. In any event, I met another fellow from my home town and he stated that some neighbors next door to him worked for an adjusting firm and he said they're always looking for men there. They had but three qualifications: they must have college degrees, be willing to relocate, and not have had any previous insurance experience. So the upshot of it was that . . . they hired me.

Other men drifted into insurance after more or less lengthy periods of work in other occupations such as accounting, teaching, and even automobile mechanics, finding dissatisfaction or failure there. One of the best adjusters I came to know had been fired as an English teacher because he refused to retreat from a decision to assign Dreiser's *An American Tragedy* in his high school classes. Here are some other examples:

Well, I had been in public relations with a much smaller organization and had an accident, and the adjuster who was at that time an old man (about as old as I am now) made quite an impression on me. I thought he had a real nice job and was doing a real job for me, and I knew nothing about the insurance business and I was getting somewhat dissatisfied with too heavy an organization and having to please too many people with their own whims, and I started looking around and I called up the adjuster, as this was possibly three or four years later. I called up the adjuster and asked what must I do. He told me who to get in touch with, and I camped about the company's doorstep 'til they hired me. The supervisor . . . told me, "I had to hire you to get you off my back." He said, "I like the persistency," so here I am.

I was in the automobile repair business and I just thought

that an adjuster's life looked like a pretty good life, so I decided to get into it. I applied with Great Plains, and I've been here three years now. . . . Frankly, it was just the status at first. I was tired of getting my hands dirty.

Well, I have a degree in physical education. When I graduated from college I volunteered for the draft because it was inevitable, and I got out in February of '55. . . . It wasn't until next September until I could have gotten a teaching job, so half-heartedly I looked . . . and I got one teaching the eighth grade. . . . I immediately quit after a week because it wasn't for me, I just didn't like it. So I had nothing to do at the time, so a friend of mine, who is now an attorney, was working for Acme as a claims adjuster and he thought that they needed a man, and if I was interested in the work, he liked it, and that I should come in and see about it. I did, and I was hired. I've been here ever since. . . .

I got interested in insurance because I was very disinterested in accounting, which I was doing after I graduated from college, got a job with General Motors. Actually, I worked with General Motors when I was going to college, as a time-keeper, and when I finished they offered me a job with an advance in salary in the accounting department, and it was the easiest way out so I took the easy way out, and I found out a couple of years later that I despised what I was doing. I looked around for another job and I walked the streets of Wall Street and I walked into Acme. Acme offered me a job right away, so I took it.

Perhaps not surprisingly, many adjusters are disappointed lawyers, having attended or even graduated from a law school but being unable to pass the bar examination or to support themselves from the practice of law. However, the involvement of claims work in the law does not seem to have been of much concern to these men. They, like the former accountants and mechanics, were looking for a job and found claims work obvious and open:

> Well, after I graduated . . . I got married. I intended to go into the Navy as a lawyer, but I didn't pass the bar. I had to do something. I had a wife and I had to support her. So I—the only job I could find at the time was in claims. It wasn't the kind of job I wanted as a law graduate, but I got it anyway. I realize that I intend to stay right now.

> Well, I took the bar exam twice but bankrupted doing it, so I figured that's the end of that. . . . I wasn't going to keep repeating that bar exam. I realize a lot of people get through it after three or four times. I've known some people that must have taken it nine times and they weren't through. . . . I was just looking for a job, and I saw Mid-West's ad, and I answered it. That's how I got the job. . . . I had no idea what it was about, absolutely none. I didn't know—you know they talked about "P.D." and all this jazz?—I didn't even know the terminology.

If most adjusters never planned, indeed never dreamed, about working in the insurance field, most of them find it very much to their taste. The men in their interviews could be realistically and devastatingly critical about some aspects of their work, particularly concerning the pay and the barriers to moving up, as will be seen later. They appear to me to have been equally candid in extolling the positive satisfactions of claims work, and most of the men I spoke with were generally content with the intrinsic satisfactions found in their everyday activities. As contrasted with many jobs available to the applicant with a college education who walks in off the street, claims work appears to its incumbents and to the outside observer as extremely satisfying.[9]

Perhaps the most obvious of the intrinsic satisfactions offered

9. A survey of Acme employees and former employees found 48 per cent rating insurance employment as "excellent" in terms of a satisfying career; in contrast, 63 per cent found it "fair" or "poor" in terms of remuneration.

by claims work is the freedom and lack of supervision occasioned by the fact that the interviews and investigations it requires must be done outside of the office on a schedule that cannot be set by supervisors. The claims man is in extraordinary control of his schedule, and remarkably immune to the burdens of being supervised.

> The main thing, I like about it is, I don't think you can actually say the work, as the freedom you have. You can do your own scheduling. Although you have supervisors over you, you handle your own cases and you are not told to be someplace at a certain time or punch in at the office in the morning, or anything like that. You set your own schedule. Sometimes you work nights. There are a lot of night calls, and that's what I like most about it. You know if you have a late night you don't have to get up at seven or eight in the morning. You can get up at nine or nine-thirty. It's like having your own business, to a degree.

Along the same lines, a supervisor says:

> Where the man is in the field, if it's a nice day and he wants to play golf in the afternoon, we don't care. I don't think the Home Office cares, because that man might work until eleven o'clock at night, and he knows he is going to have to make up this time, and he knows that he is going to have to work on Saturday, he might get a call on Sunday. And there is where you are your own boss to a certain extent.

A second theme apparent in the interviews concerning intrinsic satisfactions is that of challenge. At its best, claims work is diverse and exciting, and the men appreciate this aspect of it:

> And you know yourself, many times you're relaxing, even on a Saturday, and you get a case. Gee, you're dying to find out the facts, so you get into the car and you go get it, you know? . . . To do something different, this is where you get your kicks. You have the opportunity to do it in

this type job. There's nobody behind you saying, "Look, you gotta do it this way or you gotta do it that way." All they say to you is "Go out and get it done!" But they don't say how to do it. So you go out and all the little tricks you can do, different ways of doing it, and you can do it over a cocktail bar. . . . You can do these things so many various ways, but you don't become stagnant.

When I was over at ———— Corporation, I was working in a chemical lab. Now this is surprising because I did major in psychology. However, this was a job that was open at the time, and I did take it. Now, there, this was a job. I began work for instance at eight o'clock and quit at quarter of five, and I would be working in the lab, working with various chemicals, working on instruments or with instruments, and you didn't get much time to talk to anyone, and you were, in effect, in solitary. . . . and there were promotions, but there is just so much you can learn about chemicals and their make-up, whereas concerned with insurance there's unlimited opportunity to discover the different products, and to make acquaintances with other people, and there are so many different problems. This is what I mean by a career versus a job.

As has been noted also in the case of the police,[10] claims men prefer the bigger, more difficult, less routine cases, even though these may require a great deal more time and effort:

It gives you a feeling of doing a better job when you're having a tougher claim. . . . I mean, you try to do a better job because you know it's going to be a sticky claim in the future, if not the present. Small claims are more or less routine type—regular automobile, regular property losses. You get into a bigger claim, a fatal claim, something like that, it's much more interesting.

In passing, I would like to note that whereas most adjusters viewed the adversary facet of claims negotiation as part of the

10. See Jerome H. Skolnick, *Justice Without Trial: Law Enforcement in Democratic Society* (John Wiley, 1966), especially Chapter 7.

challenge of the work, and thus welcomed it, a few men listed this as one of the negative features of their occupation. Typical of the attitudes of this small group is the following:

> I suppose this is true of dealing with people in any situation, but I think more so in claims because people are after money and this is a real sore point with them, as well as the psychological aspect of accidents seems to have an emotional factor. They are very much emotionally involved in the outcome. It's a matter of "face" many times, even more than money. So that there are these frictions with people that come up in claims: they want more money, or they want money when you can't pay them money.

Another theme often noted in the interviews at first seems like social consciousness, but on reflection it appears to me to represent a liking of and appreciation for power. Facing the claimant, the adjuster has the ability to "help" or deny the need for help, and his considerable discretion does in fact give him a degree of power not often met in jobs of a comparable status level.

> Well, the good points are that you can do something for somebody when they have a loss or a tragedy. . . . You can help them.

> [I like] the constant association with the people. Generally many of them have considerable problems in the extent that they have a situation involved with their car or the sidewalk or their kids—and they look to you for rectifying their problem.

> I think it is very interesting and challenging work. You have a lot of money, the power to give a lot of money to people, and it's on your shoulders to see that it is distributed as fairly and as quickly as possible. On the other hand, those that aren't deserving of payment from the insurance company, you've got to find out if there are people involved like that. In other words, you can do people a lot of good and it is up to you to see that you do this fairly.

The theme is perhaps put most simply and clearly by a recent college graduate with a major in philosophy:

> Like I'm some sort of god in my job, deciding who is right and who is wrong, and helping the poor slob.

The sum of the large number of intrinsic satisfactions in the adjuster's job gives to these men a sense of status that is very likely not present in many similarly situated jobs. Many adjusters like to conceive of their jobs as "professional," and they probably have in mind such similarities to the traditional professions as freedom from supervision, autonomy, variety and challenge, and power. Other men compare their jobs with those of business executives, which they resemble in terms of responsibility and discretion. To return once more to the interviews:

> The difference between an employee of General Motors, even in the executive capacity, and an adjuster of Acme is the difference between day and night, as far as real executive privileges are concerned. Like I said, this is an executive job without executive pay.

> A claims representative is about as close to a professional position as any I know of.

> . . . I can be an individual. . . .

However, the adjuster's job is neither executive nor professional in most senses. The adjuster's room for discretionary decision is considerable, like that of the policeman,[11] but in both cases the discretion is not thoroughly legitimized. Adjusters and policemen exercise much discretion largely because it is difficult to employ traditional and effective techniques of supervision with workers whose jobs involve physical separation from supervisors and consequent control by the employee over his supervisor's information. The high social status and responsibility for mastering a special body of knowledge that characterize professions [12]

11. See Skolnick, *op. cit.*, Chapter 4.
12. See Everett C. Hughes, *Men and Their Work* (Free Press, 1958), pp. 33–34.

are denied adjusters, who are recruited without special training and who rank near the bottom in a poorly paying industry.

The disparity between an executive or professional self-image, fostered by unusual working conditions, and the pay and status that characterize an ordinary white-collar job, produces a degree of ambivalence among many adjusters. Low salary is a frequent complaint, and this is understandable in the light of executive and professional self-definitions. An employee survey made by Acme found that almost half the claims men were dissatisfied with their past pay raises; 90 per cent believed that the company should have done more to adjust pay to the cost of living and more than a third believed the company paid them less than employees in other similar lines. These findings occurred despite a high level of satisfaction as indicated on such items as interest of the work (only 1 per cent found the work "seldom" interesting) and preference for the company as a place to work.

Adjusters also experience insults to their sense of status within the company even more than without. The entire claims department is often considered a "junior" partner in the company, perhaps because it is seen as spending money while sales and underwriting are seen as bringing in money.

> For many years [the claims] department was placed in the basement or in space that the production department could not use. In recent years, better office space has been provided and the claims manager has been moved to where he is more available for consultation and advice. However, salaries paid staff adjusters are still below the scale used in other departments, as well as below salaries paid outside industry for jobs that require less education and training.[13]

This combination of great intrinsic job satisfaction with an ambiguous status and low income is associated with a striking lack of ambition on the part of claims men. Management sees the adjuster's job as the first step on a ladder of opportunity offered by the company, leading to executive positions. Since many companies promote from within, and the insurance indus-

13. Arthur Campbell, "Re: Avoid Unionization," *Insurance Adjuster,* October, 1967, pp. 23–24.

try is growing, the opportunity for promotion may in fact be great. In management's eyes, a lifetime adjuster is a hiring mistake.

Many claims men see things differently. In another parallel to the professions, they are hesitant to trade the intrinsic satisfactions of their jobs for executive duties.[14] They feel that to move to a supervisory position involves a qualitatively different type of work, intrinsically less attractive than field work, and that the additional pay and status offered are insufficient compensation for this exchange. In particular, the claims men feel that part of the increased salary attached to supervisory work actually is illusory, because supervisors must forego the advantages of having company cars and expense accounts, which are valued perquisites of the men in the field. Supervisory work offers no more security (three quarters of claims men felt their jobs to be secure for as long as they wanted, according to the Acme survey), and is more restricted by office routine than is field work. The attraction of intrinsic satisfactions is indicated by this man, who turned down a promotion:

> I would prefer to stay outside, really. I like to work with people. I look forward to meeting people of all walks of life, and over the years I've done outside work for such a long period of time that this office work does not appeal to me one bit. I would prefer to be on the outside doing what I'm doing.

The necessity to move and to break the ties of kinship and friendship is also a deterrent to accepting promotion. This factor appears along with additional ones in the following statement by a man with many years of field experience:

> Well, of course there is a ceiling on the salary and the title, if you are interested in such things, which I am not particularly, to which a field man can attain. But your next step from my job, let's say, would be as claims super-

---

14. The situation is reminiscent of the hesitancy of college professors to assume deanships, and the reluctance of many trial lawyers to assume judgeships.

intendent, which entails many things which are not particularly appealing to me. We get back to our desk job
again. You must, at least to the present day, you must
transfer to the regional office . . . which I don't particularly
care to move to. As I say, you have your desk job, you
have your supervisor literally standing behind you, and his
supervisor and so forth on up the line. It seems to me you
would be more back in the position of a glorified office
worker. In that position of course you do supervise six to
twelve men, I suppose, but then that means becoming involved with their personalities and their headaches and
their shortcomings and so forth, trying to straighten them
out through the mail and through occasional personal visits.
It also means of course moving your family, uprooting your
family, which I have done twice in the past five years
now. And my experience with that has been that while
it was my own initiative that I made the move, I don't
want to do it again, now that I am here. Of course, this
attitude could change, naturally. As you get older perhaps
you'll get tired of chasing claimants, pounding on doors and
working odd hours and so forth, but presently I would not
be particularly interested.

Finally, a great many men believe that the ladder of opportunity for them does not really go very high in their companies,
particularly if they lack the law degree. This perception may in
some cases merely be a rationalization for one's own limited
ambitions, but it is very generally held despite the efforts of
higher management to counteract it. Typically, career adjusters
see their job as leading to no higher position than that of first-
level supervisor, or of manager of a claims office. The following
quotation is somewhat extreme, but it is revealing:

I don't really think I'll go real high. because I don't have
that type personality. I don't have—I have initiative, but
I don't think I have that much. . . . I've found people have
to devote an exceptional amount of time to their job to go
really far, and I think when you do that you deprive a lot

of time from your family. I don't feel I want to have to do that.

A man who thinks of himself as more ambitious perceives the limitations to his expectations as being external:

> The claims field has always been a dead-end field. . . . For what I use as my yardstick is Eddie ＿＿＿. He's supposed to be a fair-haired boy, a rocketing success, and he's just standing still.

In many ways these observations about the claims man's job parallel those made in several studies of the police patrolman.[15] Both occupations present work situations with a great deal of intrinsic satisfaction such as variety, challenge, and power over others, and a great deal of necessary but nonlegitimized discretion. Both are fields with great visibility and open recruitment and great security, yet members of both occupations experience problems in the area of relative pay and status. Low levels of ambition, appearing as reluctance to leave field work, are again common to both. As will be shown, there are parallels in social and political attitudes among the incumbents as well. These parallels exist in spite of considerable differences in social origin, education, specific job requirements, and the objective opportunity structure. Police work and claims work have in common the fact that they both are subordinate positions in the general enterprise of maintaining the legal order. Although these positions are not professional, as are the positions at the top, they partake to a modest degree in the prestige and power of the total enterprise; indeed, many of the frustrations of men in these positions may be traced to implicit comparisons between their own status and remuneration and those of other members of the enterprise, who are dependent on the lower echelons to handle their routine problems.

Claims work—and perhaps police work and other similar oc-

15. See Skolnick, *op. cit.;* David H. Bayley and Harold Mendelsohn, *Minorities and the Police: Confrontation in America* (Free Press, 1969); Arthur Niederhoffer, *Behind the Shield: The Police in Urban Society* (Doubleday, 1967); and James Q. Wilson, *Varieties of Police Behavior* (Harvard University Press, 1968).

cupations—can be viewed as a refuge from the "rat race." It provides to those of modest talents some of the perquisites of the successful in our society. It permits but does not demand mobility, and pits against the strains associated with mobility a pleasant, secure existence that can honestly be evaluated as preferable. To the intellectually and personally capable but not unusual man, to the masses of routinely competent graduates of our increasing numbers of colleges and universities, jobs like this may solve the problems created by the meeting of heightened aspirations with the brute fact of limited room at the top.

Attitudes and Values

The adjusters I interviewed were to a high degree conservative, both in their general sociopolitical outlook and in their specific orientation to the issues associated with claims work. A general conservative outlook is indicated by results of the mail questionnaire. In response to a question concerning how the respondent would describe himself politically, the answers were as follows: solid conservative, 9 per cent; moderate conservative, 46 per cent; middle-of-the-road, 24 per cent; moderate liberal, 19 per cent; and solid liberal, 2 per cent. The claims men were nearly as conservative on this question as were, predictably, the managers and executives, 69 per cent of whom described themselves as solid or moderate conservatives. Specifically relevant to the claims field are attitudes concerning drivers' responsibility for accidents. The formal tort law is grounded on the assumption that accidents result from the failure of drivers to use due care, and that both moral and legal responsibility can be assigned in each case. As this view has been challenged by much recent research on accident causes, a five-item scale was put into the questionnaire in order to separate the group into those more and less in agreement with this assumption, so that the consequences of this belief could be studied. The intended comparisons could not be performed because too few adjusters indicated opposition to the fault concept. The questions, and the percentage in agreement with each statement, are listed below:

1. Most accidents are caused by factors over which people have little control. (1.2 per cent agreed.)
2. Driver error is a much larger factor in accidents than vehicle failure or road defects. (97.9 per cent agreed.)
3. It is possible to get people to drive much more safely than they do. (90 per cent agreed.)
4. People whose driving causes accidents should be punished in some fashion. (85.5 per cent agreed.)
5. Safety campaigns are pretty much a waste of effort. (14.1 per cent agreed.)

Such sentiments were frequently expressed in the interviews, expecially in discussing proposed alternatives to the present manner of handling claims, such as no-fault insurance. Most of the men bolstered their opposition to change on moral grounds, as the following excerpts illustrate:

I think when a person causes an accident, if he has to sustain a loss due to his negligence, due to his carelessness, inattentiveness to the road, things to this effect and he actually caused the accident—if he has to suffer for it, that's his problem. Compare that to the person who is completely innocent in the accident—a person sitting at a traffic light, he comes up and gets rear-ended by a guy who wasn't paying any attention to the road, paying any attention to the conditions around him—why should he be made to suffer?

I don't believe we should be rewarded for our mistakes. I don't think we're going to win in the long run if we take that attitude.

I think the fact that he went through a stop sign and caused pain and suffering to someone else—because he was too darned impatient to wait—[justifies denial].

In the opinion of many students of highway safety, there is no evidence for any deterrence of dangerous behavior due to civil liability. The assumption of deterrence has become especially doubtful as insurance coverage has spread, for the consequent financial obligations are now those of an insurance company, and not of the dangerous driver. However, the majority of the men seemed to believe in the existence of a deterrent effect in the civil liability system. This belief accords with the aforementioned belief in moral responsibility for accidents. Here are some examples:

> I think if you don't place the fault on a man who's not paying the proper attention, then what's he got to lose, to a certain extent? It's like the thought of, "Well, if I don't like my car, why should I get too concerned?"

> If [the driver] knows he's going to paid anyway, whether or not he's right or wrong, "Look out, everyone, here I come!" This is a safety point, rather than a payment point.

An additional argument put forth by adjusters in support of the fault principle concerns protecting the policyholder from a blemish on his record, or increased costs of insurance.

> If an insured is responsible then it's another question, but if they're not responsible I can't see paying the company's money and possibly resulting in a charge to the policyholder's record where this would reflect on the future premium, and it's not fair, it's not just.

Other claims men defend their devotion to the legal status quo on more pragmatic grounds, which seem closer to the truth. Typical is the man who objects to compensation as follows:

> Well, I think my dissatisfaction probably springs forth the same as would come from a sailor who is suddenly thrust into Fort Dix. . . . I'm fifteen years in the business, and you learn certain basic legal principles, you set down your work habits, your work patterns, and suddenly—it would be like the Pope saying that birth control is okay. I think it's just a natural rebellion of a change of something that's been usual, and it's repugnant to an old time claims man to have to go out to some drunk who rammed the rear of your policyholder and was injured.

A minority of claims men—a small minority, indeed—read into their experiences of investigating and settling claims a rather different message:

> I would say on the whole the people who have accidents are just average people who made a mistake. There are chronic violators, but you'll find these people are weeded out of the good companies. . . .

This position leads some of the men to prefer the doctrine of comparative negligence, in which payment is distributed according to the degree of "fault," to that of contributory negligence, in which no payment is made if the claimant has shown any lack of due care:

> The typical guy who gets in an accident should not have to pay the price of all those lost wages and all those medical bills, just because he was a little negligent.

An extreme and unusual opinion, appearing in a letter to the editor of a claims man's journal, sets the position of the majority in context:

> Fault is irrelevant unless we wish to punish, and it is punishment for an aberration, a lapse of judgment, or the implication of intent.

The adjuster's job requires him to take a suspicious view of claims and of claimants. Many of the men I knew had developed a skeptical attitude toward the motives of the claimant public which is in keeping with a philosophically conservative outlook. For instance, while driving by a boatyard, one man mentioned the fact that claims for boat damage tend to coincide with the end of the boating season, when bills for storage have to be met. In a business district, he stated that the better the times for business, the fewer the claims, and conversely when business is bad, fire claims mount. Another man noted that when home losses are reported, he always looks for additions to the house, such as refinishing the basement or adding a porch, which might produce a need to assert a claim for a theft or other type of loss. A third adjuster who does much hospital liability work sees the patient's need to pay hospital and doctor bills as the source of many claims of malpractice and hospital liability.

This suspicion does not necessarily lead to antagonism. To the contrary, I was frequently impressed with the way in which claims men were both wary and tolerant of the human weakness they got to know. They saw their job as being to deflate or to deny invalid claims, but not to remonstrate with or chastise the claimants. The adjuster typically believes that few people cut false claims from whole cloth, but that nearly everyone exaggerates his loss. This exaggeration is expected, and the adjuster sees his job as being to reduce the valid claim to an appropriate size. The claimant discovered in an exaggeration is the rule, rather than the exception, and nothing is to be gained by embarrassing him. Even more is this the case when exaggeration is expected but dishonesty cannot be proven, as in the case of subjective pain and the "whiplash injury."

Fairness

The attitudes considered above are reflected in the way in which the adjuster performs his job. He believes in the validity of the formal law and endorses its assumptions concerning fault. He believes that claimants will distort the evidence and exaggerate their losses, and that it is his responsibility to counteract the distortion and exaggeration before considering payment of the claim. Furthermore, the adjuster understands that he represents one side of the negotiation table, and that his job is to purchase releases and close claims for the minimum dollar cost:

> I found after a year of being a claims man that people are not being treated equitably, and [my supervisor] said: "Well, that's what your job is. If we wanted somebody to be equitable we would have hired a judge. Your job is to save money on some of the claims to allow us to have the money available to pay for the other claims which we feel just have to be paid because of the way it's presented and before it goes to a jury."

You *are* adverse to them and you do have a psychology in your mind that you are not going to pay it if you are not liable. . . . You are looking for a defense so you go out with this in mind: if I don't owe it I'm not going to pay; if I do owe it I am going to pay the minimum. . . . So you are against them, and although people take different stands on it and try to sell themselves and be friendly, they have to understand you are against them. I have told this to people sometimes. They will say "Are you on my side?" Nope, the name of the game is to get a release of my insured's liability.

However, it would be inaccurate to depict the adjusters I knew as concerned solely with minimizing claims costs, as the following stereotype suggests:

. . . the casehardened mind of a veteran claims man, trained to look upon a victim . . . as an adversary and a suspect, to be resisted and fought with one outcome representing the most ideal solution: denial of liability, on strictly legal grounds which are treated as if they were completely synonymous with moral grounds.[16]

There may have been a time in the past when the average claims man congratulated himself on denials and niggardly settlements arrived at through quasi-fradulent tactics, but this would be a gross caricature of the claims policies and practices that I observed at Acme, Mid-West and Great Plains. In another parallel with the professions, which are marked by codes of ethics, the work of the claims man appears to be strongly affected by ideas concerning fairness, which modify the pursuit of low settlements.

The fairness standard is well exemplified in the handling of a small fire claim that I observed. A fire in a waste basket had

16. Arne Fougner, "Rehabilitation and Insurance—A Partnership in Progress," address to the American Academy of Physical Medicine and Rehabilitation and the American Congress of Physical Medicine and Rehabilitation, Dallas, Texas, 1963, quoted in Robert E. Keeton and Jeffrey O'Connell, *Basic Protection for the Traffic Victim: A Blueprint for Reforming Automobile Insurance* (Little, Brown, 1965), p. 32.

damaged a small portion of a one-piece linoleum kitchen floor in a modest home. The floor had been laid six years previously, at a cost of $85.00. The home owner wanted a patch over the burned part, but was having difficulty in locating the pattern. The adjuster told him that the material today would cost about $100; he suggested that a patch would not satisfy the insured, and that a new floor covering would be needed. The insured disagreed, apparently under the false impression that his rates would be raised, and this reason was detected by the adjuster, who knew that the policy provided for replacement of the entire piece of linoleum without a penalty. As the insured was unwilling to accept the adjuster's suggestion of a completely new floor covering, the latter proceeded to "discover" additional trivial damage associated with the fire, in order to boost the payment. The adjacent baseboard had been slightly scorched, and the adjuster pointed this out. The insured said that he could fix it himself, and the adjuster offered $10 to "help you fix it." The paint on a metal cabinet had been scorched; the insured said he was planning to scrub it, and the adjuster suggested spray paint, for which he allowed an additional $10. The adjuster also added the value of the burned wastebasket. He then told the insured, "Go ahead and do what you can." The insured asked, "If I do the whole floor is it going to cost me?" The adjuster replied, "No, I figure $110. You do what you feel is necessary."

In a fire claim, of course, the adjuster is dealing with the company's own policyholder, whose repeated business may depend on settlements that appear fair. In liability claims, the claimant is not the customer, and the impression of fairness produces no direct business benefits for the company. Nonetheless, adherence to fairness standards pervades the handling of bodily injury liability claims. The sentiments expressed in the following quotations were general in all of the companies studied:

> We are not in business to chisel the public, I don't feel. I feel that we are in business to justify a settlement. If we know it is worth $20,000 then let's pay $20,000. Let's not

be noted for cheating our people. We didn't get to be the largest insurance company in the world by cheating people.

I don't think a good settlement is taking a release for $100 on a claim that is worth perhaps $1,500 and coming back with a big smile on your face and saying, "I knocked this one off for $100." I don't think that's a good settlement. I think that hurts the company more than it does actually help the company.

I wouldn't make the settlement for any company taking somebody. I don't believe in doing it. I came up the hard way, and I don't do it.

The concept of fairness used by the claims men seems to have two major referents. On the one hand, fairness indicates mutual satisfaction of the claimant and the company. I term this the "contractual" meaning of fairness.[17] It does not bar a settlement for amounts considerably lower than either the potential value of the claim in court, or the maximum that the company would pay out of court, although a claimant's grudging acquiescence to a settlement would presumably not fit this definition. In the words of one adjuster, a settlement is fair when there is "an equitable relationship between the company and the agents that represent the company and also the insureds of this company:"

> In other words, I think in order to accomplish a job here you have to satisfy a good many parties: first of all, the company; secondly, the agent; and thirdly, in many times, a claimant seeking damage recoveries who may not have any personal or financial interest in the company, but you still have to satisfy him. . . . In other words, I'm satisfied with any settlement, whether it be a loss or a claim, if I think it has been settled fairly in respect to the company's position,

17. These terms were suggested by Philippe Nonet.

and in respect to the claimant's position, and we close the case out with everybody happy.

But the case of the burned linoleum cited above indicates that fairness may mean more than mutual satisfaction, and so it would appear to most of my informants. The second meaning of fairness is approximation of the settlement to an absolute value, often expressed by adjusters in the words: "what the claim is worth." I term this the "principled" meaning of fairness. The meanings are related by the claims man's expectation that all parties ought to be satisfied with a settlement for an approximation of what the claim is worth.

The minimum measure of the worth of the claim would seem to be the out-of-pocket losses experienced by the claimant. These items, such as doctor and hospital bills and lost wages, correspond roughly to the element of legal damages known as special damages. In routine cases, a claim is said by adjusters to be worth its special damages, and the adjuster's goal is to settle for no more, but also no less, than these specials, reduced by the amount of other insurance benefits, such as Blue Cross and Blue Shield. As one informant put it, "The minimum settlement value would be the actual expenses; you couldn't ask the man to reduce his special damages." [18]

In the run-of-the-mill case, the adjuster hesitates to pay for pain, suffering, and inconvenience—the general damages of formal law. Asked to define his goal of paying "what's coming to them," another man had this to say:

> Well, usually the out-of-pocket expenses, and there are a few people that—today, more and more each day—have heard about the term "pain and suffering" and expect to be compensated something additional for it, but they don't know how to express themselves. . . . I don't educate them to the point that I tell them dollar-wise what they're getting. So as long as they're satisfied in their own minds, and as long as it's a fair settlement, there's no reason to ques-

---

18. The formal law, of course, allows no reduction in special damages on account of other insurance or collateral benefits. Adjusters deliberately ignore this fact.

tion it. They might feel in their own minds that they're getting something for pain and suffering, where on the other hand they may be entitled to something for transportation expenses that they haven't even mentioned. So if I know in my own mind that dollar-wise this is a good settlement, and although they may be high in what they ask for pain and suffering, I can allot a portion of this to another area. I do it without educating them to the point that I'm telling them, "Why, you have it coming to you for transportation expenses!" or whatever.

The combination of a reluctance to pay less than special damages with a reluctance to pay more is demonstrated in this tale:

At the time of the accident he had a broken hand so he was out of work. In the accident he received a broken leg. So he would have been out 6 weeks with the hand and he was in a cast 13 weeks with the leg, so he had an extra 7 weeks' wage loss that he didn't realize he was entitled to. In addition to this, they just gave me bills from the hospital and the doctor, and I knew he had prescription bills, and I kept saying, "Well, don't you have some other bills?," and they said they had some drug bills, were they covered? I told them they were. I asked them if they had anything else. I can't remember what else they thought of then, but they didn't mention the wages at all, and I brought it up and I said, "I know your son will be out of work for five or six weeks after the accident anyhow because of his broken hand, but he was out additional extra time," and they didn't know that was covered either. So I got the specials up to $815. The specials were there, it was just a question of bringing it to their attention. . . . Actually, all these people wanted were their specials and, like I say, they were willing to close it out for what they thought they were entitled to.

These comments on value apply to cases in which the adjuster believes that the liability situation is unfavorable to his insured.

As liability becomes more questionable, the claim becomes "worth" less in the adjuster's eyes. When there are strong doubts as to the insured's negligence, or when there is evidence of contributory negligence on the part of the claimant, the adjuster will define the claim as one "for compromise." [19] Even here, however, the adjuster is reluctant to pay less than medical bills. If a claim is worth anything, barring special circumstances it seems to be worth the doctor and hospital bills accumulated by the claimant, provided these are not paid by other insurance.

The principled conception of fairness encompasses an allowance for general damages in claims that are more than routine. The following comments apply to situations in which liability lies clearly on the insured, and injuries are neither totally subjective (the "whiplash") nor merely trivial (cuts and bruises):

> When it is a clear-cut case of liability and you owe it, then I don't think the person should be satisfied with just the specials, and we should pay more in all fairness to the parties involved.

> Our job seems to be to pay that person a reasonable amount, settle that claim for specials and something over and above for his pain and suffering.

> I think a man should be entitled to something above and beyond the specials, and I think it's our company philosophy to try and compensate him for it.

Faced with the adjuster's rhetoric of fairness, a cynic might well point to the fact that courts also have standards of fairness, and a release given for compensation disproportionate to the injury could be disregarded by the court, were suit to be filed later. I do not think that this fact is an important consideration in the settlement of claims. Most claimants who would accept disproportionately small settlements because of ignorance probably would hold their peace thereafter for the same reason. Furthermore, a settlement would have to be disproportionate

19. See Chapter 3.

in the extreme before a court would overturn an otherwise valid release. In the few cases that did develop in this manner, the adjuster could renegotiate the settlement, while savings in the balance of such cases would remain undisturbed. My observations have convinced me that the insurance companies could secure lower settlements on a great many claims, were it not for ethical constraints on the behavior of adjusters as expressed in these pages.

The claims man's pursuit of fairness is facilitated by the fact that the managements of the companies studied have declared support for this principle. Management support may have multiple origins: like many other industries, insurance is public-relations conscious, and it is also subject to governmental supervision by Commissioners of Insurance who license the companies to do business in the various states. Moreover, the higher management in the companies I studied contains many men whose personal ethics support the sentiments expressed by the adjusters. On the other hand, few executives would approve the stretching of company policy and occasional gross violations of company rules that adjusters engage in to realize their ideas of fairness. I have seen adjusters advise claimants to see a doctor and obtain a bill, so that they could pay, for "bodily injury," an amount which they could not otherwise pay for a damaged car because of restrictions on the evaluation of property damage. Executives have assured me that this behavior if known would result in dismissal of the adjuster, not only because it violates the rule but because it presents the temptation to make further and unwarranted demands. In the terminology previously introduced, I would characterize management's ideas of fairness as primarily contractual, whereas the adjusters lean toward the principled conceptualization of fairness. The following tale, in the claims man's own words, is a typical case:

> I had a case where, I guess about eight or ten months ago, this was a colored family. They live right off Girard Avenue, about 17th and Girard. . . . It was a knock-down case [a car hitting a pedestrian]. The kid was three or four years old. . . . So I went down there the first time, I guess

within the 24 hours after I got the claim, and I talked to the mother of the child and I told her who I was and that we would be responsible for the case, and to let us know. So I didn't see the child at the time; he wasn't there, I don't know where he was, upstairs or something. So I guess about three or four days later I get a phone call from this woman and she says she's talked it over with her husband. They had taken the child to the doctor, supposedly, and the doctor said the child was okay. Well, I went around, I guess, the following day or two days later. So I went in and this time the child was sitting in the living room there and I noticed the child's nose was bleeding, and it wasn't dripping out, I mean, the blood was coming out. So I said something to the woman about the child's nose because it was dripping on the floor and the furniture and the kid himself. So I said to the mother, I said, "Your son's nose is bleeding," and she said, "Well, yeah, it's been doing that for a while now." I said, "Well, how long has it been doing that?" and she said, "Ever since the accident." I said, "Did you take this child to the doctor?" and she said, 'Yeah, we took him the day of the accident." I said, "Did you take—did the doctor tell you to bring him back or anything about it?" and that's normally what the doctor will tell you if it doesn't appear serious at the time, if he's just shaken up or bruised a little. So she said, "Yeah," and I said, "Did you take him back?" and she said no. So I said, "Has this child's nose been bleeding a lot?" and she said, "Well, maybe four, five or six times a day it will start and the blood comes out." So at that time I knew, well, the father was there and the mother was there and I could have settled the case right there. In fact, just out of curiosity I asked them, I said, "Well, as far as a settlement figure on the case— you don't have any doctor bills, you don't have any ideas as far as settlement—what do you think would be a fair settlement on this case?" Because, normally, what we try and do is get their ideas as far as what they're looking for before we even make them an offer. So she said, "Well,

$100, $50, something in that neighborhood." And I knew when she said that, I knew in my mind, I wasn't going to settle this thing. Just by looking at the kid you knew he had some kind of concussion where the nose was bleeding or there was something bleeding inside. It wasn't just an ordinary bloody nose. So I turned around and said: "Look, before I settle anything I want you to take this kid back and I want a surgeon's report. I want you to take this child back and I want the doctor to fill this thing out. I won't settle with you till then." But let's put it this way: everybody goes around with a conscience, too, and I couldn't settle with her. To me and to the company and everyone else I think it was worth it to have the kid go back and I found out later the kid did have a concussion. They put him in the hospital. He was in the hospital about two or three weeks. Everything was taking its course. Now the case was finally settled for a lot more than the $50 I could have settled for, but in the long run I can't see myself . . . let's face it, I have to sleep with myself.

Supervision and Discretion

The adjuster's role, although intrinsically interesting and gratifying, contains a great deal of conflict because of demands emanating from a variety of other roles. Recognition of this fact is widespread among claims men, as witnessed by some humorous documents I found circulating in the claims offices:

CONSIDER THE CLAIMS ADJUSTER

His job consists of being all things unto all men—by comparison, the chameleon on a Scotch plaid had an elementary task. The adjuster is simultaneously a chiseler to the claimant, a snail to the agent, and a spend-thrift to the home office. To please all of these, he must be ambidextrous as an octopus. He must be aggressive but cautious; hard-boiled but diplomatic; frank but subtle. His only qualifications consist of being a lawyer, a doctor, an accountant, an auto mechanic, and a clairvoyant with a dash of bloodhound. He has to be at the office on time but 5:00 P.M. is only a position of the clock's hands. Sunday is a good day for interviewing witnesses. While he lives, the best break he can get is a city assignment during the baseball season. When he dies, all he can hope for is a full and binding release from all liability and he goes out wondering who will settle his claim.[20]

TO WHOM IT MAY CONCERN:

It is with regret that I have come to the conclusion that it is necessary for me to write this letter of resignation, but things being as they are, I feel that as a claims adjuster, I am a failure and will never have the qualifications needed to fulfill this unenviable, thankless, and melancholy job.

To be an adjuster, one must be courteous, diplomatic, shrewd, an expert jollier, of equable temper, slow to anger, a Sherlock Holmes, up-to-date, good looking (with honest eyes and a glad hand), a good memory, good cigars, business judgment, the embodiment of virtue and with a good working knowledge of evil; an adjuster must understand bookkeeping, banking, law, medicine, and human nature.

He must be a mind-reader, a hypnotist, and an athlete. He must be acquainted with machinery of all types and materials of all kinds and he must know the prices of everything from a shoestring to a skyscraper. He must know all, see all, and tell nothing, and be everywhere at the same time.

He must satisfy the Home Office, the local agent, the lawyer, the claimant, and the Insurance Department.

Having heard of only one man with the above qualifications, and finding that He was crucified over 1900 years ago and although we, in our daily lives, try to emulate Him, I feel that it is impossible for me to ever reach that state of perfection, so without further adieu and for the

20. From a pamphlet of the Cincinnati Claims Association.

benefit of all, I herewith relinquish all claims and titles, past, present, or future as a claims adjuster.

Very truly yours.[21]

Adjustment can be fairly regarded as the balancing of demands from various role partners, generally supervisors at one or more levels, and claimants or their attorneys, with other parties entering on various occasions. The situation has been characterized by one writer as follows:

> *The Policy Holder*: "The claim is false."
> *The Broker*: "You must not penalize the policy holder. I believe him, he is blameless.
> *The Claimant*: "I am in great pain. I have expenses. Think of my wife and family who look to me for support."
> *The Claimant's Attorney*: "A great injustice has been done my client. *Res ipsa loquitur*. Besides, the law in all its majesty favors our cause."
> *The Company Claims Supervisor*: "How are the closings coming this month? It's wise to be fair and fair to be wise. See my memo on the file and complete the 23 items of further investigation suggested." [22]

The balancing of these demands is greatly facilitated by a relatively unusual feature of claims work: the adjuster has considerable control over the information according to which he is judged by his supervisor. The adjuster is answerable to his supervisor principally through the medium of the file, which he himself devises and the contents of which he controls to a very large extent.

At first glance, the supervisory structure of the insurance company claims department might appear rather thorough. Taking Acme as an example—and the other companies differ mainly in detail—a first-line supervisor is concerned with a mere five or six men. At the time of the study, claims coming into field claims offices from agents, brokers or, on occasion,

---

21. From an anonymous typewritten bulletin board notice.
22. Morton Miller, "The Adjuster's Job," *Insurance Law Journal* 505:69, 1965.

directly from claimants, passed over the Assistant's Manager's desk, where he made the judgment as to the potential import of the case. Cases potentially involving bodily injury or involving property damage likely to exceed $500 were assigned to a claims man generally on the basis of the territory in which the claimant lived. Other cases, judged trivial, were handled by mail and telephone, and are outside the scope of this book. If a case initially judged trivial later appeared to be more serious, it would then be assigned to one of the claims men in the same manner. At Acme, all lines of insurance claims were handled by the same adjusters, whereas Mid-West and Great Plains had specialized personnel for automobile bodily injury claims.

At the time of the study, each adjuster at Acme had one supervisor to whom he reported concerning all claims assigned to him. Cases would be reviewed periodically, at least once within the first month and later at the supervisor's initiative. The supervisory conference was based on the claim file, the original of which was kept in the office, with duplicates of relevant materials being carried by the adjuster in the field. As new materials were acquired, they would be deposited by the adjuster in the office claim file.

Apart from the original "first notice" information identifying the claimant, the insured, and the number of the policy involved and containing a sketchy summary of what took place, everything in the claim file was obtained or created by the adjuster in the field. The adjuster would come to the office one day per week to update his files, review them with his supervisor, and accomplish other office tasks. The balance of the week he worked almost entirely at home or in his car, checking the office every few hours by telephone for messages and any new assignments that might require immediate action. A claims man's presence in the office on any day other than his regular day was taken by management as a sign that he had too little work. The adjuster was expected to be in the field.

Much of the bulk of the file consisted of adjusters' memos, written in longhand, describing information received and actions taken in the field. There were also two standard reports, copies of which went to the Home Office claims department, that had to be completed within 30 and 180 days, respectively. In addition, the file contained statements taken by the adjuster from the insured and the claimant, copies of bills, records, legal papers, and disbursement receipts, and a closing form indicating the disposition of the case.

In broad outlines, claims supervision consists of seeing that any payments made by the company are justified by the file— i.e., by documents evidencing the liability of the insured and the extent of the loss. The documents most relevant to liability are the statements of the parties, which contain among other things recitals of the events leading to the accident.[23] Bills from doctors and hospitals and statements from employers form the principal evidence for the extent of the loss.

Significantly, the collection and presentation of this information are to a great extent under the control of the adjuster in the field. Although a witness giving a statement will generally read it carefully,[24] the claims man—being cognizant of the consequences for apparent liability of various assertions that can be made—has a limited degree of freedom to manipulate the consequences through manipulating the written assertions. Likewise, he has a limited ability to affect the appearance of damages by requesting or failing to request various bills, by indicating his opinion of the impression that the parties' testimony might make at trial, by evaluating the degree of pain actually suffered by the claimant, and by the general tone of his memos. Furthermore, in the conference with his supervisor he is able to interpret the data to a certain extent, heightening some points and lowering others by selective emphases, explanations, amplifications and omissions. The standard 30-day and 180-day reports also allow the claims man a degree of freedom and of art. For example, it is he who indicates that a case is one of "questionable liability" or "no liability" for the purpose of the form and thus of supervision.

In sum, the supervisor exercises control not over the real

23. See the description of the statement in Chapter 3.
24. Supervisors advise new adjusters to make deliberate errors in the statement so that they may be corrected by the statement-giver, indicating that the statement was thoroughly read.

world, but over the file, and the file may be influenced by the adjuster's personal need to minimize the conflict element in his role. Only rarely does the supervisor get to the real world without its being filtered through the adjuster. A claimant's complaints, for example, may be directed to the supervisor, and offer an independent perception of the adjuster's behavior. It will be shown below that the adjuster's discretion generally leads to more liberal payments than a supervisor would prefer. Since complaints generally concern denials or payments that appear parsimonious to claimants, it is unlikely that the ability of the supervisor to control the adjuster's liberality is much enhanced by his hearing of complaints. Another circumstance in which the file may be bypassed is through the mails, which pass over the supervisor's desk. To illustrate, Acme had a rule that a personal visit was to be made by the adjuster to every claimant. Frequently, under pressure of a heavy case load, claims men would violate this rule and mail their cards with the request for the claimant to call, and on occasion the latter technique backfired when the card was mailed to the wrong address. It would be returned by the Post Office, and would reach the adjuster with a note of censure from the supervisor. Since most claims work was done in person in the field, the supervisor's scrutiny of the mail was also seldom important in controlling the adjuster's presentation of the file. On the whole, the adjuster's discretion in the matter of the file was limited mainly by his conscience and by the experience of supervisors in a wide variety of claims situations over the years.

The use that adjusters make of their discretion can be best understood by analyzing the strains in their relations with supervisors. The most important of these comes from pressure to close the files. Official policy in all three companies studied was to close claims files as expeditiously as possible. The rationale is exemplified by the following statement in Acme's *Adjuster's Manual:*

> Early investigations are necessary other than for the purpose of preserving the true facts: they are increasingly important in permitting the claim department to liquidate

its obligations before otherwise unscrupulous claimants have been coached in padding their damages and otherwise rendering an equitable disposition of their claims difficult or impossible.

An Acme supervisor cites additional reasons for speedy handling of claims:

Of course you know the public often accuses the insurance company of the delay in settling a claim. Practically speaking, when we put the money in the reserve, that's money we can't use. The sooner we dispose of that file, the better off we are. If there is going to be a saving on that reserve, we have to get that money back in circulation and make some money on it. If there is not to be a saving, if we are going to pay exactly what the reserve is, we want to get rid of the file. Each time somebody takes it out of the file cabinet, somebody looks at it, somebody types in it, there's a lot of expense to it and to any insurance company. So it behooves the company to get rid of the file as quickly as possible.

These statements of policy are translated into pressure on adjusters to close their files expeditiously. Such pressures are more effective than are the pressures to close files cheaply, for the reasonableness of a payment must be judged against the facts of the claim, which are presented in the file over which the claims man has significant control. The adjuster's economy is judged on a case-by-case basis, where special circumstances are always relevant. In contrast, the adjuster's efficiency in closing files is judged on a total-caseload basis. The pile or drawer of open files provides physical evidence of the ability of the adjuster to handle his load, and special problems that a supervisor must admit as relevant to the handling of an individual case can be ignored when one is talking about forty cases. Moreover, open files are likely to lead to complaints to managers and supervisors, whereas very few files closed with payment ever present further difficulty to the claims man.

Adjusters are thoroughly cognizant of this situation. When

asked how they could make their work easiest and least burdensome, the nearly invariable answer was to close cases quickly:

> If you take your time about it . . . chances are you're
> going to devote a lot more time to that claim than it
> requires. You'll get complaints. Many of the supervisors
> will be unhappy about it and in the long run you'll be
> working a lot harder on that particular claim.

> If you don't get on a claim they'll contact the agent, and
> the agent would be calling you, so the best way to be lazy
> on this job is do your work first.

> It goes back to that old pending list, which is the list
> that you have for your monthly claims that you close out.
> They judge you on that numerical basis. . . .

Succinctly put by one man, "Closing files, two words, describes
our job in the ultimate—closing files!"

A consequence of the pressure to close files is that claims men
often seem to search for a way to make a payment on the claim.
Contrary to the common impression, the typical adjuster is not
fixated upon the goal of denying claims; his fixation is rather
on terminating them, and in most cases the easiest way to do
so is to make a payment. The adjuster may prefer denial, but
when faced with a situation in which the file can be made to
support a payment, and in which the adjuster is convinced that
a denial would not close the file, he desires to make a payment: "I find it the easier way to adjust a claim . . . to look
for a way to pay it, rather than wait."

The principal problem in paying and thus closing claims is to
be sure that the payment can be substantiated, i.e., to produce
a file that will satisfy the supervisor that the claim deserves payment, and that enables the adjuster to close the case. In the
routine case, damages are the lesser part of the problem, although it is difficult to justify a significant payment without
doctor bills, and unsophisticated claimants at times have to be
coached to secure these bills. Higher management would greatly
disapprove of the behavior described in the following quota-

tion, but such behavior is common because it solves the adjuster's problem in presenting his file:

> Suppose they got a little problem with the neck or something. You can say they had a terrific whiplash and dizziness and nausea and the whole route. Write this in your report, give them a couple of extra bucks, they are real pleased with your settlement and they sign the release.

An apparently more difficult part of the problem of presenting the file concerns liability, but in the words of one man, "It's very easy to fabricate liability—anybody can fabricate liability to get rid of a file":

> You can color your statement and the taking of it so that you minimize contributory negligence, which is our biggest factor in making a denial, but depending on how you want to word it. Regardless of how the claimant says it you know how you have to word it to get it through to make a payment or a denial.

I recall, for instance, the liability claim of an eighty-year-old school teacher who fell on the steps outside of a funeral home. The adjuster deliberately omitted certain photographs of the steps from the file in order not to raise the issue of contributory negligence with his supervisor. In another case, an equally aged claimant fell over some barrier stones in a parking lot, which the claims man arbitrarily described in his memo as having been improperly placed. The adjuster who handled these cases explained to me that the amounts being requested by the claimants were modest, and that in view of the age of these claimants their claims might be serious if they were not promptly closed.

In my experience, the files seldom contained sheer fabrications, but the adjusters frequently yielded to the temptation to describe and label a claim as of questionable liability, thus justifying some payment, rather than as of no liability, which would commit them to denial. The case-by-case basis of supervision and the claims man's control over the file made it impossible for supervisors to detect and control the discretionary behavior described here. The adjusters argued that not only was such behavior easier on them in their work, but that it saved the company money in the long run by preventing large numbers of suits. I believe that they were right in a large proportion of cases, and perhaps their supervisors and higher management might agree as well. However, the latter were never given the opportunity to know of or judge what their subordinates were doing.[25]

The unusual weakness of supervision and consequent degree of discretion in claims work raise the possibility of more serious delinquency. Arguably, exaggerated impressions of liability or injury inserted in a file to justify closing a case may be in the interests of the employer, albeit against his rules. No such argument can be raised in favor of the "payoff," which some metropolitan attorneys allege to be necessary for adequate settlements from some adjusters.[26]

I spoke of the matter of payoffs to the men with whom I had established the closest rapport. Most of these agreed that "there's no control and there is much opportunity." These men had freely discussed with me such sensitive matters as their padding of expensive accounts. I believe they were frank and open when they stated that offers to share in a liberal settlement were often made by auto repair shops, and occasionally by attorneys, but that they had never accepted such offers, nor did they know of anyone who did. In fact, they claimed, the payoff is a subject of occasional joking—when a man comes to work in a new car someone may say, "I see your ten per cent is coming in handy" —but there is a complete absence of serious discussion of the topic:

> Like I said, nobody really wants to talk about it because

25. Police patrolmen are also isolated workers who are supervised from a distance. See Skolnick, *op. cit.* The general problem of controlling discretion in this situation is treated by Kenneth Culp Davis, *Discretionary Justice: A Preliminary Inquiry* (Louisiana State University Press, 1969).

26. One attorney explained that though an estimate is not possible, "many" adjusters can be "taken care of." The going rate is a ten per cent cut of the settlement, which the attorney said he was willing to pay provided he got "value" for his money. For example, this attorney settled a case that in his opinion was worth $1,200 for $6,000, of which $600 went to the adjuster.

nobody really wants to bring it up, because it's one of those tight subjects. You just forget about it. It comes to you, and if you don't take it, you forget about it and let it go.

The embarrassment, the feeble jokes, and the lack of communication among claims men concerning the payoff recall the atmosphere that surrounded cheating among my fellow students in college. Cheating was recognized as a serious offense, that was very hard to rationalize as being "noncriminal," [27] yet we all understood the ease with which it was committed and the terrible inducements that some students felt. We believed, without really knowing, that very few students cheated. However, the matter was seldom discussed, perhaps because of the dilemma that such knowledge would pose for the listener: there would be strong pressure to bring such a serious matter to the attention of the authorities, countered by the demands of loyalties to peers and the feeling that there, but for the grace of God, go I.[28]

If the payoff is in fact rare among adjusters, and I have no evidence that it is otherwise, one important deterrent may be the fact that adjusters often deal repeatedly with the same attorneys and repair shops, and to accept a payoff at one time creates the potential for blackmail in the future:

> I think one of the main things, if a person is basically honest and it comes up in front of him, is he doesn't want to give the other person something to hang him on. In other words, let's say you go into an attorney's office and he comes out with little hints here and there, you more or less get the idea that the attorney's offering you something or a percentage. It might be good to get it right

27. See Donald R. Cressey, *Other People's Money* (Free Press, 1953). His thesis is that embezzlement becomes possible for people who lack a criminal self-conception if they can define the act as noncriminal or as beyond their control.

28. See Samuel A. Stouffer, "An Empirical Study of Technical Problems in Analysis of Role Obligation," in Talcott Parsons and Edward A. Shils (eds.), *Toward a General Theory of Action* (Harvard University Press, 1954), pp. 479–496.

then, let's say, but what's going to happen six months from now when you get a questionable case and the attorney starts throwing this to you: "Well, look, remember six months ago when you did this?"

The Adjuster's Approach to Claims

Let me summarize the chapter to this point. I have shown that adjusters come from a wide variety of social backgrounds and come to their jobs in insurance principally through coincidence. Once at work in the claims department they find that the job has great intrinsic satisfaction: autonomy, challenge, power, and security. Although the job of the adjuster is neither executive nor professional, some of the characteristics of these higher status jobs adhere to claims adjustment.

Adjusters are overwhelmingly conservative, both in general and in their specific agreement with the law of negligence. Their liking for working with people is tempered in the field by a job-induced distrust and cynicism. On the whole, the typical claims man is predisposed to resisting claims, a stance that is in harmony with the short-run business interests of the organization that hires them.

This predisposition is counteracted by several factors. Prominent among them is a devotion to fairness, an unwillingness to "chisel," which in the specific case becomes an unwillingness to pay less than the out-of-pocket losses of the honest claimant. Added to this are the pressures from the supervisory hierarchy to close claims expeditiously. These pressures are generally more urgent than are the pressures to close claims with the lowest possible payment. They are also more difficult for the claims man to evade through his control over the file. It is far easier to argue that a given payment was justified than that a given delay was necessary. Over and above these routine supervisory pressures are pressures from claimants, with whom the adjuster must maintain rapport or control, to accede to their definitions of value. Plaintiffs' attorneys and other interested parties are similar sources of pressure to pay, and all can affect the claims man directly by complaining to the supervisory hierarchy.

Adjusters are therefore not—stereotypes to the contrary— resisters of claims. Their goal is not to deny or pay the lowest settlement possible, regardless of other considerations. Rather, the claims man may be envisioned as a sharp but decent buyer of commodities. His orientation is above all to consummate the purchases, with prices being a secondary consideration. He is willing to buy various qualities of goods, to be sure on different terms, but there are relatively few items for which he is unwilling to make some small payment. His goal is a low price per item, but a fair price, and one that will be high enough to avoid frequent delays in the sale. Rather than resisting the transactions, he wants them to be supported by documents that will provide him and his superiors with evidence of value received. If the intangible claim can be nailed down with doctor bills, statements from employers, and similar documents, the adjuster is a willing buyer.

This stance feeds into the claims man's professional self-conception. Unmitigated claims resistance would make his task a time-consuming and stressful one. His sense of freedom and of power would be compromised. Moreover, such a stance could be forced on the adjuster only through an expensive and difficult program of field supervision; indeed, it might be altogether impossible.[29]

The Claimant and the Insured

In this section I will briefly discuss two additional roles in claims settlement—those of the claimant and the insured. As one would expect, the claimant is a major actor in the drama of settlement, and he will reappear throughout the remaining chapters. In contrast, the insured has a mere "walk-on" role. Although he is intimately involved in the accident that begins the claim, and it is his report that sets the claims handling procedure in motion, he rapidly fades from the scene and will seldom reappear in later chapters.

In describing the claimant and the insured I will rely princi-

29. For a similar conclusion concerning the police, see James Q. Wilson, *op. cit.*

pally on the reports of others. My research design did not focus on these roles, and although I met many claimants and a few insureds when accompanying adjusters on their rounds, my personal knowledge has been limited in depth and representatives. All claims originate in accidents, but not all accidents produce claims. Following the language of Keeton and O'Connell,[30] I use the term "victim" to designate someone who has experienced injury in an automobile accident. A claimant is a victim who presents a liability claim to an insurance company. The insured or defendant is the person against whom the claim is formally made. From the legal point of view, he is a defendant and the claimant is a plaintiff. From the insurance company's point of view, he is an insured.

The language of these definitions would suggest that the victim initiates the claim by presenting demands to a driver's insurance company. In actuality this is seldom the case. The claim is usually initiated by the insured, who is required by the conditions of his insurance policy to notify the company if he has an accident. The company could perhaps merely note the incident in its records and wait for the claimant to bring his demands, on the theory that sleeping dogs may lie. In the companies studied, however, all people reported as involved in an injury-producing accident were treated as potential claimants and were approached by an adjuster as quickly as possible. Among the reasons for this procedure are: (1) the assumption on the part of the insurance company that most victims do in fact make claims, that delay in approaching the victims increases the likelihood that the claimants will have retained attorneys, and that represented claims are more expensive to settle; and (2) the need for investigation of the claim while physical evidence is fresh and the memories of witnesses are relatively clear. The need for investigation also rests on the assumption that a claim will be made.

I have not been able to find any factually grounded estimates of what proportion of injured people would present claims if left to their own devices. Apparently, few if any reputable insur-

30. Keeton and O'Connell, *op. cit.*

ance companies are willing to take the risk involved in finding out. Some evidence is available suggesting that most victims today do make claims. In New York City, for instance, a study by Hunting and Neuwirth found that 87 per cent of people injured in accidents reported to the State Bureau of Motor Vehicles made liability claims.[31] The Michigan study does not tell how many victims filed claims, but about half of all victims either hired lawyers or received settlements without hiring lawyers, so the proportion making a claim may very well be in the neighborhood of the New York City figure, despite other differences in these populations.[32] On the other hand, the Osgoode Hall Study in Toronto found that only about half of the injured made a claim.[33]

The scientific literature suggests that some classes of victims are more likely than others to make claims. Zeisel, Kalven, and Buchholz, for instance, compare the number of accidents and the number of claims in different jurisdictions, and find that in certain areas—notably the cities of New York, Philadelphia, and Chicago—the claims rate is high relative to the accident rate.[34] Metropolitan residence may thus be associated with victims' making claims. Hunting and Neuwirth report the conditional probability of a victim's making a claim to be higher with greater damage, a feeling of blamelessness, previous experience with claims, discussing the accident with others, and high socioeconomic status.[35] The adjusters I interviewed were generally of the opinion that Jews invariably would claim, and that ministers and schoolteachers—low-income, high-prestige people —were particularly insistent claimants. Inasmuch as the great bulk of victims make claims, these differences are relatively un-

31. Roger Bryant Hunting and Gloria E. Neuwirth, *Who Sues in New York City?* (Columbia University Press, 1962), p. 8.
32. Alfred F. Conard, James N. Morgan, Robert W. Pratt, Jr., Charles E. Voltz, and Robert L. Bombaugh, *Automobile Accident Costs and Payments: Studies in the Economics of Injury Reparation* (University of Michigan Press, 1964), p. 154.
33. Allen M. Linden, *The Report of the Osgoode Hall Study on Compensation for Victims of Automobile Accidents* (privately printed, 1965), Chapter V, p. 11.
34. Hans Zeisel, Harry Kalven, Jr., and Bernard Buchholz, *Delay in the Court* (Little, Brown, 1959), Chapter 20.
35. Hunting and Neuwirth, *op. cit.*, pp. 10–12.

important. Given prevailing insurance company practices, it takes a positive act on the part of the victim *not* to make a claim. I have seen victims in the Pennsylvania Dutch country refuse to accept payment, producing no little problem for the adjuster who therefore cannot close his file as required with a signed release of liability.

The nature of the losses sustained by victims has been amply documented in several studies.[36] The best and most recent figures are those of the Michigan study, which show that about 1 per cent of the total population sustains some economic loss due to injury-producing automobile accidents in a given year. Most of the losses are trivial: in Michigan in 1958, more than 60 per cent were less than $500, and fewer than 10 per cent were more than $3,000.[37] These estimates, based on statements by victims, are probably liberal. The routine claimant has suffered minor injuries and minor economic losses: cuts and bruises, a sore neck, and at most a day or two at home from work. At the other end of the scale, a small proportion of losses—2 or 3 per cent in the Michigan study—exceed $10,000, and many of these are tragic, involving disfigurement, paralysis, and death. Claims of this sort are rare and, as will be shown, they are treated differently from routine claims.

An important difference among claimants concerns whether they handle the claim themselves or through an attorney. Negotiation and settlement procedures differ considerably in the two situations.[38] Most claimants handle their claims directly with adjusters. In the Acme files, 1,601 of the 2,216 claimants were unrepresented. The Michigan study found that only 12,000 of 86,100 victims hired a lawyer.[39] Hunting and Neuwirth found two thirds of claimants in New York City to be represented, but the New York area is known to be unusual in this respect.[40] The Acme files, the Hunting and Neuwirth study, and the Michigan

36. A detailed discussion of these various studies appears in Keeton and O'Connell, *op. cit.*, Chapter 2.

37. Conard *et al.*, *op. cit.*, Fig. 4–2, p. 152.

38. See Chapters 4 and 5.

39. Conard *et al.*, *op. cit.*, p. 155.

40. Hunting and Neuwirth, *op. cit.*, p. 8; but see Zeisel, Kalven, and Buchholz, *loc. cit.*, for an indication of the uniqueness of New Yorkers in making claims.

study show representation to be strongly associated with the size of the claim. Almost half of the "seriously injured" victims in Michigan hired lawyers.[41] The Acme files also show that living in a city is correlated with hiring a lawyer. Hunting and Neuwirth report correlations between representation and all factors that are also correlated with making a claim, except for social status, which is inversely correlated with representation.[42] The adjusters in their interviews for this study asserted that representation was related to ethnicity—Jews and Italians were believed to elect representation in an unusual proportion of claims—and to residence in specific local communities—those populated by what adjusters defined as a "striving" middle class.

When a claimant is represented by an attorney, he is no longer a visible participant in the settlement process. His first instruction from the attorney is not to discuss the case with anyone, particularly not with a representative of the insurance company. Although from time to time he may be "resurrected" by the attorney, usually as a negotiation ploy,[43] he plays no further role. The unrepresented claimant, of course, is the adjuster's major role partner. A great deal of the adjuster's work is directed to maintaining the claimant's unrepresented status, closing the claim without the intercession of an attorney. This is called keeping the claim under control. The behavior of the "controlled" claimant will be analyzed in passing throughout the remaining chapters of this book. At this point, I shall only sketch my understanding of his viewpoint, based on the field observations and on Hunting and Neuwirth's questionnaire.[44]

The claimant's understanding of his rights and obligations is generally vague and imprecise. When he makes a claim, he is looking for payment of his actual losses plus, in Hunting and Neuwirth's words, "a little gravy." He desires a simple, mechanical payment of his claim, and views any delay as a hardship deliberately imposed by the insurance company. He does

41. Conard *et al.*, *op. cit.*, p. 183.
42. Hunting and Neuwirth, *op. cit.*, pp. 8–10.
43. The ploy is to depict the claimant as unreasonable; see the section on the attorney that appears later in this chapter.
44. Hunting and Neuwirth, *op. cit.*, pp. 8–10.

not understand the rule of contributory negligence, and when this is explained to him he strongly disagrees with it. His understanding of and liking for the rule of negligence are only slightly greater. The claimant is often uninformed in evaluation and unskilled in negotiation. At times claimants will request so much that the adjuster will deliberately relinquish control, trusting that it will be easier to negotiate with an attorney than with an unreasonable claimant.

Adjusters, like salesmen, know that the claimant is not an isolated individual, and that he experiences pressures from others around him. These pressures are not as structured as those faced by the adjuster in his role as employee, but they must be acknowledged and managed by the adjuster. Family, friends, doctors, employers, policemen, and others are all potential sources of influence over the claimant, and they are expected to advise the claimant to refuse any offers an adjuster might make and to seek representation. In consequence, an adjuster's job often involves negotiating with parties other than the legal claimant or his formally authorized representative. A fortunate or sophisticated claimant can use these parties to obtain significant bargaining advantages in coming to an agreed settlement.

The role of the insured in settlement is extremely limited. He initiates the claim by notifying the company of the accident, and he presents his version of the accident in a signed statement. Because his cooperation is required by the insurance contract, he may be called on for further information at later times. Otherwise, unless the case promises to go to court, in which case the insured must be a witness, his role is minimal. The only exception to this statement is probably the unusual case in which an insured with considerable assets becomes involved in an accident where the damages are likely to exceed the limits of his insurance—the maximum amount that the company is obligated to pay on his behalf. In such a case the insured may be expected to take an active role in settlement negotiations. These cases are extremely rare, and I never had a chance to know of a particular instance or to observe one.

In the ordinary case, the role of the insured is described by Hunting and Neuwirth as follows:

Who are the persons really interested in the lawsuit? Theory says that it is the man who is injured as the plaintiff and the man who caused the injury as the defendant. The fact is that the real interested parties are the injured man and his attorney (whose fee is almost invariably a portion of the client's recovery) and the insurance carrier of the man who injured him. . . . The defendant himself has no financial interest in the case; he has paid his insurance premiums and will pay them in the future.[45]

Similarly, the Michigan study finds "that the defendant is best characterized by his lack of involvement in the litigation process, evidenced by both his lack of knowledge about the outcome of the case and by the small amounts of time and money he is required to invest to reach the settlement."[46]

The case is perhaps overstated. Many insureds become psychologically involved in the settlement of claims against them, feeling that they have a stake in the matter because of increased premiums following a settlement, or on grounds of "principle," denying responsibility for the accident. An illustration concerns a woman who experienced an accident in an intersection. She had emerged from a street controlled by a stop sign, and as far as the adjuster could tell she bore the entire legal responsibility for the accident. In her report of the accident, the following language appeared:

The operator of Vehicle 2 [the claimant] received a summons for driving without a license. . . . Vehicle 2 was sufficiently far away from Vehicle 1 to turn. . . . The operator of Vehicle 1 [the insured] is very familiar with the roads she was driving on because she drives on them every day.

The adjuster predicted that the most difficult part of handling this claim would be explaining to the insured why payment was made.

The principal reason for the minor role of the insured in

45. Hunting and Neuwirth, *op. cit.*, pp. 22–23.
46. Conard *et al.*, *op. cit.*, p. 309.

claims settlement is that he lacks any institutional means of bringing pressure on the adjuster. Unlike the claimant, who can withhold cooperation, the insured is committed by contract and by economic interest to being a compliant witness to the facts of the accident. He possesses nothing of value to the adjuster except his story, and when that is given he leaves the stage.[47]

The Claimant's Attorney

In this section I shall try to parallel the information presented above concerning the adjuster with similar information on the claimant's attorney. Acme files showed slightly more than one fourth of all claimants to be represented and, as noted before, representation was proportionately more frequent with higher losses. Where special damages exceeded $200, more than half the claimants were represented. When a claimant retains an attorney to handle his claim, he is instructed not to discuss the claim further, and dealings with the adjuster leading to settlement are conducted exclusively by the attorney. Negotiation and settlement take different forms under these conditions, as will be seen in later chapters. Among the factors responsible for these differences are the attitudes and work pressures of the attorneys. These factors will be explored here. In my own estimation, the information available to me concerning attorneys was less adequate than that concerning adjusters. I interviewed far fewer attorneys, though at the same length as the adjusters. Moreover, it was difficult to interview a representative sample of metropolitan attorneys. I drew a random sample of Harrisburg area attorneys from the claims files of Acme, and each of the twelve attorneys who were approached for an interview agreed, all but one being extremely cooperative. A sample of 25 attorneys was drawn in a similar fashion from the Long Island office of Acme, but cooperation was very poor. Many of them excused themselves on the grounds that they never handled negligence cases, although their names appeared as representing

47. Conard *et al.*, *op. cit.*, found that two-thirds of those claimed against did not know the outcome of the claim. The same was true of one-third of those who had been formally sued. See pp. 279 and 292.

claimants in the files of an insurance company. In the end, I interviewed whichever metropolitan area lawyers would agree to talk with me, making no attempt to get a representative sample. I take the high refusal rate to be a valid item of data for the study. In conjunction with information obtained in the interviews and from the social science literature, it suggests that metropolitan lawyers may have more things to hide than lawyers practicing in a small city.[48]

At least since the publication of Jerome Carlin's *Lawyers on their Own* and Erwin Smigel's *The Wall Street Lawyer*,[49] it has been common knowledge among students of the legal profession that the bar is highly stratified. At the top of the legal profession are the men who as partners in large law firms advise the rich and powerful and help in great measure to shape the basic institutions of society. Smigel shows that these men generally originate in the top levels of society and partake of elite schooling and legal education. They are professionals in all the traditional senses: highly skilled, extremely responsive to the ethics of their calling, and well rewarded in money and prestige. At the bottom of the legal profession, generally practicing alone and not in firms, is a different kind of lawyer. Carlin shows a tendency for these men to originate from lower levels of the social structure, from among recent immigrants and nonprofessional parents. Their education is non-elite, culminating in legal training at a proprietory or a lesser Catholic law school, often taken at night while the student is engaged in nonprofessional work during the day. Their legal skills are marginal, their rewards in money and prestige are minimal, and their orientation to the ethics of the bar is, at best, pragmatic. Their clientele is a personal one, composed of lodge brothers, neighbors, and relatives, and their work is shaped by the needs of

48. Compare Jerome E. Carlin, *Lawyers on their Own: A Study of Individual Practitioners in Chicago* (Rutgers University Press, 1962), with Joel F. Handler, *The Lawyer and His Community: The Practicing Bar in a Middle-Sized City* (University of Wisconsin Press, 1967).

49. Carlin, *op. cit.;* Erwin O. Smigel, *The Wall Street Lawyer: Professional Organization Man?* (Free Press, 1964). See also Handler, *op. cit.;* Jack Ladinsky, "Careers of Lawyers, Law Practice, and Legal Institutions," *American Sociological Review* 8:47, 1963; and Hubert J. O'Gorman, *Lawyers and Matrimonial Cases* (Free Press, 1963).

the common man—real estate, wills, marital cases, small corporate matters, and negligence. Much of this work is not professional in the traditional sense, but is closer to brokerage, and it meets with severe competition from subprofessionals such as realtors and bank trust officers. This is the dissatisfied and hungry end of an extremely varied occupational spectrum.

The men who handle automobile accident cases come from a variety of points on the spectrum, but a large proportion appear to come from near the bottom. This assertion can be supported by various facts: negligence is the single most common specialty among lower level lawyers, according to Carlin. In contrast, the great Wall Street firms may assign an associate to handle the occasional negligence case that falls into the personal lives of their business clients, but such cases are not sought. Additional support comes from the fact that the Acme files show 81 per cent of all attorneys representing claimants to be practicing as solo lawyers. The concentration of lower level lawyers in the negligence field occurs because actions in negligence—unlike, say, the law of trusts—can befall the small as well as the great—and the contingent fee, which is virtually universal in the negligence area, makes the little man's claim as interesting to the lawyer as the big man's claim.[50] A real estate closing can yield a lawyer future negligence business as well as or better than an argument to the Federal Trade Commission.

Cross-cutting the stratification of the bar is another dimension of the practice of law: specialization. The sample of attorneys interviewed in the study was too small to yield precise estimates, but it is clear that a substantial minority of the claims encountered were handled by men whose work was virtually confined to negligence matters.[51] Within this group were those whose entire practice was representing claimants, and those whose principal practice was representing defendants but who from time to time would represent a plaintiff. Some of the specialists I interviewed

50. Daniel P. Moynihan estimates that perhaps a third of the legal fees of the American bar come from litigation over automobile accidents. See "Changes for Automobile Claims?" in Robert E. Keeton, Jeffrey O'Connell, and John H. McCord (eds.), *Crisis in Car Insurance* (University of Illinois Press, 1968), pp. 1–9, at p. 2.
51. O'Gorman, *op. cit.*, finds a similar situation in divorce work.

appeared highly skilled, and were renowned in the community for their effectiveness. Others seemed to have specialized in negligence for want of other business:

> They don't come to me with their real estate or corporate matters although I am equally [competent]; so it seems to me, not by choice any longer but by necessity, I have become confined to the practice of negligence.

Most of the attorneys I spoke with obtained their negligence cases in the course of a general legal practice. Attorneys in general practice estimated that negligence work provided them with from 20 per cent to a third of their total business. The balance of their work was in the lines of real estate, wills and estate planning, and marital disputes. Many of the general practitioners I interviewed declared that they never tried cases and would call in specialized trial counsel in the event that a negotiated settlement could not be obtained.

In short, the attorneys I interviewed were a heterogeneous lot, probably because the universe of attorneys handling negligence cases is a heterogeneous one. Stratification and specialization were evident in my sample, even though it was small and not randomly chosen. Although there is much more to be learned about the attorneys handling negligence cases, I can note here some consistent similarities and differences between attorneys and the adjusters with whom they negotiate, since these comparisons help to further understanding of the settlement process.

In origin and educational background the lawyers I interviewed seemed closer to the Carlin solo practitioner model than to the Smigel Wall Street lawyer model. Virtually all the Harrisburg attorneys had attended Dickinson Law School, the only local law school, which is not affiliated with a university. Their class standings in law school ran the gamut from valedictorian to the lower third. What most clearly distinguishes their career backgrounds from those of the adjusters is the amount of planning that went into their occupational choices. Even when practiced at a low level, law is not an occupation into which one falls by chance; indeed, the achievement of a low-level practice may be the culmination of enormous effort and self-denial on the part of the attorney and his family. Contrast the following typical career description of a lawyer with the preceding descriptions by claims men:

> I knew I wanted to be a lawyer. I knew that when I was . . . 14 years old. And in my high school yearbook it says I wanted to be a trial lawyer, so that it all followed right through, then, and I wanted to get into law school as soon as I could. So I transferred into law school from Dickinson College as soon as I had enough credits, and went straight through the law school in two years—it was a three-year course—sold storm windows and brick siding while I was in law school, and when I was in college I worked in a restaurant at night tending bar, and waiting on tables during the day. But the Dean of the law school didn't want me to be occupied with that while in law school, so I canvassed door-to-door selling brick sidings and storm windows in the communities around central Pennsylvania.

As noted above, most of the lawyers interviewed were not negligence specialists, but had handled negligence cases as an aspect of a general practice. Some of these general practitioners found the work unpleasant, though a necessary part of their practice. Negligence work may be easily regarded as brokerage, rather than the profession of law, as the following reaction illustrates:

> To me it's demeaning to haggle, and unfortunately this is what it has come down to on whether it be a $1,000 case, a $5,000 case, or a $10,000 case, or even more than that. It's still the same type of haggling. . . . I'd consider it similar to a push-cart type of operation where I remember my mother going into the streets and saying, "Well, I'll give you . . . ten cents for it," and the other saying, "I'll give you five cents for it," and somewhere along the line they would compromise the thing. This is what I resent. That I don't like!

However, most general practitioners and all of the specialists viewed negligence work more favorably. A principal reason is that, relative to other types of ordinary legal work, negligence is lucrative and makes individual practice possible. Moreover, negligence, like criminal practice, fits a traditional "Clarence Darrow" view of lawyering in that trial work is involved and the party represented can be characterized as the underdog, but, unlike criminal practice, negligence work yields a worthwhile income to the lawyer. The following considerations are quite typical:

> I graduated from Yale Law School in the class of '59 and after being discharged from the Army some six months later I came to New York because I wanted to do what involved a considerable amount of trial work, number one, and representing people as opposed to corporations or even businessmen. (I don't consider businessmen as people, I guess, at least not in their business lives.) . . . In the criminal field I found that most of the criminal lawyers who I ran into were just an unfortunate lot who had to wander around court to pick up $50 fees here and there, $100 fees here and there, or who represented people like gamblers on a retainer basis. . . . I discovered after a little investigation that the Legal Aid Society were representing so many of the people who I would have wanted to represent that there was no way for me to break into the criminal field unless I wanted to work part-time for Legal Aid. I must say that I still have a basically selfish motive, and I do want to have a private legal practice which would be successful, and I do not want to go to work for any organization or agency. So this really left negligence as the only thing or kind of thing, I should say, that covered or satisfied all the areas which I was interested in . . . .

In detail, the satisfactions mentioned by the attorneys were very similar to those mentioned by the men on the other side of the table, the adjusters: challenge, excitement, variety, working with people, and independence.

Attorneys obtained their negligence cases in various ways, depending on whether they were general practitioners or negligence specialists. Negligence cases were obtained by the general practitioners mainly as a consequence of other, previous legal services rendered to a client who now happened to have a negligence claim. I did not further interrogate the general practitioners on the source of their clientele, although in passing there was mention of friends and relatives, political activity, a good local reputation, and above all, recommendation by other clients. The specialists obtained a large proportion of their cases from other attorneys, usually personal friends or law-school colleagues, who would either make the referral immediately or would refer the case once negotiation attempts had broken down and the need for trial seemed evident. The chief reason for referral, according to the men I interviewed, was the referring attorney's dislike for trial work and not the difficulty or complexity of negligence law.

Negligence specialists also obtained cases from nonprofessional sources. In Harrisburg, a member of the best-known negligence firm pointed to that firm's reputation in the community as a means of obtaining new clients directly. Another lawyer mentioned "one or two doctors" as an occasional source of clients. The principal nonprofessional source mentioned was previous clients, who referred their friends and acquaintances to a lawyer who had obtained a satisfactory settlement for themselves.

The use of "ambulance chasers" or paid nonprofessional sources of referral was not acknowledged at all in Harrisburg, and only one metropolitan lawyer confessed to using them. Adjusters, on the other hand, believed that referral of claimants to certain lawyers through a network of paid laymen such as policemen, hospital orderlies and other people likely to come into contact with the injured, was a fairly common practice. The situation is said to be routine in the Chicago area:

> Almost all serious personal injury cases are chased, and estimates of the number in which a chaser contacts the injured party run as high as 95%. Over half the claims

presented for personal injuries of any degree of seriousness are probably handled by these [chaser-using]
lawyers.[52]

My research methods were not geared to making an estimate of the
extent of chasing, which is a very sensitive subject because it is
specifically prohibited by Bar Association rules. The reluctance of
metropolitan lawyers to be interviewed may be interpreted as
evidence that such formally unethical behavior is not uncommon
in the metropolis.

It is not clear to me that ambulance-chasing, to the extent that
it exists, is necessarily an evil. The attorney for a chased client
has an investment in his client's case, to be sure, but such an
investment is inherent in any case governed by the contingent
fee, which is in the United States the near-universal means of
compensating attorneys in personal injury claims. For the attorney to maximize his investment, it would seem that he would
in general try to maximize the claimant's settlement. Moreover,
since the amount of the contingent fee is fairly standard, there
would seem no reason to suspect that the net settlement for the
"purchased" client need be less than the one to the client obtained without a chaser. The client's interest would be harmed
by the chaser system only if it were the less competent attorneys
who were involved in it, and the more extensive the system, the
less likely this is to be the case. The insurance company pays
more because, as will be shown, represented claimants have higher
recoveries, but this fact alone is not unjust. On the contrary,
the supplying of representation to those victims who might
otherwise be unrepresented may seem to some observers to be
a salutary development, increasing the use of legal services and
benefiting innocent victims as a group against the guilty.

52. "Comment: Settlement of Personal Injury Cases in the Chicago
Area," *Northwestern University Law Review* 47:895, 1953, at 899. This
article was later cited in the appellate court case of Morris *vs.* Pennsylvania
Railroad Co., 10 Ill. App. 2nd 24, 134 N.E. 2nd 11 (1966) and in Kenneth
J. Reichstein, "Ambulance Chasing and the Legal Profession," *Social Problems*, 13:3, 1965.
53. See Reichstein, *op. cit.*, especially p. 9.

The attorney's relationship with his personal injury client has struck some observers as being of a different order from the relationship usually envisaged between client and attorney. Hunting and Neuwirth, for instance, suggest that there might be a degree of exploitation here that is not found elsewhere in legal work:

> So we find that the traditional attorney-client relationship of trust and reliance, the intimate counselor and adviser usually thought of when "attorney and client" is mentioned, is far from the relationship that often exists when the client is the victim of an automobile accident. There, instead, we find two strangers who deal with each other only in passing. The client may be, in the eyes of the lawyer, only the source of a piece of lucrative "raw material" to be processed to a settlement while the lawyer is, in the eyes of the client, only a necessary professional aid in extracting from the insurance company enough money to compensate him for expenses and suffering.[54]

The use of the contingent fee bears on this question. Virtually all employment of attorneys by bodily injury claimants is governed by contingent fee agreements, which entitle the attorney to a percentage of the total recovery in the event that he obtains a settlement. The percentage is usually a flat figure, such as 33⅓ per cent, but some contracts stipulate a decreasing percentage for higher settlements—for example, 50 per cent of the first $1,000, 33⅓ per cent of the next $5,000 and 25 per cent of the balance—and other contracts specify an increasing percentage in the event that suit is filed or trial is undertaken. The claimant pays nothing in the event that his claim is unsuccessful but, as will be shown in Chapter 5 below, this is a most unlikely event. In the large majority of cases, according to the Acme files, a claimant who has provable economic loss will recover something, and the average recovery of represented claimants ranges from $1,800 to $5,000, depending on the type of lawyer. These figures

54. Hunting and Neuwirth, *op. cit.*, p. 109.

suggest an average return to the attorney of from $500 to $1,500 per claim represented.[55]

The contingent fee would seem to produce a strong congruence of interest between the attorney and his client. A higher settlement for the claimant results in a higher fee for the attorney. However, three opportunities for conflict of interest seem apparent.

The first opportunity is more likely to occur for the negligence specialist, who negotiates on a repeated basis with the same insurance companies. His goal of maximizing the return from any given case may conflict with the goal of maximizing returns from the total series of cases he represents. His negotiating opponent may, for example, plead for a lower settlement in one case and offer in return more consideration in another, yielding the attorney a larger sum of fees in total. Failure to oblige might additionally create more difficulty in obtaining settlements in the future. I have seen "trades" made in the settlement of a number of cases, testifying indirectly to this conflict of the lawyer's interest with that of some individual clients.

A second source of conflict of interest springs from the fact that the costs of trial may be borne proportionately more heavily by the attorney than by the claimant. Some contingent fee contracts make no allowance for additional compensation to the attorney in the event of trial, and other contracts allow only a modest increase in the percentage, which in small cases yields a negligible dollar amount. In a certain group of cases, then, trial might be profitable for the claimant and unprofitable for the attorney. Most of the attorneys said that they would try a case at the client's insistence, but their advice as to whether to accept a settlement offer or to proceed with trial could possibly be affected by their personal interest. The settlement could be

55. The popularity of the contingent fee with the public is indicated in the experience of one Harrisburg attorney who offered each new client a choice between the standard contingent fee and his regular hourly fee on a win-or-lose basis. He stated: "The interesting thing is there never has been an occasion where anyone has been willing to hire us on a time basis to represent them in a personal injury case, even where we have advised them that their right to recover is clear, and it's only a question of how much."

recommended more because of what it would save the attorney than because of what it would net the client.

A third source of conflict of interest is the attorney's business and personal needs for funds at certain times. He may, for instance, prefer an early, low settlement in order to meet personal emergencies or to obtain tax benefits.

I wish to stress that I have no evidence that these possible conflicts of interest are frequently realized, nor that the attorneys tend to prefer their own interest over that of their clients. These conflicts are merely potential, and in my opinion are overshadowed by the common interest created by the contingent fee. Apprehension of these possibilities may underlie the lack of confidence between the client and the attorney suggested in the above quotation from Hunting and Neuwirth.

I did observe an absence of claimants during meetings discussing settlements and this might be interpreted, at least by the claimants, along the Hunting and Neuwirth lines as evidence of a distant and possibly exploitative relationship between the attorney and the client. My impression is that convenience and —more important—certain bargaining advantages lead to exclusion of the claimant from settlement negotiations. To anticipate later discussion, the attorney may secure some leverage with the adjuster by depicting the claimant as an unreasonable and unrealistic type who can be barely controlled in his desire to take the case to court, and who can be expected to give his grudging approval only to the very highest offer that the adjuster can squeeze out of his reluctant supervisor.

Feelings of exploitation by one's attorney may also be rooted in a claimant's unrealistic expectations concerning settlements. The delays intrinsic to investigation and negotiation can also produce feelings of exploitation, particularly when the claimant has pressing financial needs.

If the attorneys' relations with their clients were at times strained, on the whole they found it easy to get along with the adjusters. Attorneys generally believed adjusters to be competent in investigation and evaluation, although only a few of them thought that adjusters were "fair" as they understood this term. The highest compliment paid to an adjuster would seem to be that he was realistic. Cooperativeness and preparedness were among the other compliments offered. On the other hand, some attorneys accused adjusters of bad faith bargaining. This accusation referred to the belief that adjusters for some companies were unable to make binding agreements, or that they unjustifiably delayed settlement to increase their bargaining power.

In fact, the adjuster's ability to conclude an agreement is limited. In the companies I worked with, the limitation occurred in different ways. Great Plains and Mid-West put specific dollar limits on the settlements that each adjuster could make without consulting his supervisor. Acme had no such limitations, but the responsibility of the adjuster to his supervisor in fact required much the same degree of consultation. The men were theoretically free to write a check for any amount, but large settlements would be made only with supervisory approval. The necessity to clear an agreement with a supervisor, whether formal as at Great Plains and Mid-West or informal as at Acme, resulted in bargaining power for the insurance company that was very frustrating to some attorneys. An adjuster could come to a tentative agreement with the attorney only to have it rejected by his supervisor, in which case the adjuster could credibly plead that his hands were tied and that a new, lower agreement would have to be reached. Understandably, attorneys sometimes suspected pre-arrangement of this type of event, and believed that the original bargaining had been in bad faith. Sometimes they were right. An ingenious group of men in one small field office frequently "teamed" together, presenting one adjuster as a "supervisor" whose role was exactly to shave marginal amounts from settlements tentatively negotiated between the other and various attorneys. These tactics led to complaints such as the following:

> How can they attempt to negotiate a settlement when many of them come to see you without any authorization to do so? This is one of the first questions that I ask an adjuster: "Are you authorized to negotiate a settlement in this case today, or are you here to pick my mind and de-

termine what is in the file?" If that is the case, then we are talking about pre-trial discovery, which I do not feel is fair.

Paradoxically, in the light of the strong pressures on adjusters to close cases, attorneys frequently perceived adjusters as sources of delay. I find that the following comments overstate the truth, for in the ranks of field claims men and supervisors as well as among home office executives there is great concern for closing files expeditiously. On the other hand, it is true that a front-line worker in a bureaucracy is unable to act as independently and thus as quickly as a single claimant and his adjuster. Cases of any size must be reviewed by supervisors, and very large claims cannot be paid without review at two or more levels. Furthermore, in selected cases delay may well be a tool of considerable power, and on occasions it may well be used consciously to lower the settlement, as these lawyers suggest:

> They're using [delay] as a bargaining tactic, and also the companies are holding onto their money and using it in other areas. They have the investment potential of the funds that they now have as well as the interest it draws while it's in their hands; and for that reason we were informed, we were advised, that it's to their advantage not to dispose of their funds but to hold on to them as long as they possibly can. Not only that, with delay there is more difficulty encountered on trial: plaintiffs die, witnesses get lost. A case suffers from delay while litigators lose interest, and I think the companies take advantage of these factors and take deep consideration of it when they withhold negotiation and settlement of cases until actual trial.

> [Some companies] would approach the case from the standpoint: "We're going to rely on our ability to delay this for three years, to wear down the plaintiff. We're going to rely on our expectation that the plaintiff, when the chips are down, will not want to go into open court and be subjected to the problems that arise there and

rely on every technical defense available and ultimately beat down the settlement to the lowest level." There's an element of this approach in every adjuster's approach. It seems inevitable, but with some it's much less harsh than others.

As with all negotiation patterns, the interaction between the attorney and the adjuster has a large component of common interest. Both parties desire a quick disposal of the claim, and both wish to avoid the costs of litigation. Moreover, the attorney and the adjuster share a knowledge of values of personal injury claims, based on familiarity with large numbers of such claims previously negotiated. They are united as well in their familiarity with the tacit rules of negotiation, and in the knowledge that because future dealings are likely, adherence to these rules can be demanded.

To sum up the attorney's approach to claims, the contingent fee creates an identity of interest with the client that is rather unusual in the practice of law. This close personal interest in the case protects the claimant in dealing with a lower level attorney, with far more effect than a code of ethics. However, reliance on effective professional ethics is still necessary in those instances where a conflict of interest with the client nonetheless develops. Examples are offers by an insurance company to trade high settlements on some cases for lower settlements on others, cases in which accepting a settlement as against trial may be profitable for the attorney and unprofitable for the client, and cases in which settlement at a given time may be differentially favorable to the attorney and his client.

The attorney's interest in the claim is generally opposed to that of the adjuster, but this conflict is modified by a common orientation to values created by intimate knowledge of settlements in similar cases, by the possibility of having to negotiate future cases together, and by a common desire to avoid time-consuming and expensive litigation.

3. Investigation and Evaluation

THIS CHAPTER examines how the parties to a bodily injury claim investigate and evaluate a claim, and the following chapter describes the process of negotiation. The separation of investigation and evaluation from negotiation is analytical and is to a considerable degree artificial. The same activities are often relevant to all of these aspects of settlement. For example, a visit of an adjuster to a claimant for the purpose of taking a statement may be defined as investigative, but the statement and other transactions during the visit will help to form an evaluation; furthermore, the visit provides an opportunity to negotiate and perhaps even to close the claim with an agreed settlement.[1] Problems experienced in negotiation will in turn indicate the direction for

1. The first-call settlement—involving taking a statement, ascertaining expenses, obtaining a release, and delivering a draft in settlement, all during the initial visit with the claimant—is considered by the claims department to be highly desirable in the routine case. It provides the claimant with a prompt and assured payment, enables the adjuster to close the file, and avoids the costs associated with representation by an attorney.

further investigation and will also affect the evaluation of the claim.

Bearing these reservations in mind, the following procedures can be described as primarily investigative.

First Notice

As a general rule, a claim first comes to the attention of the insurance company through notice by the insured, rather than by the claimant.[2] Having experienced an accident, the insured will in the normal course of events telephone his agent—the man who sold him the insurance, and whom he thinks of as representing the company. The agent will notify the company's claims office, again generally by telephone, and a written memorandum of the telephone call will start the claims process. The first step is to verify coverage, to ascertain that the particular driver and vehicle are protected by a valid insurance policy. Claims are then reviewed by supervisory-level personnel to determine whether they are likely to be serious enough to warrant assignment to an adjuster, or whether they may be handled by mail or telephone. At Acme, for example, claims would be assigned to an adjuster if they appeared likely to involve damage to property exceeding $500, or injury to any person, except where there was clear evidence of no liability. The following comments were among those made by the Assistant Manager of an Acme claims office as he made the determination to assign a claim to an adjuster ("outside"), or to handle it by mail ("inside"):

> The insured nicked another car while backing out of a parking space. The claimant asserts $167 property damage, no ailments: inside. . . . An assigned risk did $900 to his own car, injured passengers. He claims Vehicle 2 ran a red light. Set up as outside because you can't tell who ran the light. . . . The insured has $75 damage and says the claimant has none: inside. . . . Assigned risk—these are

2. The insured has a contractual duty promptly to notify the insurance company in the event of an accident. Failure to provide this notice exposes him to possible denial of coverage. In practice, coverage is seldom denied, even though late notice may be quite prejudicial to the company's case.

usually lulus! Hit the claimant when he swerved to avoid a cat. There's nothing more to talk about, injuries all over the place, our driver a junior operator. I hope the claimant is a cat-lover: outside. . . . Our man parked, hit by another car: inside. . . . Backing out of a parking space, scraped rear fender of Vehicle 2: inside. . . . Hit in rear, we owe it. No injuries, '62 Pontiac, a fairly heavy auto. Take a chance and set it up as inside. They will write the fellow and tell him to send in an estimate of damages. Who knows? You can't set up an and assign everything. . . . Patrolman issued a summons to No. 2. Throw it into inside. . . . Damage was $229. Driver 2 turned left in front of insured: inside, on the assumption that it's his fault. You can always guess wrong, but if a guy's going to an attorney he will probably have one by now. . . . Vehicle 2 cut in front causing Vehicle 1 to slide into Vehicle 3. Both claimants have written letters to the insured saying he's at fault, but neither claims injuries and property damage doesn't seem too great, so let it go at inside. . . . Here we guessed wrong, set up as inside and get a summons. Maybe we shouldn't have made it inside. He doesn't tell us what happened. If we'd have read this a little closer we would have set it up for outside. Probably we hit him in the rear. There's no description of the accident. The blanks in the estimate of repairs should have tipped me off. I have to guess at the passenger of the plaintiff; I think she was a passenger in Vehicle No. 2. Set up a claim for Driver 2 as well. . . . Boy on a bicycle collides with a car. Set it up as outside. $100 damage to right front of our car; he must have done a good job on the bike. . . . Insured tried to avoid hitting an animal, ran into a pole. No collision coverage, so we couldn't care less: inside, unless there was property damage, but we'll just let it set. We don't know what kind of pole it was or whose it was. . . . Don't know who the claimant is. The insured just says he ran into the rear of No. 2. Make it outside, because the damage to insured's [*sic*] car is over $100. . . .

The particular adjuster to receive the claim will be determined by such matters as who usually handles the territory involved and who has the skills (and settlement authority) commensurate with the apparent seriousness of the claim. In the ordinary course of events, a single adjuster will handle the claim from this point onward.

Procedures of Investigation

The first notice will usually identify the insured and the potential claimant or claimants, and will give some minimal information concerning the accident. The adjuster will give priority to investigating the claims that appear most serious. His first action is most often to interview the insured and then the potential claimant.[3] In some cases this procedure ends the investigation except for accumulating information on the injury. The story may be such a simple one that further information will not be expected to yield sufficient reward:

> Now I just saw something this morning where at an intersection our insured . . . said, "I did not see the stop sign." There is no investigation necessary here.

> I frankly don't have that much of a real understanding of physical evidence, impacts, measurements and skid marks and this kind of thing. I've never got involved in it and I don't find the time—and I don't think most of us do— to really get involved in that sort of thing. Again, the consensus seems to be, among most adjusters that I know, that in nine out of ten cases most of this is superfluous anyway. The only time you're really going to need this is where you have a real solid liability question and you're playing for big stakes, and these cases don't come up very often. So most of this I tend really to shy away from, and to try to reach a conclusion as quickly as possible.

3. Most of the adjusters followed the practice of interviewing the insured first. A claimant will not grant an interview if he is represented; thus there are many claims in which an interview can be obtained in the days immediately following the accident, but not subsequently. If only one claimant interview can be obtained, adjusters hope to base their questions on the story related by the other side. The insured can be reinterviewed to iron out discrepancies, since he is obligated by his insurance policy to cooperate, whereas the claimant may become unavailable.

The keystone of the standard investigation is the statement, obtained from the insured, the claimant and the witness, and focusing on the occurrence of the accident and the damage suffered. Statements serve two distinct functions: for negotiated settlements, they provide the claims man and his supervisor with material on which to base evaluation, and in the cases that go to trial they freeze the testimony so that the defendant may prepare his case with certain matters taken for granted. A statement is not ordinarily admissible in evidence in litigation, but it can be used to impeach contradictory testimony, showing that what a witness says under oath is different from what he said earlier.[4]

Statements are usually not directly dictated by the interviewee, but are written by the adjuster in a coherent fashion, based on responses to a series of questions. "It is the adjuster's absolute responsibility to take an intangible, incoherent and spotty story and, without changing the contents or the personal idiosyncrasies, convert it into a legible written account that will be clearly understood by even the dullest jury member."[5] The following record of all questions asked during one statement-making session illustrates the procedure.

> Your age?
> Did he [the other driver] claim any injury?
> Your wife's first name? Any children living in the house?
> How many boys? How many girls?
> Who are you employed by? What line of business? Where is it located?
> Your driver's license and registration? How long have you driven? How many miles per year do you drive on the average?
> What day of the week did the accident occur on? What time of day?

4. See Harry B. Otis, "Role of Statements in Claims Investigation," *Insurance Adjuster*, July, 1966, pp. 14–16. A disadvantage of using the statement in evidence is that should the party not admit having given it, the adjuster must testify to its origin, thus acknowledging before the jury the existence of insurance.

5. Norman C. Eddy, "Signed Statements," *Insurance Law Journal* 445:85, 1960, p. 86.

How many lanes were in the road? At that point the road
is straight and level, isn't it?

At five o'clock was it just getting dark? Had you any lights
on? Which? How would you classify visibility: good,
fair, poor? It wasn't raining, was it? How fast were you
going? The passenger was on the right? What was her
name and address? Was anyone wearing seat belts? What
type of gas station [was on the corner]? How far from
the corner was the point of impact? When did you first
see him? That would put you 90 feet from the corner?
What kind of car did he have? Make? Color? You applied your breaks immediately and couldn't stop? What
part of the front of your car was dented?

Did the other driver own and operate the car?

You swerved to the right?

The third car, the witness: Owner? Address? Make?

Where did your car finally stop? You had been in the right
lane and the third car in the left lane?

Any police on the scene?

What happened after you stopped?

What were your injuries? Her injuries? Cut or bruised?

Any medical or hospital treatment required immediately?

Both cars drove away under their own power; no towing?

Did you go to a doctor? Which? The witness you
mentioned?

This example suggests the contents of a typical statement. The
interviewee—claimant, insured, or witness—is decisively identified; his driving skill or lack of it is implied; the accident is
definitely located in time and space; the speed and direction
of both vehicles is estimated; conformity or lack of conformity
to safety laws is stipulated; passengers and witnesses are named
and identified, and their injuries estimated—all in a document
which is carefully protected from hearsay and other impediments
to use in possible litigation. The statement is given evidentiary
value by having the interviewee read it and sign it, usually in
the form: "I have read the above statement of -- pages, and
it is true and correct." In some of the offices, routine statements

are recorded over the telephone. These are not rewritten, and do not need to be signed because the statement-giver's voice is adequate identification.

Statements are the heart of the insurance company's investigation. In some cases, a statement or two may terminate the investigation, particularly under the following conditions: where liability appears to be clear from the statement of the insured; where the claimant's statement indicates a lack of liability on the part of the insured, and there is a witness statement to corroborate it; and in cases in which the injury and the demand appear quite limited. The investigation is most likely to be continued where liability appears to be questionable and where large amounts of money are at stake.

Another source of information utilized in investigation is official documents. In the New York offices, much reliance was placed on the accident report form required to be filed with the State Department of Motor Vehicles, and a photocopy was routinely requested. This material was not available in Pennsylvania, but the Harrisburg area offices had access to police investigatory reports, which were difficult to obtain in New York. In general, these documents covered much the same information as statements. In cases of any significance, a routine search of previous claims is made, using the Index System, a countrywide clearing house for records of personal injury claims.[6] Reference of a claim to the Index System will obtain photocopies of cards representing previous claims made under names similar to that of the claimant. The information contained on the cards is minimal, but more can be obtained by writing the reporting company. The use of the Index System provides some degree of control over the practice of claiming twice for the same injury, and the report of a large number of previous claims may alert the adjuster to the possibility of fraudulent activities such as the simulation of accidents.

The extent of damages requires investigation in any weighty

6. See H. Laurence Ross, "Insurance," in Stanton Wheeler (ed.), *On Record: Files and Dossiers in American Life* (Russell Sage Foundation, 1967; Bernard L. Hines, Jr., "Fake Claims Snagged by Record Reservoir," *Insurance Adjuster*, January, 1970, pp. 28–29.

claim. Receipted bills from physicians and hospitals are furnished by the claimant or his attorney, but the adjuster's investigation will generally include an independent physical examination by a defense physician, and the obtaining of detailed medical and hospital records. At the time of the statement, in the case of an unrepresented claimant, authorizations are obtained for physicians and hospitals to release these records to the insurance company. The company will routinely offer to pay modest fees for the records, and the adjuster will try to coax recalcitrant doctors and hospitals with the suggestion that payment of their bills will be facilitated by his payment of the claim.

An important element of most investigations is an accident diagram, which is usually constructed initially from reports contained in the statements. Where the investigation is to be more than routine, or where physical characteristics of the site would seem to have some bearing on the case, the adjuster will visit the site and take measurements and perhaps photographs for the sake of accuracy of the diagram. Photographs are also used on occasion to verify property damage and injuries.

Basically, the same procedure is followed by the plaintiff's attorney in conducting his own investigation. Negligence specialists frequently contract this work to private investigators, whereas general practitioners on the lower levels do the work themselves. This fact accords with Carlin's general thesis that much of the work of lower level attorneys does not involve strictly legal skills, but work of a more pedestrian order.[7] Some attorneys report that they vary the contingent fee by charging the claimant for part of the investigatory costs.

The attorney's investigation generally takes place at a later date than the company's because of delay in retaining counsel. Such delay may be considerable, as when a claimant attempts dealing directly with the adjuster, retaining counsel only when his case is denied or the adjuster's final offer appears too low. This delay creates a considerable disadvantage for the plaintiff's attorney, as compared with the insurance company, which investigates all cases to some degree immediately upon receiving

7. Jerome E. Carlin, *Lawyers on their Own* (Rutgers University Press, 1962).

notice of an accident. Attorneys thus find that their investigations are often not as good as those of the companies when it comes to determining liability. At a later date it is harder to locate witnesses, and temporary physical evidence such as skid marks has disappeared. On the other hand, the attorney has much better access to medical materials than does the adjuster, and his file is likely to be stronger with respect to damages.

Taking statements, obtaining forms and documents, and occasionally visiting the scene of the accident constitutes the whole of the routine investigation of injury claims on the part of both the adjuster and the attorney. A small minority of claims is investigated further, especially where fraud is suspected, in which case the adjuster's techniques resemble those of a private detective. An example is the situation in which disability is suspected of being exaggerated, and a neighborhood check is conducted:

> It would be mainly in a bad injury in a built-up case where you feel that the medical bills which were submitted were extensive, and you have to evaluate them, so you make a neighborhood check. You check the neighbors about the person's activities, try to ride around the house a couple of times and catch them. I had a case where a guy had a back injury with two or three hundred dollars in medical bills, all various types of treatments. Seemed odd! I rode around the house and caught him fixing a flat tire once. You can't fix a flat tire with a bad back. . . . I walked up to him and said, "Are you so-and-so?" He said, "Yes," and I handed him my card. And his lawyer called me and they dropped the case. That happened once but I have a couple of cases with extensive bills now where I will have to make a neighborhood check to discover the condition of the house, try to find out where she works, check out where she works, try to check on her social activities. Maybe she is a bowler; where does she bowl? Check any league records: if she has a bad back injury she can't have been bowling. Where does she go on vacation? What type of work does she do? You can usually find a neighbor that

doesn't like your claimant and they are glad to squeal if they think the claimant is trying to cheat. They will tell you everything you want to know. Check banks; if she's in debt or back on payments, Retail Credit. If they are in debt they want more money and might build up the case. Check liens, hospital liens. Mainly it's the neighborhood. Kids are the best people to check with because they are the most honest. You can't hold them for anything but you get the information from them.

To emphasize, the neighborhood check is not routine. Most adjusters I interviewed stated that they had never made one. Investigations are tailored in their thoroughness to the risk embodied in the claim. As explained by the president of an adjusters' training school:

Even if there were enough hours in one day to conduct a complete investigation on every assignment, it would be economically unsound to do so. The busy adjuster learns that he must settle in most cases for information adequacy rather than completeness. He obtains sufficient facts to justify, make and act upon his decision. The majority of claims are disposed of without arduous nit-picking over every detail.[8]

On the other hand, when fraud is suspected, investigation will go further yet in the hands of special organizations designed to protect their insurance industry members from criminal exploitation.[9]

Evaluation of Liability

The evaluation of the claim proved to be one of the most difficult subjects to learn about in the course of the study, particularly where the adjusters were concerned. This problem re-

8. Benjamin Horton, "Judging the Merits of Investigation," *Insurance Adjuster*, April, 1969, pp. 60–61.

9. An example is the stock companies' Claims Bureau. See N. Morgan Woods, "Fraudulent Automobile Insurance Claims," *Police*, September-October, 1961, pp. 15–17.

flected the difficulty of the adjusters themselves in describing how they obtained their ideas of value. It is true, as adjuster after adjuster told me, that "every case is different," yet every experienced man, if pressed, could set a dollar value on any given claim. Some of them, no matter how hard pressed, could not explain how they reached the figure. I believe that one source of the problem lies in the reluctance of management and supervisory personnel to provide broad, general rules, through fear that unintelligent application of these rules would result in unrealistic estimates in individual cases. In consequence, the evaluation of claims by adjusters seems to be based on informal information-seeking among first-level supervisors and colleagues with experience. These rough procedures are not inevitable; the attorneys base their evaluations partly upon study of awards given by juries in similar cases in their jurisdictions,[10] and in one claims office a privately compiled record of settlements was circulated by the manager for the use of his adjusters. This apparently rational procedure was not used in any of the other offices, and I think the more typical procedure is described as follows:

> I don't do a strong investigation into individual—into past —claims, but I will take a group of files with similar accidents. I won't come in and pull all those files, but I'll scan over them. I'll talk it over with [my supervisor], I'll talk it over with [a fellow adjuster], I'll talk it over with my brother-in-law with a different company, I'll talk it over with any adjuster I see. If I feel that I'm having a problem with a claim, I'll go up and say, "Gee. I have one here where this fellow . . ." and they'll always say, "Well, I had one similar to it . . ." and I'll get all the information on what other people have done. . . . I go to the Northeastern [Pennsylvania] Claimsmen's Association meeting. We get thirty or forty men up there once a month for a general meeting, a dinner, a discussion. You'll go up to a fellow and you'll, if you have a problem . . . say, "What do you think

10. *Personal Injury Valuation Handbooks* (Published in series by Jury Verdict Research, Inc.).

of this?" and you explain it to the man, a man that you
know has experience.

Evaluation of a claim depends on understandings concerning
the liability of the insured and the injuries and other damages
suffered by the claimant. Just as evaluation is intimately linked
with negotiation and investigation, so the question of liability,
though logically prior, is intimately linked with all other aspects
of evaluation, and the separation made here is analytical.

The formal law of negligence liability, as stated in casebooks
from the opinions of appellate courts, is not easily applied to the
accident at Second and Main. It deals with violation of a duty
of care owed by the insured to the claimant and is based on a
very complex and perplexing model of the "reasonable man,"
in this case the reasonable driver.[11] Moreover, in the vast majority of accidents it would be erroneous to characterize the
driving of either the insured or the claimant as "unreasonable,"
a fact that has gradually altered the law's ideal driver into a
hypercautious, pokey, and infuriating roadway menace. It is
not with this intellectual model, however, that claims men must
deal. In their day-to-day work, the concern with liability is
reduced to the question of whether either or both parties violated the rules of the road as expressed in common traffic laws.
Taking the doctrine of negligence *per se* to an extreme doubt-
less unforeseen by the makers of the formal law, adjusters tend
to define a claim as one of liability or of no liability depending
only on whether a rule was violated, regardless of intention,
knowledge, necessity, and other such qualifications that might
receive sympathetic attention even from a traffic court judge.
Such a determination is far easier than the task proposed in
theory by the formal law of negligence.

To illustrate, if Car A strikes Car B from the rear, the driver
of A is assumed to be liable and B is not. In the ordinary course
of events, particularly where damages are routine, the adjuster
is not concerned with *why* A struck B, or with whether A
violated a duty of care to B, or with whether A was unreasonable or not. These questions are avoided, not only because they

11. See Chapter 1, pp. 13–18.

may be impossible to answer, but also because the fact that A struck B from the rear will satisfy all supervisory levels that a payment is in order, without further explanation. Likewise, in the routine case, the fact that A was emerging from a street governed by a stop sign will justify treating this as a case of liability, without concern for whether the sign was seen or not, whether there was adequate reason for not seeing the sign, etc. In short, in the ordinary case the physical facts of the accident are normally sufficient to allocate liability between the drivers. Inasmuch as the basic physical facts of the accident are easily known—and they are frequently ascertainable from the first notice—the issue of liability is usually relatively easy to dispose of. In fact, many adjusters claim to be able to predict the matter of liability with considerable accuracy from the moment they **receive the notice of the accident. I interpret this as evidence of** the mechanical and superficial way in which liability is determined; and if endless squabbles and large numbers of court cases are to be avoided, mechanical and superficial formulas are a necessity here as elsewhere for the vast bulk of routine cases. The following quotations are illustrative:

> You can almost tell when you get the report of the accident whether or not your insured is responsible, simply on how the accident happened. Right off the bat you know which way you're going to go. My idea is to try to get out and close the case as fast as possible, and if your insured admits making a left turn in front of somebody, or admits hitting somebody in the rear end, you know right away that he was negligent, and the only other question is whether or not the claimant was contributorily negligent.

> A lot of times—I would say 75 per cent of the time—once you get the [first notice] report you can pretty well determine the liability, you see. Because what it is, it's a rear end job: "A car stopped in front of me, I couldn't stop and I hit him." These are probably 20 per cent of your injury claims, but I don't know, I'm speaking off the top of my head on that. Or, "I failed to see the red light," or "I'm new

in the area, the bushes were hiding the stop sign and I went through the stop sign." Now, on something like this— a red light or a stop sign—to determine unquestionable liability on our part, we have to determine first of all any negligence on the other party, and the main issue is speed; and that is pretty rough to determine, unless skid marks speak for themselves or a witness that says, "I don't know how fast the car was coming, but it was going like blazes," in a 25 area, or say the damages themselves.

In other words, although the formal law may put the question of negligence in difficult terms, the law in action finds that the basic diagrammatic facts of the accident are usually sufficient to answer the question. Since negligence lawyers usually act on the same assumptions, this routinization of the matter of liability allows the handling of large numbers of claims with relatively little expense and delay.[12] The price paid is reduction of any meangingful consideration of fault, and the substitution of mechanical presumption for scientifically based investigation. However, no insurance system can undertake the latter on a routine basis, and this is not said in criticism of the adjuster. The main critical bearing of this observation is on the premises of those who believe that some more traditional understanding of fault is meaningful in the automobile insurance system.

Perhaps the classic accident with which the adjuster deals is the rear-end collision. In my sample of files, these formed the basis for almost half of all claims. A strong presumption of liability on the rear driver governs the handling of these situations, and in the routine case very little investigation is made. A typical example concerns an adjuster whose entire knowledge of a claim consisted of the information that the claimant had been driving the forward car in a rear-end collision. As we approached the office of the attorney handling the claim, the adjuster confided, "It's a rear-ender. If I don't pay it, somebody will." In a serious case, the adjuster may search for criticisms of the stop of the forward driver, but these are seldom expected

12. Compare David Sudnow, "Normal Crimes," *Social Problems* 12:255, 1965.

to yield more than minor negotiating points. In one such case I observed, the forward driver on a country road stopped short to avoid running over a mother duck and a row of ducklings filing after her. The adjuster took the position that this driver ought not to have stopped for mere ducks, and thus was contributorily negligent. In general, this kind of claim would not be resisted.

The controlled intersection furnishes another class of clear liability cases. When the claimant is favored by a stop sign, the case is routinely paid; in serious cases an attempt is made to establish that the claimant was speeding. When the claimant is favored by a green light, liability is also assumed. However, these cases require somewhat more care, for frequently both drivers will claim that the control was green when they entered the intersection. Here is the advice of one supervisor in this situation:

> Always cover [in the statement] the color of the light as they approached the intersection. Ninety per cent of the time, the fellow that approaches and the light is green is the guy who goes through the red light. Put yourself in the other guy's position: Suppose they're both approaching an intersection. The light is green for our man and red for the other fellow. Ordinarily, the fellow that has the red light as he approaches is not going to continue right through the red light. Well, what happens to the fellow with the green light as it turns yellow and he figures that he still has time to get through, so he keeps going and it turns red, and he's just about entering the intersection when it turns red and this other fellow's turns green, and he goes through, so he tries to beat the light and hits him. That's usually the way they happen.

Another case in which liability is generally assumed is the left turn in front of oncoming traffic. The best defense would be that the oncoming car was speeding. Similar is the U-turn. Finally, entry into a main highway from a driveway or side road is treated much as an intersection controlled by a stop sign. The principal kind of accident in which liability questions are troublesome is the collision in an uncontrolled intersection. Typically, state laws assign right-of-way to the car on the right and to the car first into the intersection. The former condition gives few problems in investigation, but there is frequently gross conflict of testimony on the latter. The speed of the vehicles is also an issue in this type of accident since it affects liability directly—speeding may constitute negligence—and it also has a bearing on the meaning of the configuration of vehicle damage for the question of who arrived first in the intersection. However, though the questions are more difficult to resolve, the process of routinization appears here as well. It is parodied in the following "suggestion for increasing traffic fatalities":

> In any case in which actual damage results to a vehicle from a collision, let the judge find that the harm was caused by that driver who with the front of his car hit the rear of another car. Since front and rear are vague terms, use the center of the car as a dividing line, so that he who has the damage anywhere forward from the center line of his vehicle is the criminal.[13]

Similar problems are met in other types of accidents. Head-on collisions and side-swipes, for example, involve disputes concerning where on the roadway they took place. For the proclaimed reason of previously established trust, and for the additional reason that it is in the company's interest, adjusters will side with the insured in disputed cases, in the absence of adverse testimony by police or uninvolved bystanders.

The relationship of liability conclusions to accident configurations can be documented statistically. Table 3.1, based on Acme files, compares the opinions of adjusters concerning liability with a rough categorization of accident configurations by coders instructed in the above reasoning. The liability opinions were contained on forms filled out by adjusters when the case was six months old. (Because the forms were occasionally missing, and because a proportion of cases settled before six months, the total

13. Gerhardt Mueller, "How to Increase Traffic Fatalities: A Useful Guide for Modern Legislators and Traffic Courts," *Columbia Law Review* 60:944, 1960, p. 965.

Table 3.1. Relationship between adjuster's opinion of liability and accident configuration

Adjuster's opinion of liability	Accident Characterization												
	1. Rear-end collision, insured behind		*2. One-car*		*3. Intersection, claimant favored*		*4. Miscellaneous, claimant favored*		*5. Rear-end, claimant behind*		*6. Miscellaneous, insured favored*		*7. Miscellaneous, favorability unknown*	
	No. of cases	Per cent	No. of cases	Per cent	No. of cases	Per cent	No. of cases	Per cent	No. of cases	Per cent	No. of cases	Per cent	No. of cases	Per cent
Liable	267	85	51	52	106	77	38	84	7	8	8	6	9	13
Not liable	25	8	23	23	7	5	1	2	73	88	90	64	12	18
Questionable	21	7	24	24	25	18	6	13	3	4	43	30	46	69

number of cases does not equal the full 2,216.) The accident configurations were coded from descriptions and diagrams contained in each file. Although the categorization is gross and based on sometimes flimsy data, the relationships evident in the Table give strong support to the adjusters' claims that the eventual decision as to liability can be predicted from minimal information concerning the accident configuration. Table 3.2 below condenses the material in Table 3.1; the categorization in the heading will be used hereafter in this study as the principal measure of "apparent liability," and the Table testifies to its validity as reflected in the opinions of adjusters.

Table 3.2. Relationship between adjuster's opinion of liability and apparent liability based on accident configuration

	Apparent Liability					
	1–4, Likely		5,6, Unlikely		7, Questionable	
Opinion of liability	No. of cases	Per cent	No. of cases	Per cent	No. of cases	Per cent
Liable	462	78	15	7	9	13
Not liable	56	9	163	73	12	18
Questionable	76	13	46	21	46	69

The taking of a statement provides the adjuster with an opportunity to nail down liability, and some of the questions asked the interviewee are specifically directed to this matter. I never observed an adjuster to misquote or distort a claimant's remarks for this purpose, but the adjuster will be sure to include in the statement materials that he knows to be admissions of contributory negligence, which the unrepresented claimant will very likely not recognize. Here are detailed examples from the interviews:

Well, we have a series of questions that we ask claimants. They don't know the significance of the answers and most of them are truthful, and they will give you the answer, and this many times is not the type of answer or the type of result they would like to get. . . . In regular auto collisions, one of the questions would be: "When you saw the other car for the first time, how far away was the front of your car from the other car? State it in feet, yards, car-lengths, or whichever way you can do this best." And they will often say that they saw the car a pretty good distance away. . . . I often ask things about the obstructions that may have been present between himself and the other car. They'll often come out and say they don't know, that maybe another vehicle parked at the curb, or it may be a high hedge, and they'll come out and say things that are not physically present at that intersection. They say it was wide open, you could see for a great distance, or as I mentioned before I ask them when they saw the other car for the first time and many of them have come out and said, "I didn't see the other car until the collision occurred," and then you ask them why he didn't see the car, and he can't give you an answer.

Two things that get them in the most trouble: One is the statement, "I assumed." "I assumed that he was going to stop." "I assumed that because I had a green light I could proceed on it." These "assuming" statements that they just assumed their right of way, even in uncontrolled intersections where there is no absolute right of way . . . I think this is one big factor. And the other one is people seem to think if they didn't see the other party that it's a help to them, this gives them the excuse to proceed, and they say, "I didn't see them," and many times they did. They may just have gotten a glimpse of the headlight a hundred feet away, but they'll say, "I did not see the other car," and of course immediately the question is, "Why didn't you see it? You didn't see it because you were not looking." . . .

> Another factor is making wild estimates without thinking about it. [My advice is] if they do have to give an estimate, to give a broad range of estimates; instead of saying, "I was going 35 miles an hour," [say] "I was going somewhere between 25 and 40," or do not be tied down for future situations. . . .

Many a claim has lost most or all of its value because an unrepresented claimant has wanted to put material into the record that he erroneously believes exculpates him. The claimant may believe that he should not be blamed for failing to take evasive action to avoid a car that he did not see, but the adjuster knows that the fact of not seeing the hazard is generally taken as an admission of negligence. Likewise, an assumption concerning the behavior of the other driver—"I assumed he would stop!"—may be relied on by the claimant to rationalize his own behavior, but the assumption, no matter how reasonable, may be without legal foundation and hence be interpreted as negligent. In his desire to rationalize his own action, the claimant manages to trap himself into admissions adverse to his cause. Perhaps one of the reasons that represented claimants are found to recover more than unrepresented claimants is that their attorneys' advice not to discuss the accident with anyone protects them from making admissions of this type.

Evaluation of Damages

The discussion of damages in claims adjusting proceeds on two different levels, depending on the seriousness of the case. On the one hand, there is the routine case, most commonly the whiplash or neck sprain, in the discussion of which great emphasis is placed on the cost of medical services as a basis for estimating value. Distinguished from the routine case by the presence of residual impairment and disfigurement is the serious case, which is discussed in a different frame of reference, that of potential value in front of a jury. Routine cases are investigated very superficially, and their evaluation is relatively mechanical and conventional. Serious cases tend to be investigated more deeply, and their evaluation is more subtle and far more generous.

A common indication of a serious case is the presence of scarring. The following report is illustrative:

> It was with a young girl who was 31 years old. She had 118 stitches in her face; of course, she had other stitches in her legs and arms, too, but what they paid on that case, counting the plastic surgery fees and everything else, it came pretty close to the policy limits. Now this is a girl who worked for the Navy Department, and what she did was advertise for the Navy for the WAC's or the WAVE's. She used to go to these recruiting centers and interview young girls. Well, a young girl goes in there and is interested in the WAVE's, they don't want to go in and see somebody who is all scarred up. They want to see a fairly nice-looking person, at least a well-kept person, and scars take away from a person's looks, more or less. It detracts something away from them. And this had quite an effect as far as settlement of the case. It more or less concerned the amount of scar tissue that was on her face. It more or less ruined her advertising for the Navy. Anyway, she's still in the Navy with another job. I know that she did lose that job as far as a recruiting officer.

In addition to scars, a serious case can be marked by amputations and prostheses, the use of braces, limping, impairment of sight or other senses, and similar residuals. Needless to say, death cases are treated as serious cases, but they pose different and generally less perplexing problems than the other serious cases. Moreover, they are generally evaluated at less than cases bearing residual impairment and disfigurement for live people.[14]

The evaluation of the routine case is strongly affected by understandings common to both adjusters and attorneys concerning an appropriate relationship between settlement and the degree of injury as measured by medical bills. This can be termed the

14. There are several reasons for lower evaluation. Among them is the fact that a badly injured person may be better able to appeal to a jury than can his survivors. Furthermore, medical costs are limited in a death case, and the economic loss involved in the death of, say, an infant or an old person may be trivial. Recovery in death cases may also be limited by statute.

formula method of evaluation. The hospital and physicians' bills are totaled, and are multiplied by an arbitrary coefficient—typically from two to five, depending on the practice of the area—to yield an agreeable figure for the intangibles of the case, the pain and suffering and inconvenience. With represented claimants, a figure of three times the medical bills is sometimes described as allocating one third to the lawyer, one third to the physician, and one third to the claimant.

The formula method is by no means always avowed. Its legitimacy in the abstract is frequently challenged by both attorneys and adjusters. Its apparent meaninglessness can be illustrated by comparing hypothetical cases with identical doctor bills, the one being trivial and the other incapacitating, or by citing the absurdity of paying three times the surgeon's bill to compensate for a lost eye. These disavowals, however, are based on cases to which experienced men would never apply the formula method. The method is applied only to injuries that are either trivial or undeterminable, as in the case of the whiplash. Nor is the formula applied blindly. The constant by which the bills are multiplied will vary, and, more significantly, adjusters must satisfy themselves as to the nature of the bills. For instance, X-rays will be dismissed by statements such as: "I'll be damned if I'll pay for your movie pictures." Repeated treatments for sprains will be disallowed as physical therapy rather than medical expense. Here, according to the adjusters, is how it works:

> They call it a rule of thumb; for want of a better term, I'll use that. Three times the medicals plus loss of wages, plus the car damage, plus whatever incidental damages they might have, but the basic charge for increase over actual damage is your medical. If a fellow has a hundred dollars worth of medicals and he pushes hard enough—let's say he's got a hundred dollars worth of medicals and two days lost wages and car damage—before I would let him go to an attorney I would go up to three times the medicals, plus the other expenses, not tripled—now this is on cases of clear liability.

Assuming you're dealing with reasonable specials, assuming that you're dealing with all other factors being equal, (and there's so few cases that fit this) I believe you can use that method, but there has to be so many other factors that are the same. I believe that it's fallible to use it as a god. . . . You cannot use it as a god because it's so—there's so many things wrong with it. For instance, I use it with attorneys where it works to my favor, where you get real small specials, then I'll talk this three times the specials. If he has built-up specials then I tend to play it down. I don't mention it or I don't bring it up because it's grossly wrong. It's useless to use it on some cases, I mean a man's hand is severed or something of this nature. I have a case now where a man's leg was amputated above the knee and he doesn't have any specials. Now here again you do have specials because you're talking about wages for the rest of his life, but if you were talking three times medical, which many times they do, it would be ridiculous. . . . I use it and I don't use it, but I would say that for the average run-of-the-mill case is to have it in the back of your mind and not being tied to it. It can be helpful, especially for a new adjuster who doesn't know where to start. He has no idea where to go. We occasionally mention this to him, but we say, "Don't think this is an authorization or that you can always use this 'cause it will throw you way off in many cases."

A supervisor gives this example of estimating what a claim will cost: [15]

Let's go back to that carpenter that made $200 a week, that had a fractured leg. This was a case of liability. This is all we know at the end of 30 days. We were trying to estimate what his special damages are going to be. A carpenter with a fractured leg is out of work for 16 weeks at $200 a week, unless we can prove or substantiate otherwise, making it about $3,200 in lost earnings. The attorney [estimates a] hospital bill of about $400, medical bill of

15. This is a rather large case to be treated by the formula, and the multiplier applied to the medical bills is somewhat larger than usual.

about $400 estimated and the loss of earnings of $3,200. . . .
Now we can only assume that this fellow is making a good
recovery, a full medical recovery, and after four months
will be back to doing exactly what he was doing prior to
the accident. I would take that $400 medical bill, multiply
it by five, making it $2,000, add on the $3,200 and add
some to take care of any complications and I would probably put $7,500 on this case. . . .

Attorneys sometimes deny that they use the formula method
in any cases that they handle, attributing its use to the adjuster,
and hinting that it indicates a nonprofessional approach.

I had an adjuster practically stand on his head trying to
impress me with the fact that he doesn't use the rule of
thumb, three and a half times expenses, but every time I
looked at his lump offer on the case I came out with this
three and a half times expenses, and this is wrong. I think
they should be taught and impressed with the fact that
you can't analyze a case in that direction.

In amusing contrast is the same accusation directed by an
adjuster against attorneys in his area:

Generally, in this area here, if you talk to an attorney, you
can talk to an attorney until he's blue in the face and he
won't admit that he's, say, four or five times the specials.
He talks the type of injury and things like this, it's true,
but still, when you've got a little claim and he evaluates it
in numbers, he takes medical bills, he multiplies them by
four or five times. Generally, that's what you end up settling for.

In my opinion, both "accusations" are correct. The key to
simple and rapid agreement on the part of attorneys and adjusters is that both sides understand that, in a routine case, a
multiple of medical bills that appear to be in proper relation to
the claimed injury forms a reasonable basis for evaluating the
total claim. The formula method is mechanical and artificial, but
it is efficient as a means of disposing of a large workload of

claims. Moreover, even when some aspects of a claim are unusual, and are specifically taken into account in settlement, the formula method provides a starting place for negotiation. It indicates a general standard with which a specific settlement may be compared, and from which a planned deviation may depart. The elements of general damages are evasive and difficult to measure and, to repeat an old question, who can provide a valid translation of pain, suffering and inconvenience into money? Yet this is the promise made by the law of torts, and it is acknowledged by all parties that these general damages are worth something. Perhaps the wisdom of Solomon could provide the ideal evaluation of every case, but in a situation in which ordinary men, albeit specialists, have to handle large numbers of rather routine claims, the formula method provides a simple, efficient evaluation that does not seem unjust. To a party who denies the validity of this method, the negotiator may reasonably put the question, "If not this, then what?" This is a most difficult question to answer, and in the routine case the effort involved may not be worthwhile.[16]

Discussions of cases labeled serious, primarily on the grounds of residual impairments, appear rather different from discussions

16. The formula method of evaluation, appropriately qualified, is specifically endorsed in the practical literature. Witness the following:

> Most lawyers will seek five to seven times the specials depending, of course, on the amount presented. A good rule of thumb for the claims man when dealing with the claimant directly is one to two times the specials. . . . Lawyers should be offered approximately one to two-and-one-half times the true special damages [Jack R. Artstein, "Analyzing Special Damages," *Insurance Law Journal* 496:261, 1964, p. 265].

In the same vein, compare the following two quotations from the same article:

> The fallacious method of making settlement for 3 or 4 times the 'specials' is expedient in all the derogatory senses of the word [John R. Foutty, "The Evaluation and Settlement of Personal Injury Claims," *Insurance Law Journal* 492:5, 1964, p. 8.].

> Despite the inadequacy of 'rule of thumb' settlements in cases of insured liability a settlement of 2 to 3 times the medical expenses added to the special damages is usually a desirable settlement, and is usually equitable in cases where no permanent partial disability or future medical care is anticipated [Foutty, *op. cit.*, at p. 10].

of routine cases, and I believe that different considerations are operative in evaluation. An important reason why one might expect this to be so is that these are cases which, if not settled, have a realistic chance of being litigated. Routine cases frequently would be worth so little in court that the costs, including the attorney's time, rule out recourse to litigation, except where extrinsic matters such as the parties' bargaining reputations are at stake. The value of routine cases before a jury may thus be considered irrelevant to evaluation for settlement. In contrast, the serious cases can generally be expected to bring a verdict sufficient to justify the expense of litigation, and the trial value or value before a jury becomes a central concern in evaluating such cases for settlement.

The value that a claim might have before a jury usually appears to be considerably in excess of what adjusters ordinarily define as fair, and adjusters tend to blame the differential on such illegitimate considerations as sympathy for the claimant and dislike for the insurance company. However, the relevance of trial value is generally admitted:

> Always in the back of your mind is the question of what would happen if they secure counsel and what would happen if this case were taken to a jury. We do have some experience. If you've been around in claims for a while you eventually will reach the point where a number of cases have gone to trial—just a small number—but you get some experience in what a broken leg for trial is worth; as compared with a broken leg for an older man, you learn there is a difference because children heal better.

As with settlement value generally, there was no systematic procedure for instructing claims men in trial value in any of the offices I studied. "You learn" what various types of injuries and various liability situations may bring, but the tools used by the attorneys, notably the Jury Verdict Reports *(Personal Injury Valuation Handbooks)* for the jurisdiction involved, were seldom used by claims men. It may be for the purpose of keeping evaluations conservative at the level of the adjuster that the companies do not encourage the routine consultation of trial data.

Considerable discretion is needed in interpreting data such as those contained in the Jury Verdict Reports. Settlement value is discounted from jury value according to several considerations, which will be explored below, and an unsophisticated user of jury data might well overevaluate his case.

In evaluating the serious case, a large number of variables are taken into account. Among these are the obvious out-of-pocket costs, along with an allowance for the pain, suffering, and inconvenience of the claimant. In addition, evaluation of the serious injury claim includes attention to aspects of the case that, while formally irrelevant to value, would be expected to exert influence if litigation were in fact undertaken. Among these are the sympathetic or antipathetic characteristics of the parties who might appear: the claimant, the insured, and witnesses. Age, race, sex, and occupation are said to be relevant, as well as more subjective attributes such as the over-all impression of veracity. The reputed skill of the attorneys and the nature of the court in which the case might be brought are also considered. The literature contains several listings of factors that may affect the value of a case before a jury and that hence require attention in evaluating a case for settlement.[17] The following typical statement relates the factors considered by one of the attorneys I interviewed:

> Of course, this is terribly difficult because we are dealing with making a guess as to how a group of 12 people are going to value. It's hard to explain how we go about it. In this office, of course, after we have the file developed to a point where you can make an intelligent analysis of it, what we do in determining what we think the case is worth and what demand to make and so forth, we ordinarily get together and review and file and then we inde-

17. See, among others, Taylor H. Cox, "Some Guides or Factors in Evaluating a Personal Injury Claim," *Insurance Counsel Journal* 25:209, 1958; John C. Elam, "Settlement Procedures," *Insurance Counsel Journal* 28:602, 1961; Wilbur W. Jones, "Evaluation and Settlement of a Personal Injury Damage Claim," *Insurance Law Journal* 440:559, 1959; Patrick Magarick, *Successful Handling of Casualty Claims* (Prentice-Hall, 1955); Raoul D. Magura, "Evaluation and Settlement of Personal Injury Claims," *Insurance Law Journal* 441:639, 1959.

pendently make an appraisal of it, and see how we come
out. . . . You have to look at your client from all points of
view: the type of person that he is, the type of job that he
has, the type of people he meets. A cut on the head which
may leave some scar may be worth practically nothing to
a truck driver and worth a good deal more if your client
is a salesman who has to meet the public or a woman who
runs a beauty and charm school or whatever. I think sometimes the intangible thing—you talk about scars and the
broken leg and how much time is in the hospital and how
much time at home—these things are important. I think,
though, that of equal or maybe of greater importance are
the things that are not quite as easy to observe. The demeanor of your client—whether or not you think if you
went to a jury that the jury would consider the client some
kind of crank; and, unfortunately, at times you find people
with very genuine injuries that you don't think could make
anyone believe it hurts. . . . At times the evaluation of the
case is influenced by the doctors that are involved. I know,
for instance, that if I got a plastic surgery problem and if
Dr. Harding in Harrisburg says it is bad, I know the insurance companies are going to listen, but if you have a
doctor who is not highly regarded, then you have a problem. And some doctors are difficult to work with in court.
Some doctors can minimize a very serious injury before a
jury by giving them a lot of mumbo-jumbo that they don't
understand. . . . Sometimes if you've got an intelligent
client with a decent demeanor who is able to explain to
somebody in a convincing manner how it was and why it
hurts, that's worth more than the doctor's testimony. There
are some people who can live through a perfectly excruci-
ating pain sequence and when they tell you about it, you
don't get the message; even in the office you don't get the
message.

The basis, then, of settlements in serious cases seems on both
sides to be an estimate of the likely recovery of the claimant
before a jury. Although the attorneys go about it more rationally,

both sides come to this estimate by comparing a given case in its many dimensions against other, similar, cases that have gone to trial. However, jury value and settlement value are not the same thing. The jury value is initially discounted by the savings in cost to the claimant by not proceeding to trial. A Harrisburg attorney analyzes it thus:

> Let's say I figure a case is worth $10,000, and I could probably get $10,000 from the jury. I know that first of all my fee to my client is going to have to be higher because I'm going to have to try the case, so we take that and make an adjustment for that right away. We know also that we're going to have to be higher because we're going to have to pay extra witness fees, so I deduct those, and then my client may have to miss work for a couple of days, and we discount that. I know we may have to pay witnesses who will be missing work: I discount that and then I may throw in an additional couple of hundred dollars for just the fact that you put under the heading of the uncertainty of the jury's behavior—and then the resulting sum would be the sum I would be willing to settle for, because what you're really interested in is how much your client is going to walk out of the courtroom with in his pocket, not what headlines he is going to make or what, how big a verdict he's going to get. It's how much is he going to have left after everybody's paid that counts.

Significantly, the company as well as the claimant saves by the negotiated settlement: less time is needed on the part of adjusters and supervisors, and considerable legal fees may be avoided. However, for reasons that will be discussed in the next chapters, it is the claimant who yields a discount for settlement.

The calculation of a likely jury value as a basis from which to negotiate a settlement is certainly more complex and more sensitive to the particular aspects of a given claim than the procedure used in routine cases. It is closer to the formal law's mandate of individualized justice. However, even this procedure is subject to routinization. The attorney's comparison of the claim with "similar" cases appearing in the Jury Verdict Reports is one example of this tendency. Another is furnished by the use of various published formulas, the best-known being the Sindell formula, which is contained in a set of materials sold to negligence attorneys.[18] The Sindell formula allocates 50 per cent of the value of the case to liability considerations, and divides the balance equally according to injury, age of the plaintiff (value correlates negatively), "type" of plaintiff (appearance, intelligence, wealth, etc.), "type" of defendant, and actual loss (special damages). The total number of points or percentages accumulated by a given claim is applied to a figure representing jury verdicts in similar cases to yield a suggested settlement value. Formulas like this are clumsy and give a false impression of precision. They are not in practice nearly as helpful as they might seem at first glance. However, they symbolize the strain toward simple and efficient procedures in the face of a complex and difficult task.

Evaluation of the Represented Claim

Over and above the considerations cited so far, the fact that a claim is represented by an attorney has a direct effect on evaluation. A claim that is handled by an attorney is valued higher, for purposes of negotiation and settlement, than one handled by an unrepresented claimant. Some insurance personnel, to be sure, will deny this, often vehemently as in these words: "Because we happen to have one of the best known negligence attorneys on this case in the United States, to me has no bearing on the value of the case at all." Such statements are, however, very rare among candid adjusters, and seem to be made mainly as public relations or wish-fulfillment gestures. The more common statement is exemplified by: "Let's not say it's worth more. . . . Let's say it's going to cost more. No matter how you slice it, it's more money," or "On the claim where I paid five

18. *The Sindell Negligence Folio* (Lawyers and Judges Publishing Company, n.d.). See also Ben W. Swofford, "Evaluating Damage Claims," *Insurance Law Journal* 412:273, 1957. The Sindell Formula is followed in Daniel G. Baldyga, *How to Settle Your Own Insurance Claim* (Macmillan, 1968).

hundred dollars to the claimant I'd pay seven or seven hundred and fifty to an attorney, which is understood." The increment in value is typically considered to be enough to pay the attorney's fee of one fourth to one third of the settlement, and to produce little or no net benefit to the average claimant: "They're still going to . . . end up getting the same amount I offered them in the first place."

Various reasons are suggested by claims men to account for the superior value of a represented claim. Perhaps most frequently cited is the fact that an attorney brings to the claim the knowledge and the desire to obtain payment for all legally accessible damages. The unrepresented claimant may well be ignorant of his right to payment for pain, suffering, and inconvenience—the general damages in law. He may feel that his right to compensation extends only to "my back pay, my hospital bill paid, my doctor bill paid, and a hundred dollars." In such a case, with liability likely, "You hand him a check right now. You don't argue with him. You don't even discuss it. You say, 'That's very fine, I appreciate it, that's reasonable,' write him a check and leave it with him." In other instances even a knowledgeable claimant will, because of ethical or religious scruples, forego compensation beyond out-of-pocket losses. Considerable numbers of such claimants were reported in the Pennsylvania Dutch area. The nearly universal contingent fee effectively prevents attorneys from relinquishing rights to payment for intangible damages.

Another reason for the increased value of represented cases lies in the degree of control that an attorney can exercise over the appearances of both liability and damages in the claims he represents. As noted earlier, many claimants forfeit recoveries by making statements that can be construed as admissions of contributory negligence, which are signed and placed in the adjuster's file. The represented claimant will not be allowed to give statements to the adjuster, and his testimony in depositions or at trial will be guided by the attorney's advice concerning the implications of language like "I didn't see him until we collided." One claims man who thinks that the ordinary claimant would do better without counsel nonetheless concedes:

Sometimes these contributory negligence angles where I can get a good, strong statement from the claimant, this is enough to turn him down. If I can never get a statement from him I have to begin negotiation without this, and [if] I don't feel that I have a strong enough investigation to warrant a turn-down then I will make a compromise settlement. Now this effect, it works better for the claimant in that he comes out to the advantage he at least gets some payment on the claim.

Some control is also exerted by the attorney over the amount of damages, through increasing within reasonable limits the amount of medical treatment, time lost from work, and similar expenses related to a given injury. As discussed above, special damages serve as the basis for much claims evaluation. An evaluation formula of three times the special damages makes each $100 increment in doctor bills worth an additional $200 in payment for pain, suffering, and inconvenience. Moreover, "lost wages" are recoverable even if the worker has received sick pay for his time off the job. The claimant whose medical bills are paid by Blue Cross and similar coverages can obtain more extensive treatment at little or no cost to him, while increasing the value of his claim by a sizeable multiple of the medical charges. The situation presents a strong temptation to the attorney and claimant to "build" the claim by obtaining unnecessary treatment or staying away from work longer than necessary. Patently unreasonable "building" will not succeed, but it is very difficult for the adjuster to argue, for example, that treatment should have been administered by the family doctor rather than an expensive specialist. Thus, most claims will support a modest amount of "building," and attorneys may take advantage of the opportunity.

To build up his case [the attorney] will tell his people [to say]: "I'm not fighting the Bar on this. I talked to my attorney and he said I might stay home for a few weeks, especially since I get paid salary anyway," to lend credence to the claim that he was so badly hurt that he couldn't go to work. Or else they'll send him down the street to the general practitioner for two or three visits to check on his neck—they'll do that, and then they'll send him to an orthopedist for an examination which will cost us $50; and then, for those headaches that the fellow has been having, they'll send him to a neurologist and that will be another $50; and then to a radiologist. . . . Here we are talking about a case that, if the attorney wasn't there, might have accumulated $50 in medical bills and gone back to work. With the advice of the attorney, he would have stayed away from work and gathered up about $300 to $400 worth of medical bills and a couple of hundred dollars worth of lost pay. So if the attorney is on the case you set your sights a little higher when it comes to reserving a claim.

Another advantage of the attorney comes from the commitments he makes when he agrees to represent a client. The adjuster knows as well as the attorney that a represented case must be paid off in "real money," and not just a token payment:

If we had a claimant in an automobile accident and we went to that claimant and said—let's say he had a $5 medical bill—and we said to him, "We'll give you $10," and he said no. He turns around and gets an attorney, and the attorney begins suit; we cannot go to that attorney and say, "We'll give you $10." So once he gets an attorney we have to go up somewhat.

Moreover, in a case in which an attorney is retained after previous direct negotiation between the claimant and the adjuster, settlement will generally not be possible at a figure that nets the claimant less than the adjuster's last offer:

The attorney has to justify his fee that he charges his client, you see. Originally, whatever I offered the client obviously is out. Whatever consideration the attorney is getting, it would probably have to be at least the basic amount plus the fee. At least that much!

These commitments by the attorney to his client are effective because *both* sides know that the attorney is in trouble with his client if he cannot meet them, and that therefore he cannot accept a negotiated settlement that violates them. The anticipated negotiation strength given by this commitment raises the adjuster's evaluation of the claim.

A related negotiation strength of the attorney comes from his own investment in investigating and processing the case, an investment that is increased in claims that are "bought" from a chaser. As one highly placed executive conceded, "Ambulance-chasing lawyers *must* collect something." Another advises:

> Although the potential settlement value of the injury is not markedly increased by the entrance of an attorney into the picture, the adjuster should realize that he is now dealing with someone who probably has a general idea as to the value of a claim, and further, that an attorney seldom realizes a profit in handling a claim settled for less than $1,000. As this is the case, an offer of payment of the claimant's special damages or a fraction of the mid-point value would not only be an insult to the attorney, but often a bar to further negotiations.[19]

In those situations where claims negotiation is a repeated matter—where an attorney and an adjuster expect to deal with each other in future cases as well as the instant one—it is possible that a higher evaluation may be given to a claim, particularly to one that is marginal. An attorney frustrated in his commitment to his client, or one who is forced to handle a claim at a net loss, may be a bitter and more formidable opponent in future negotiations. If future negotiations are expected, the effect of the previously mentioned factors may thus be strengthened, thereby increasing evaluation. This situation is more likely to occur in smaller communities, where the plaintiff's bar and the adjusting staffs are less numerous and better known to each other.

These considerations lead to a final point with respect to the effect of representation on claims evaluation: the threat by an attorney to go to trial is a credible one. It is much less likely to

19. John R. Foutty, *op. cit.*, p. 14.

be a bluff than is the similar threat by an unrepresented client, who may cool off after a few days, or who may well be cooled off by attorneys when he seeks the necessary representation. The credibility of the trial threat is enhanced as the attorney goes through the preliminary stages—filing of suit papers, taking depositions, pre-trial conference, etc.:

> I think as a claims man you have to appreciate the fact right away that there are more than one set of values for a claim. I think you have to wear two hats, because when you're talking about [a claim with a contributory negligence defense] I think that good business and good ethics dictate that I have to take your word for it if you're my policyholder, but I think that I also have to be practical about the thing, and if it comes to the point where a complaint has been filed and there's a possibility of its going before a court of arbitration or a jury, and our experience with that judge or this lawyer or this county or this particular court has been adverse in the past, I think you have to weigh the monetary value a little bit differently and maybe go ahead and pay 25 or 50 per cent.

In sum, the fact of representation causes an adjuster to evaluate a claim more highly than when it is unrepresented, for the various reasons sketched above. This summary fact requires the qualification that claims are more or less amenable to exploitation by the procedures cited, and attorneys are more or less capable of this exploitation. A claim hampered by admissions of liability by the plaintiff and numbers of adverse witnesses is not likely to be evaluated seriously by an adjuster, regardless of representation. Visible but simple injuries, such as lacerations, are much less amenable to control by an attorney than are more subjective complaints, such as the whiplash injury. The unknown attorney will have less of an effect on evaluation than will the specialist whose desire and ability for trial are known in the claims office, but perhaps he will have more of an effect than the attorney whose ineptness is a known quantity:

> For instance, you have attorneys who may be tax attorneys,

and they happen to pick up a [bodily injury] case around income tax time; and then you have your regular negligence firms that are top-notch plaintiff attorneys. You can go in to this tax attorney, that just simply might have the case because he picked it up, and you know he's not going to try it, or if he does try it he's going to have to get an associate counsel and split the take, so you can negotiate with him on a different level than you can with the top-flight negligence attorney.

Evaluation in Cases of Questionable Liability

Liability is the formal legal basis for any claim, and thus for any payment by an insurance company under a liability policy. A claim without liability is formally a claim without any value at all. Moreover, the common law is clear to the effect that a person is liable or not liable for an injury to others: he cannot be partially liable, even though he may have contributed only one factor to the total complex of factors that produced the injury. Either a driver's contribution to the accident was so small or so distantly related to the injury as to excuse him in the eyes of the law, or else he is fully responsible, despite the fact that his action was not alone sufficient cause for the injury.[20]

In formal law, then, an individual is either liable or not liable for an injury, and the insurance company is therefore responsible either for the total damages or for nothing. However, a claims adjuster seldom is able to proceed in accordance with this model. Questionable liability may not exist in the formal law, but it is the adjuster's daily experience.

A principal source of questionable liability is the uncertainty that is inherent in recreating the past and distant event that is to be evaluated. The automobile accident is an excellent example of this problem, which so preoccupied Jerome Frank.[21]

20. A consequence of this legal arrangement is that several different individuals may find themselves liable for the total damages experienced in a single accident.

21. Jerome Frank, *Courts on Trial* (Princeton University Press, 1949); also, by the same author, *Law and the Modern Mind* (Coward-McCann, 1930).

The experience of an accident is novel, traumatic, and sudden. It is all over within a matter of seconds. The recall of such an event over a long period of time is extraordinarily subject to biases and distortions, unintentional as well as deliberate. Although physical evidence may be of some help in recreating the accident, it is seldom unequivocal. The problems that confound a judge or jury in applying legal definitions of negligence to an accident are present as well for the adjuster. Some cases may be relatively clear-cut: the claimant and the insured say essentially the same things, their version is confirmed by a reliable witness, and it is in conformity with available physical facts such as the pattern of damage to the vehicles, skidmarks, etc. More commonly, recitals of the accident differ and the physical facts are ambiguous. The opposing versions of the accident lead to different liability conclusions, and neither presents a completely convincing case.

This source of questionable liability is related to Frank's critical position of "fact skepticism." Another source is related to the position of "rule skepticism," i.e., doubts as to whether a legal outcome is obtained by a simple-minded and naive application of black-letter laws, be it in the courts or in the situation of negotiation. The adjuster experiences this most clearly in cases of apparent contributory negligence, in which the claimant seems to have contributed significantly to his own injuries. The formal law of most states bars any recovery in this situation. On the matter of contributory negligence, adjusters are profound rule skeptics:

> Well, the law says that contributory negligence is a bar to recovery. If you and I were in an accident and I'm 90 per cent at fault and you were 10 per cent at fault, your 10 per cent is supposed to bar you from recovery. It doesn't any more, because courts and juries by precedent [*sic*] have changed all that.
>
> You can't apply contributory—the law of contributory negligence as it's written—because it's not the law as it operates in the day-to-day operation, as it operates in the courtrooms. It's not the law.

Both factual uncertainty and contributory negligence present serious evaluation problems of a similar kind. In theory, a decision ought to be made—as to which version of the accident is more convincing, or as to whether the claimant's conduct significantly contributed to his own injuries—and one of two consequences should follow: either payment at full value or denial of the claim. A meritorious claim warrants compensation for all damages sustained, and an unmeritorious one warrants no "charity." Acme states its official policy as follows:

> An inherent rule of the Claim Department is that unmerited claims shall be resisted and that the cost of defense shall not affect our decision with respect to the payment of unwarranted claims. Cases which clearly qualify for payment should be paid with the utmost promptness and cheerfulness.[22]

As a matter of experience, departure from the formal law in these situations is virtually universal in the negotiated settlement. The pressures of negotiation and of the organizational situation of the adjuster profoundly affect evaluation and settlement in a manner not predictable from the formal law. In the following pages I shall discuss the effect of questionable liability on claims evaluation. In this discussion I shall follow the practice of most adjusters in treating uncertain negligence and contributory negligence as presenting the same problem.[23]

To be sure, adjusters occasionally speak of questionable liability in a very formalistic manner, citing doctrine and maintaining that the formal rule alone determines their behavior:

> On contributory negligence, if the other party is just 1 per

---

22. *Acme Adjuster's Manual*, p. I-1.
23. The distinction as well as the similarity between the two situations is well expressed by an adjuster as follows:

> A contributory negligence case should be an uncontrolled intersection, two cars approaching at the same time from different directions, and they collide; neither has a stop sign or a stop light. . . . Questionable liability [uncertain negligence] could be possibly where two drivers are approaching the same intersection controlled by . . . a traffic light, and they collide, and each one says that the light was green.

cent negligent, I myself would turn the claim down. Even though the insured is 99 per cent [negligent], if the other party contributed to the loss, then I would prepare myself to defend the insured in a court of law.

Statements like this are most frequently made by adjusters with very little experience. They may be the basis for bargaining, particularly with an unrepresented claimant. They do not describe the behavior of most claims adjusters faced with a determined or represented claimant. More commonly and more realistically one hears:

In New York there is contributory negligence, but there is no comparative negligence. Strictly, there is no comparative negligence, but in effect I think there is.

Pennsylvania is a contributory negligence state, and if you want to be technical, no settlement, compromise or otherwise, should be made with a person whom you think is contributorily negligent. But as a practical matter, on the other hand, you do have situations where our insured is more at fault, in our opinion; therefore you want to try at least to make a settlement and get a release of the claim . . . which is contradictory to your contributory negligence thinking.

Significantly, this pragmatic position is limited to bodily injury claims. Adjusters speak much more formally, and are quick to deny claims with questionable liability, where property damage only is involved. The bulk of cars are covered by collision insurance, which means that the sum at issue in the typical property damage claim is the deductible, commonly only $50 or $100. If a claim is "sewed up" as one of property damage only, as by a signed statement to the effect that no injury was experienced, the adjuster will deny, with the explanation to the claimant being either in terms of the contributory negligence rule, or in terms of an "obligation" to believe the insured when there is a question of his word against that of the claimant.

The pragmatic position in bodily injury claims has two roots: negotiation pressures and organizational pressures. Where bodily injury is involved, a claimant can convincingly threaten that he will obtain representation in the case of denial, and an attorney can credibly claim an intention to take the case to trial and a possibility or probability of winning with damages being computed on the basis of the formal law, i.e., without diminution for questionable liability. It is commonly believed in legal and insurance circles that a case wth enough merit to be put to a jury will generally receive some recovery, and that judges are loath to declare cases insufficient as a matter of law. A plaintiff's attorney comments on the insurance company's risk in litigation:

> They're running the risk of getting to a jury, namely that the court will allow the case to be decided by a jury rather than by them as a matter of law, on facts which are clear. Once it's to a jury, then an insurance company has a serious problem of persuading them that—no matter whether it was total negligence or not—persuading them to deny a badly injured person some compensation.

In any event, a claim that an adjuster believes will be taken to trial will be regarded as destined to incur costs of defense on the order of $500 to $1,000, disregarding any award to the plaintiff. Although these costs are borne by the company and not by the adjuster, claims men are keenly aware of them and cite them as reasons to make payments in cases of questionable liability. Here is an example:

> Now, if I find contributory negligence on a driver, and say his wife is injured; now if she were to sue our driver we would bring in her husband and she can't sue her husband in the state of Pennsylvania. But supposing their damages were $150, and you've got one of those hardheaded guys— I've had them and you know them, too—"It's not the money involved, but the principle, and I'll spend $5,000 to sue you for that $150." Now for us to be present that one day in court and win it for $150 and spend $300 for our attorney, it's not worth it to us. So we will say to this man: "O.K., you file a complaint for your $150. Tell you what I'll do. There's no question that you were contributorily

negligent"—he might not understand a word, may have talked an attorney into handling the case on a daily rate, I don't know—"We'll give you $100 to forget about it." The attorney is glad to get rid of it, he talks his client into it, they take it. We don't owe it. To save money, we pay it.

In my estimation the more important root of the pragmatic approach to questionable liability is organizational pressures. Although negotiation pressures are cited as frequently by the adjusters in explaining their willingness to compromise, the extra costs involved in standing on one's rights would not be felt by them directly, but by the company as a whole. It would be difficult to criticize the behavior of an adjuster who stood on these rights, as by doing so he would be following official company policy: "Millions for defense, but not one cent for tribute." I find the assertion that compromise saves money to be convincing in the usual case, but it also smacks of rationalization for behavior that departs from the rule book but makes the adjuster's life easier.

The principal pressure felt by the adjuster on a day-to-day basis is the pressure to close files. Most claims offices are understaffed, and virtually every adjuster or supervisor I questioned believed the case load to be a heavy one. The necessity to handle one's case load, by closing files, was constantly stressed at supervisory meetings. Moreover, the adjuster with a growing set of files was easy to pick out and admonish. Complaints of delay would come in from claimants and attorneys, and from the regional and home offices if reports were delayed. Failure to close files would be difficult to explain, in contrast to explaining a single settlement figure, particularly since through control of the file—its description of liability and injuries—the adjuster can make a wide range of settlement figures appear reasonable. Moreover, none of the companies I studied make a practice of computing the general level of an adjuster's payments and comparing them to a norm. In short, the pressure to close files is heavy and hard to resist, whereas the pressure to keep payments low is less constant and easier to handle. Since perhaps the first lesson that an adjuster learns in the field is that the quickest way to close a file is to pay it, the organizational pressure to close files provides a strong incentive to allow value to cases of questionable liability:

> The attitude that the upper echelon takes is that they want you to take the word of your insured, if it's just a question of the insured versus the claimant. Well, you're restricted along that narrow line, which means that you have a larger pending list and claimants list. If that situation develops too much, where you have case on case of contributory negligence, and your files are piling up rather than closing out, then I think it's almost psychological that you're going to pay some contributory negligence situations. . . .

The attitude was stated most frankly by an experienced adjuster in a metropolitan area: "At any time I have contributory negligence I would like to pay. . . . I'm closing out contributory negligence cases."

In sum, adjusters generally treat questionable liability in bodily injury claims as a factor to lower their evaluation, but not to extinguish value. There is variation from office to office and from adjuster to adjuster in how this is done. Impressionistically, departure from the formalistic approach seems greatest in the metropolitan offices, and among adjusters who have been employed longest and who are the most legally sophisticated. The new employees, the supervisors, and the more naive men seem more ready to endorse formalism in this matter.

The exact manner in which increasing doubts over liability affect evaluation is hard to ascertain, as claims men themselves find it difficult to explain. Adjusters discuss degrees of questionable liability in two types of language. They may talk about the proportion of liability on the insured, especially in cases involving contributory negligence. They may, alternately, speak of the chances of winning a case if it were litigated in court. The latter sounds more realistic, and avoids the direct refutation of the formal law of contributory negligence that is inherent in the former language, but its realism is compromised by the fact that adjusters seldom spend much time in court, and the estimates of chances of winning seem to have no firm basis in experience or statistics.

Recognizing the crudeness involved in estimating degrees of questionable liability, I shall propose a model of three zones of doubt as to liability, and suggest first that a slight degree of doubt serves merely as a "talking point" and does not affect the adjuster's evaluation; second, moderate doubt as to liability reduces the case to one of "compromise," amounting to at least special damages, but deliberately short of a hypothetical "full value"; and third, where doubt is severe the case becomes one of "nuisance," possibly justifying payment in relation to defense costs rather than in relation to injuries sustained. The relationship between degree of doubt and evaluation is not a simple one-to-one inverse correspondence, as I had suspected at first. Rather, on the one hand, a claim can support some degree of doubtful liability without serious diminution in value, and on the other, even a large degree of doubtful liability may not extinguish a claim completely. The black-and-white, liability-or-not model of the law means very little in the world of the claims man. Most bodily injury claims are of the gray shades of questionable liability and nearly all have some value.

The typical case of slight doubt might be where the insured makes a left turn and collides with a car headed straight through the intersection in the opposite direction. A common charge in this situation is that the claimant driver was exceeding the speed limit. Adjusters tend in practice to have little faith in the ability of this charge to reduce the payment they will have to make. In negotiating the claim they will mention the charge, but "you will use it only as a negotiation tool and not seriously be trying to talk down the value of the case." A claimant's attorney puts it more strongly: "Once you get it [the chance of winning] over 60 per cent it's the same thing as a victory, to my thinking."

A more interesting matter is the situation of moderate doubt, as in the uncontrolled intersection accident; neither driver has a stop sign or a traffic light, and they collide in the middle of the intersection. Several traffic code rules may be relevant to such an accident—priority to the right, priority to the first to enter the intersection, etc.—but the situation is seldom clear-cut in liability terms, and there is almost always a strong likelihood of negligence on the part of both drivers. The formal law could seldom support an evaluation of any amount to claims arising out of the uncontrolled intersection accident, yet few adjusters would decline payment absolutely. To the contrary:

> If I figured it's an intersection accident uncontrolled, and both cars hit the front end in the middle of the intersection, it's a 50–50 proposition and I would then probably offer 50 per cent of what I would if there was dead liability over the case.

Even severe doubt as to liability does not seem to extinguish the value of a claim for most adjusters. Perhaps few would go so far as to say, in the words of one man, "I don't think there is any case that doesn't have some value to it," but statements such as the following are common, and have virtually the same effect:

> I would venture to say that most questionable cases are paid. Some of them aren't, most of them are. . . . You should have 75 per cent chance of winning the cases before you try it, I think—at least 75 per cent!

An attorney in the very conservative Harrisburg area supports this position. Although he contends that the value of a claim "really goes down" as the chances of winning in court drop below 50 per cent, he states:

> I guess the only time that a case drops to zero is where it's quite clear that there's no fault on the part of the potential defendant or defendants, where you don't have any possible liability, where the facts of the accident are clear— that they were caused solely by the negligence of either somebody you can't sue, or the negligence of the claimant. And [these cases] are very hard to find, by the way. Very often you can come up with some sort of an argument that the potential defendant had some degree of fault.

Compromise, then, is the order of the day in cases of questionable liability, understanding always that payment in these cases is a last resort. Moderate or severe degrees of doubt will be used by the claims man to attempt denial of the claim, and often he will succeed. It is only when faced by a determined claimant that the adjuster will make compromise payments. To say that a claim has value despite questionable liability is to say that the adjuster will make some payment rather than allow the claim to go to litigation.

Evaluation for compromise takes several forms. A common way of handling the matter is to diminish the "full value" by a factor corresponding to the doubtfulness of liability. For instance, to many adjusters the uncontrolled intersection accident described above would yield a claim having about half the value of the same injuries experienced in a rear-end collision where liability was unquestioned. The rationale for such a diminution would be that each party was 50 per cent responsible (reasonable, but inconsistent with formal law), or that the company would have a 50 per cent chance of winning the case if it were litigated (in conformity with law, but speculative).

Another basis of compromise evaluation is to allow the claim no more than out-of-pocket costs, or such costs plus the attorney's fee if there is representation. No allowance is made for general damages, and special damages are diminished by deducting recoveries from collateral sources such as sick pay, medical insurance, etc., which are not deductible according to the formal law. A common defense for this mode of compromise is that such an amount usually suffices to prevent litigation. If handled adeptly, the amount necessary to pay out-of-pocket costs can be quite nominal. Consider the following example:

> Where we're getting to almost, let's say a 60–40 basis of negligence, with our insured on the 60 end of it, that being the case, I would probably tell the claimant as we sat down and discussed the settlement—first of all, again, we would lay out his actual bills. There you have to be a little more insistent that actual bills means actual bills. In other words, if he has hospitalization and so forth which has paid his hospital bill, he hasn't lost anything. If he works for an organization which compensates him for part of his lost

wages—for example the Pennsylvania Railroad—he has not lost [his total salary]. Say he makes $100 a week. I think they reimburse their man—the last time I looked, at any rate, it was $10.20 a day, $51.00 a week—so he hasn't lost $100 a week, he's only lost $49; and in fact hasn't lost $49 because Uncle Sam would have taken some of that $100, and so forth. So you reduce what would have been a hundred-dollar payment. Let's say he lost one week, and you reduce what would have been $100 lost wages payment in a case of complete liability to perhaps $35 or $40 because of the contributory negligence on the part of the claimant. Now you also reduce the medical bills and so forth by the amount that has been paid by a hospitalization carrier. You also reduce his property damage figure by any amount paid by a collision carrier, so all you're talking about is his deductible; and you try, at least, to shy away from some of these petty expenses that some people will tack on—bus fare, time spent in the waiting room of the doctor's office, baby-sitters (even though it was the grandmother who doesn't charge them) and so forth. In other words you really shave it down, as it were, to the bone.

Yet a third basis for compromise is an amount less than that which litigation would entail for the company as processing costs—staff time, counsel fees, court costs, witness fees, etc. Such costs are estimated by one company at about $700 per case. This basis for compromise appears reasonable, as any case which can be settled for less than the processing cost, and which would otherwise have a very high likelihood of being litigated, represents a saving for the company.[24]

In any case of questionable liability, even where doubt is slight and the evaluation of the claim is unchanged, the presence of doubt is seized on by the adjuster as a negotiation tool. It can often lower payment, if not value in the sense of the

24. The companies are opposed to giving official approval to this policy for the convincing reason that such a policy, once known to the plaintiffs' bar, would perhaps be likely to stimulate both routine litigation and the presentation of unmeritorious claims.

amount that the adjuster would be willing to pay to avoid litigation.[25] As the following claims man implies, questionable liability can be used to counteract items of questionable damages: or, as the second quotation illustrates, payment in cases of questionable liability can be used (counter to legal ethics) to demand money-saving concessions on unrelated cases:

> Boy, it just is refreshing to have something to talk about, liability-wise, rather than walk in here and know you're dead wrong and there is no question about it. There's not even a discussion about liability, so you are talking damages, and you can go on and on about damages, but if you have something to talk about liability-wise . . . you can keep your conversation sort of hinged on this question that you have and so forth, and you just mitigate the damages as best you can with that question.

> You tend to try to pick [for denial] the ones that you think the attorney might give on and he might not push . . . or you might even swap cases; you might agree that in this case you'll go 50 per cent if such-and-such other case is settled accordingly.

The Routinization of Formal Law

The process of investigation and evaluation of claims for settlement purposes has been repeatedly found to meet a complex and ambiguous mandate with procedures that appear to be rather simplified. On the one hand there are the frequent allusions to the individuality of each case, the large number of factors that have to be investigated and taken into account in evaluation, and the unpredictability of the ultimate judicial machinery in the event of failure to settle. On the other hand, adjusters and their supervisors and claimants and their attorneys find as a matter of daily experience that they can agree on values for the vast majority of bodily injury claims despite the

25. See Philip J. Hermann, *Better Settlements Through Leverage* (Aqueduct Books, 1965).

complexity of the task. Moreover, the adjuster is able to meet the demands of his superiors to investigate, evaluate, negotiate, and settle 30 or 50 claims per month—a task that might seem impossible upon reading the formal law.

The solution to the problem is through simplifications that render the task manageable at the cost of some departure from the treatment of cases on their individual merit. The formal tort law is highly specific, and has been defended against criticism very much on the ground that it produces an individualized justice. It looks closely at the individual accident, delving deep into complex sets of legal duties through such concepts as contributory negligence, proximate cause, last clear chance, etc. It also looks closely at the specific injury, recognizing that a particular injury may mean very different things to people of various ages, stations in life, professions, sensitivity to pain, etc. This specificity is what makes the task of evaluation, investigation, and negotiation appear so complex and demanding. Indeed, when it is done with an attempt at scientific precision, the task of deciding cause and attributing responsibility can be overwhelming. The Case Studies of Traffic Accidents at Northwestern University investigated, in a three-year period and at a cost of more than $300,000, fewer accidents than many claims adjusters handle in a month.[26] As in that study, such deep investigation may be warranted for some purposes; it would certainly give a more valid basis for attributing liability than does the typical claims man's investigation. However, one could not run a reasonably efficient insurance system with the use of such time-consuming and expensive techniques as were used for that study. Adjustment of insurance claims compromises the legal mandate for individualized treatment with the need of a bureaucratic system for efficient processing of cases.

This compromise can be observed at many points in the processes of investigation and evaluation. Investigation is vastly simplified, for instance, by presumptions as to liability based on the physical facts of the accident. Accidents are thus seldom individualized to an insurance adjuster or a claims attorney.

26. See Chapter 6, footnote 23.

Rather, they are rear-enders, red-light cases, stop sign cases, and the like, and the placement of an accident into one of these categories ordinarily satisfies the requirements for investigation of liability. An injury situation that can qualify a claim as a "big case" may receive something of the individualized treatment envisaged by appellate courts. Otherwise, and most commonly, claims people on both sides of the fence see an injury fundamentally as a collection of medical bills. Similarly, evaluation is frequently a matter of merely applying the locally accepted formula multiplier to injury as measured by bills, all disclaimers to the contrary, and considerations of questionable liability merely add some mechanical qualifications to formulas established for full liability.

These observations are not meant as criticism of the good faith of the insurance industry or other parties associated in the handling of claims. Rather they are meant to put claims handling into proper context; to show that here as elsewhere—for example in handling pleas to criminal charges, or in making decisions as to whether a mental condition merits institutional commitment —a large-scale society proceeds by routinizing and simplifying inherently complex and difficult procedures. This is how the work of the world is done. This is the law, as it is experienced by its clients rather than its philosophers. Perhaps in the light of some kinds of legal philosophy it is bad law. In my opinion, such legal philosophy has lost contact with the reality of modern society. Again in my opinion, in addition to—indeed, as a precondition for—justice and equity as standards for good law, we must assume the criteria of practicability and feasibility.

4. Negotiation

The investigation and evaluation of bodily injury liability claims proceeds with the expectation that these claims will terminate not in court but in a negotiated settlement. In fact, better than 19 in 20 claims are disposed of informally through negotiation. The spirit of negotiation thus pervades the entire claims-handling process, and its tactics are empirically intertwined with the tasks of investigation and evaluation. However, negotiation can be distinguished analytically for the purpose of exploring its rules and tactics, and for delineating its relationship to the rest of the claims-settlement process. This chapter describes the negotiation of bodily injury claims. It offers generalizations that may be applicable as well to many other areas, such as business relations, labor-management relations, and international relations, where negotiation is an important mechanism for resolving differences among men.

Negotiation vs. Adjudication

"Negotiation is a process in which explicit proposals are put forward ostensibly for the purpose of reaching agreement on an exchange or on the realization of a common interest where conflicting interests are present." [1] The exchange of proposals is, of course, supplemented by arguments designed to rationalize and to strengthen or weaken the proposals, but the fundamental move in the game of negotiation remains the offer. The recipient of an offer is then faced with a continual threefold choice: to accept the offer, to accept no agreement, or to continue negotiation.[2] The final outcome of negotiation is thus either an agreement based on an offer and an acceptance, or no agreement, based on the inability of either side to make an offer that is acceptable to the other. Negotiation situations may be divided roughly into three major types depending on the consequences of no agreement.

One type of negotiation occurs in situations where no agreement simply implies a new and different negotiation. Here, opportunities to negotiate an agreement are relatively numerous and competitive. The purchase and sale of a house or a car exemplify this type of negotiation, where each side can assume the availability of many alternative bargaining partners should a given negotiation fail. The parties will reach an agreement if they are persuaded that a particular offer is likely to be at least as attractive as what they might expect from other opportunities to negotiate. The limiting case here is the totally free market where every negotiation may be expected to have the same outcome. It is likely that negotiations in this category are fragile—that they frequently come to no agreement—but the adverse consequences of no agreement are minor. The main determinants of who bargains with whom are the accidents of time and place: the person who happens to need a five-year-old sedan bargains with a resident of the same city who happens to have one for sale at the time. As the item in question becomes more

---

1. Fred Charles Iklé, *How Nations Negotiate* (Harper & Row, 1964), pp. 3–4.
2. Iklé, *op. cit.*

differentiated and specialized, the negotiation comes to resemble that of the second or third categories.

In the second class of negotiations, the consequence of no agreement may be disorderly.[3] In the extreme, the issue concerns a unique matter that must be disposed of either by agreement or by a fight—the disorderly alternative. Many kinds of international relations exemplify this case: Poland is to be partitioned, either at the bargaining table or on the battlefield. Industrial relations can be similar when the alternative to a contract is a disruptive and disorderly strike. In this case, the negotiated agreement enjoys considerable advantages over the disorderly alternative. Relative benefits include not only costs in time and money, but such matters as mutual regard, trust, and even mutual survival.

In the third class, the result of no agreement may be the determination of the issue by a formal and orderly procedure. This case is exemplified by legal claims of all varieties, because the parties can take an unresolved case to court for a formal adjudication. The negotiated settlement may be preferred for a variety of reasons, chief of which is the cost in time and money of resort to the formal alternative. In addition, the relative informality of negotiation may appear as an advantage for the parties. Negotiation not only costs less than adjudication, it uses different techniques and allows the application of different talents. Negotiation may thus be preferred by one or even both parties because they believe that they can gain something through informality. For example, they may have "false counters," maneuvers that they believe likely to be ineffective or deficient in formal procedure but possibly effective in negotiation. The informal process may also permit outcomes that are

3. Where the alternative mode of dispute resolution is disorderly or formal, negotiation may continue as a substratum even while the alternative is in process. Bargaining goes on during war, a strike, or a trial, albeit under changed conditions. It is only when the alternative procedure leads to an irreversible outcome—e.g., destruction of the enemy, or a final judgment—that negotiation must cease. Thus, many tried claims are appealed chiefly for the purpose of continuing negotiation. Negotiation under the condition of the alternative does lose much of its cost advantage, but it retains some of its secondary advantages, such as the ability to produce compromise where the alternative permits no such outcome.

unavailable in the formal process—e.g., compromise, as against an all-or-none determination of rights—yet which are preferred by both parties over the outcomes possible using the formal procedure.[4]

The negotiation of bodily injury claims falls into this last category. The negotiators are in the position of bilateral monopoly—the claimant cannot find another insurance company to be interested in his claim should he not like the offer, and the company must deal with the particular claimant, no matter how much they would prefer someone else. However, the failure to reach a negotiated settlement offers either side the opportunity to put the case into litigation. Economy in time and money is clearly a major reason for both sides to prefer the negotiated settlement. A full-scale common-law jury trial is never trivial, and it can be enormously expensive. A routine case is apt to cost each party several hundred dollars more than a negotiated settlement. The costs involved are only in part those of the courtroom—court costs, jury fees, document fees, and the fee of a trial attorney. Also important are the costs of preparation, including depositions, special investigations, exhibits, and the time of legal and paralegal personnel who must oversee and coordinate these efforts. Since these expenses are not recoverable from the opponent even if one wins the case there is a strong incentive to avoid litigation and to prefer a negotiated settlement. The analysis of the Acme files showed the average cost of defense legal fees in tried cases to be $740, compared with an average fee of $221 in all other cases where the plaintiff was represented, and only $3 where the plaintiff was unrepresented. The fees of defense physicians and other direct processing costs totaled $105 in tried cases, $72 in other represented cases, and

4. Most of the literature on bargaining in a legal context has reference to the guilty plea in criminal law. See Donald J. Newman, "Pleading Guilty for Considerations: A Study of Bargain Justice," *Journal of Criminal Law, Criminology and Police Science*, 46:780, 1956; Donald J. Newman, *Conviction* (Little, Brown, 1966); Abraham S. Blumberg, *Criminal Justice* (Quadrangle Books, 1967); Arthur Lewis Wood, *Criminal Lawyer* (College and University Press, 1967). A colleague has suggested that improvements in the formal process—increased opportunities for bail, better prison conditions, the decline of the death penalty, etc.—may be subverting the established informal process.

$4 in unrepresented cases. Also involved in trial are large un-
measured internal costs, including the salaries of adjusters and
other staff for extended periods of time.

There is in addition to monetary cost considerable delay involved in adjudication. The amount of delay involved in a civil
suit for bodily injuries can run from a few months in some fortunate jurisdictions to several years in most major metropolitan
areas.[5] Delay is transparently uneconomical to the ordinary
plaintiff, who must do without any compensation until the end
of the trial, and whose living expenses may be increased while
earning power is decreased as a result of injuries sustained. It
has been argued that, to the contrary, the average insurance
company profits from delay. These arguments are repeatedly and
consistently denied by insurance management,[6] and the preoc-
cupation of adjusters with disposing of cases quickly indicates
that, whatever the economic effect of delay on the company as
a whole, the men who control the cases ordinarily regard it as a
nuisance and strive to eliminate it. On the other hand, delay is
certainly more costly to the usual claimant than it is to the company, and it tends to make a negotiated disposition compara-
tively more attractive to the claimant.

The informality of negotiation may be regarded as an advantage to both sides over trial, considerations of cost aside. From
the viewpoint of the claimant, the formal law may appear very
favorable to the insurance company, particularly in light of the
contributory negligence rule which denies all payment to a
plaintiff who has contributed in any significant way to the accident. In fact, it would seem that very few multi-car accidents
occur without some "error" on the part of all parties, and in
theory it would seem that trial ought to yield very few plaintiffs'
awards. Though that is not actually what happens, the claimant
anticipating trial has in mind the definite possibility that his
jury will take judge's instructions regarding contributory negli-

<hr>

5. See, for instance, Hans Zeisel, Harry Kalven, Jr., and Bernard Buchholz, *Delay in the Court* (Little, Brown, 1959).

6. See John C. Phillips, "Insurance Companies are Not Responsible for
Court Congestion," *Insurance Counsel Journal* 33:426, 1966.

gence at face value and therefore render a verdict for the defendant.

From the viewpoint of the insurance company, the presence of a jury as a matter of right in most bodily injury claims makes the formal law seem a claimant's law. In most cases, contributory negligence is a jury question, and defendants rightly feel that juries hesitate to leave an injured person with no compensation whatever. Moreover, along with the fact that juries' sympathies tend to be with injured people is the fact that their discretion in making awards is very large, indeed. Pain and suffering constitute legitimate damages, and these can be and have been evaluated in the hundreds of thousands of dollars (all tax-free to the plaintiff, on the theory that these are reparations for what has been taken from him). To be sure, awards that are "excessive" can be reviewed, at additional cost for appeal, but few defendants probably agree with the courts' ideas concerning the reasonableness of general damages.

In this situation, where the formal law threatens the plaintiff with the possibility of no award, and the jury system threatens the defendant with a judgment even in the absence of formal liability, negotiation offers the advantage of permitting compromise. The claimant can eliminate the chance of no award and the defendant can eliminate the possibility of a "runaway" jury verdict by a compromise that violates the letter of the formal law but accords with the spirit of negotiation.[7]

The advantages of negotiation over adjudication in terms of lower cost and the possibility of compromise are apparent in the fact that more than 95 per cent of all bodily injury claims made against insured automobile drivers are settled by negotiation. Even among those claims represented by an attorney and accompanied by formal suit papers, the majority result in negotiated settlements. The outcomes of these claims are affected

7. In seeking compromise, the parties are behaving in accord with game theory's minimax principle. The strategy of negotiation as against trial has the best worst outcome, but it also has a less favorable best outcome. Thus, the claimant avoids the possibility of a zero outcome but gives up the possibility of a runaway verdict. Most claimants seem to prefer this strategy, but in certain circumstances this is not true. See the discussion of trial in Chapter 5.

by the special features of negotiation—its rules and tactics—which are the subject of this chapter.

Some Dimensions of Negotiation

The form of a negotiation may well be affected by the peculiarities of the situation in which it is carried out. In this section bodily injury negotiation is placed on several dimensions that are likely to shape its form, as compared with other kinds of negotiation. Some differences are noted between negotiation with an unrepresented claimant and negotiation with a plaintiff's attorney.

A first consideration is the number of parties involved. Regardless of representation, bodily injury negotiation is generally (though not always) a simple, two-party affair, even though more than two cars may have been involved in a given accident. In the latter case there is much less coordination than one might expect in the handling of related claims by different insurance companies, and each claim tends to be negotiated independently. An adjuster will usually request and obtain a contribution in a settlement involving a joint tortfeasor,[8] but his negotiations generally involve only minimal consultation with the latter.

A second concern is the balance of power between the negotiating parties. This is substantially different in represented and unrepresented claims. Dealings between two parties, one of whom is completely powerless, could not meaningfully be called negotiation, and even an unrepresented claimant possesses power through his ability to secure an attorney and file suit in the event that he is dissatisfied with his experience with the adjuster. However, as noted in Chapter 3, many unrepresented claimants are naive; they have only vague knowledge concerning their rights to recover, and they are unfamiliar with the rules and tactics of negotiation. The balance of power is more

8. The formal law provides that when an injury is inflicted by two or more people acting together, each is "jointly and severally" liable for the entire damages, and in ordinary circumstances one of them having paid the damages may not demand a contribution from the others. This is another instance of the departure of the law in action from the formal law. William L. Prosser, *Torts* (Foundation Press, 1964), at 258, 274.

equal when the adjuster deals with a plaintiff's attorney or with the rare plaintiff who is personally knowledgeable and skilled concerning the nature of his rights and the techniques of negotiation. Overall, I would guess that the combination of represented claimants and sophisticated claimants adds up to less than half of the total number of claimants, and that the power balance generally favors the insurance company.

Third, the number and clarity of issues may affect the nature of negotiation. A multiplicity of complex issues may permit or favor integrative bargaining, whereas a single clear issue usually permits only distributive bargaining in which the gain of one party is the loss of the other.[9] Negotiating a labor contract with a multiplicity of issues may permit the exchange of union recognition—perhaps crucial to the union—for a lesser increase in the hourly wage—which may be crucial to the company. Each side then feels that it has lost relatively little and gained relatively much. Bodily injury negotiation generally allows no such trade-offs. The only matter at issue is the amount to be paid for the release, and what the claimant gains the company must lose.

A fourth factor is time-orientation. Some negotiations, like those over a labor contract, adjust conditions for the future. Bodily injury negotiation is almost entirely concerned with the past, thus ruling out many types of threats and promises as effective negotiating tools. For example, although employees can threaten to change their work patterns, it is difficult to threaten the opponent in bodily negotiation with a possible change in the manner of occurrence of the accident.

A fifth and related factor is the continuity of negotiations. Relations between countries, for instance, continue over time, and mutual attitudes and bargaining reputations have effects on future installments in the relationships. Bodily injury negotiation is generally a one-time affair, particularly in urban areas where reputations of individuals and even of companies are slow to

---

9. See Richard W. Walton and Robert B. McKersie, *A Behavioral Theory of Labor Negotiations* (McGraw-Hill, 1966). Distributive bargaining concerns the division between the negotiators of resources with a fixed utility. Integrative bargaining takes advantage of the fact that the utility of various resources may be different for the different negotiators. Thus, by appropriate trades, the total utility of all concerned may be increased.

spread. There is relatively little to be gained or lost in the way of a reputation through the use and display of integrity or determination in this situation. The firmness of a commitment, for example one to go to trial, does not return as great rewards in bodily injury claims negotiation as where bargaining continues over time.

Finally, there is the previously mentioned factor of available alternatives in the event of failure of negotiation. In some negotiations, the outcome of failure is merely another negotiation. In others, there is a costly and disorderly alternative, such as war. In others, including the bargaining over criminal charges as well as bodily injury negotiation, there is the costly and formal alternative of litigation and adjudication by a court.

Comparison of bodily injury claims negotiation with other types of negotiation on these dimensions indicates that the former may be a particularly simple and rudimentary form of bargaining. The number of parties and issues is minimal, and there is relatively little interrelationship between one negotiated agreement and another. The balance of power is often one-sided, and agreements are retrospective rather than prospective in orientation. The bargaining is entirely distributive. Finally, the consequences of failure, although not trivial, are not catastrophic, so the achievement of a bargain is unheroic. The simplicity of the personal injury negotiation suggests that the rules and tactics observed here may be very basic. There is little material here that is specialized and applicable only to specific situations. Therefore, though bodily injury negotiation may strike the observer as simple, inelegant, and unimaginative, it may afford an opportunity to examine some very elementary and universal aspects of negotiation.

The Role of Expected Value in Litigation

A necessary but not sufficient condition for a negotiated agreement is that there be a range of values that all parties prefer over no agreement. This range may be defined by the overlap of the parties' resistance points, which are the points of indifference of each party between a settlement and no agreement.[10] Taking for example a buyer and a seller, the buyer's resistance point is the maximum he would be willing to pay to acquire the commodity. The seller's resistance point is the least he would accept. Where these points overlap—where the buyer would be willing to pay at least as much as or more than the seller would minimally accept—there exists a settlement range or contract zone, and a negotiated agreement is possible.

A party's resistance point is strongly dependent on his perception of the costs to him of the no–agreement alternative. In negotiating settlements of serious injury claims, this alternative is the courtroom trial, which is, as mentioned before, costly to both sides. The resistance point for each party is thus a function of his expectations of value in litigation—the amount that a jury might give, modified by the chance of recovery—and of his expectations concerning direct and indirect processing costs.[11] If each party's assessment of the likely jury award and chance of recovery is the same, a settlement range equal to the combined processing costs of both sides is logically implied. Expected value in litigation is based on understandings concerning the facts of liability and damages. Where the parties' perceptions of these facts are significantly different, there may not be a settlement range. Where there is a convergence of expectations concerning value in litigation, the settlement range will be centered on the point of convergence, and will have an extent corresponding to the combined processing costs. Figure 4.1 diagrams a hypothetical settlement range where the parties' expectations of value in litigation are reasonably close.

10. The concepts of "resistance point" and "target" are borrowed from Walton and McKersie, *op. cit.*

11. Realistically, some other considerations are involved. The negotiator may be concerned with his bargaining reputation as it will affect future negotiations, causing some preference for trial, and this may affect his resistance point. Also, the utility of money is not a straight-line function— the certainty of a small award may be preferred to a mathematically equivalent gamble for a large award—and thus the resistance point may not be strictly equal to the mathematic expectation of value in litigation. Nonrational factors, e.g., pride in negotiation skill, may also be present and affect the resistance point.

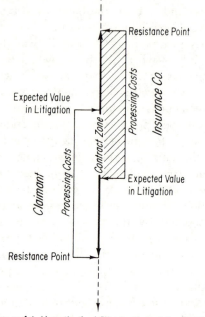

Figure 4.1 Hypothetical Illustration of the Settlement Range or Contract Zone.

The expected value in litigation is thus the most important factor influencing the general level of settlement for a serious bodily injury claim. Particularly in the early stages of negotiation, the goals of each party center on manipulating the expectations of the other concerning this matter.

The most effective strategy for the claimant is to manage the appearance of both liability and injury. First, information is generally withheld, and is released only when it can support but not limit the strength of the case. An adjuster advises:

> If you want to get the last dime . . . you begin by not cooperating with the insurance company, so they have no information to use against you. You don't give them a statement; you don't sign consent forms so that medical information can be obtained early in the picture; you

don't consent to a medical examination, etc.; general non-cooperation.

The commonly accepted paper indications of damage should be maximized. Special damages can be accumulated in the following manner:

> I have a doctor that will, at your request, X-ray every bone in your body, and he always renders a bill that's about $200 for all these X-rays, and his report is always the same— I could dictate it myself. It goes along and everything is negative, and then he puts a long page of explanation after that as to why the X-rays being negative doesn't prove anything and doesn't rule out soft-tissue damage, etc. And then the doctor that works with this X-ray may charge $100 for the first examination, which is a thorough examination to determine what is wrong with you, and then $15 to $25 for a treatment and the treatments average three to five per week. You can see that with a very simple whiplash injury you suddenly have a thousand or two thousand dollars' worth of bills.

Another adjuster adds:

> If I was a claimant—I mean if I was injured in an automobile accident—I'm sure I wouldn't go to work the next day, not because I would want to cheat anybody, but if I didn't feel like working and I'm going to be paid for it anyhow, why should I work?

Liability must also be managed, and damaging admissions must be avoided:

> There are certain key words of negligence in every state. "I didn't see the other fellow," in Pennsylvania that's the magic words. . . . When you have ice, a fall on the sidewalk, you have got to say there were hills and ridges, in Pennsylvania. You've just got to! . . . "I didn't see the other person," is really the biggest thing of all. I think a lot of claims adjusters sometimes cheat people by being a psy-

chologist and asking a question in a correct way to elicit a different answer. . . . In Pennsylvania you are supposed to be looking around to see where you are going, and having your car under control at all times, and therefore an admission that you never saw the other vehicle shows that you are not paying attention, and are therefore negligent. . . . and mostly it's not true. They did, but they don't want to admit it because to the average person seeing the other car seems to equate itself with, "I could have done something to avoid it." That's not true. . . . Most often this is true: you are at an intersection and you do look around a bit and there's the car right on top of you, and what can you do? But for some reason people, if you ask that question right, nine times out of ten you will elicit this response.

In response to these manipulations by the claimant, the insurance company can obtain a defendant's medical examination that will convert the issue of damages into a battle between the experts, thus spoiling the claimant's game. The company can further cite testimony of possible witnesses—real or imaginary —who may counter the claimant's version of liability.

Each party's approach to negotiation is conditioned not only by his resistance point, but also by his target—a point more favorable to him, which he believes to be a possible point of agreement, the best that can be hoped for. A party's target corresponds with his estimate of the opponent's resistance point. The strategies used to affect the opponent's expectations of value in litigation are relevant to both target and resistance point. If the case is redefined as potentially more costly in litigation, this redefinition should affect the resistance points of both parties directly, moving them upward. The adjuster should be willing to pay more in settlement than previously and should also expect the claimant to insist on more. Thus, his target is raised. If, on the other hand, a claimant happens to disclose a weakness in his case the adjuster will probably lower both his target and resistance point. However, the two points do not always vary together. An adjuster may have estimated the value of a claim in court at $1,000, and set his resistance point at $1,500, with a target at $500. Should the claimant indicate that he is thinking in terms of a $400 settlement, the adjuster may lower his target to $300 without changing his resistance point.

Some General Rules of Negotiation

The following rules are derived from reading the bargaining literature and observing adjusters negotiating with attorneys. They are proposed as descriptions of the understandings that guide skilled negotiators when dealing with other skilled negotiators. Failure of either party to follow these rules may result in a breakdown of the negotiations, even though there may be a settlement range within which the parties could have reached agreement.

1. Yield from an initial demand. Stated conversely, the rule is to make an initial demand that is well in excess of one's resistance point. Yielding was noted in virtually all negotiations that my students and I observed between adjusters and attorneys. This rule makes understandable the fact reported by the Michigan Study that 63 per cent of all first offers by adjusters were for three quarters or less of the economic loss, and that two thirds of first offers were for less than half what the lawyer demanded.[12]

The general bargaining literature cites an apparent exception to this rule: the Boulwareism technique (named after an officer of the General Electric Company), whereby a single offer is made and rigidly adhered to.[13] This was practically never attempted between the "professionals" we observed, but it occurred on occasions when adjusters negotiated with unrepresented claimants. Boulwareism does not seem to fit the definition of negotiation, since no exchange of proposals is involved, and it may well be considered a different "game"—called "take-it-or-leave-it." It

12. Alfred F. Conard, James N. Morgan, Robert W. Pratt, Jr., Charles E. Voltz, and Robert L. Bombaugh, *Automobile Accident Costs and Payments: Studies in the Economics of Injury Reparation* (University of Michigan Press, 1964), pp. 203, 209.

13. Carl M. Stevens, *Strategy and Collective Bargaining Negotiation* (McGraw-Hill, 1963), pp. 34–37.

could conceivably work among "professionals" only where the side employing it could build a reputation for deviant bargaining with the other side. Otherwise, the technique would fail and the negotiation would break down because of the opponent's disbelief. Because automobile claims negotiation infrequently involves the same combination of adjusters and attorneys, a bargaining reputation is difficult to obtain. The general rule of yielding is followed invariably among negotiators of automobile bodily injury claims.

2. *Balance concessions.* Concessions by one party generally require concessions by the other, although the amount need not be similar. Indeed, the amount of a concession will communicate to the other party how readily future concessions will be given. For this reason, concessions are carefully measured. A negotiator planning for a possible retreat from an initial demand of $10,000 to a final demand of $2,500 will not make a first concession of, say, $7,000, because that would leave him virtually no room for balancing concessions in the event the negotiation should be protracted.

My observations showed that negotiation moves were quite generally balanced, and that claimants yielded larger sums than did the insurance companies. Thus, the claimant's initial demand was often considerably farther from the final outcome than was the company's offer. A failure to reciprocate a concession was treated as an invitation to trial, and the granting of an unreciprocated concession (i.e., making two concessions in a row) was interpreted as a sign of extreme weakness.

3. *Retractions may not be made.* It is very difficult to make a conditional proposal in negotiation. Even a carefully guarded and qualified offer—for example, one with a time limit on it— is hard to retract. The offer exposes the fact that the party's resistance point is not thereby exceeded, and in practice the opponent will regard any offer as binding. This rule may be tested in some more complex types of negotiation, but I never saw a successful retraction in the course of my observations.

4. *Bargain in good faith.* This is a most general rule, though the concept of good faith is difficult to define. The term has somewhat the same place in negotiation that "due process" has

in litigation. To lack good faith is to subvert negotiation, and to perpetrate a fraud. The good faith negotiator must want to reach an agreement, and must be willing to follow the rules in obtaining the agreement. The bad faith negotiator uses the exchange of proposals to gain time, to obtain information to destroy his opponent's case in litigation, or for other reasons apart from the ostensible one of reaching an agreed settlement.

These rules create the familiar pattern of high demands and low offers, the distance between them diminishing with the passage of time in a reciprocated fashion. At some point it may become manifest to the negotiators that a settlement range exists, and thus that an agreement is possible, in which case the problem shifts from that of determining or creating a settlement range to that of determining a specific point of agreement within this range. This problem will be discussed below. On the other hand, a considerable separation of positions coupled with trivial concessions may make manifest the fact that a settlement range does not exist, and the claim will have to be litigated.

Some Tactics of Negotiation

Within the context of these four general rules, the "game" of negotiation proceeds with a variety of tactics. The tactics of negotiation have been variously labeled in the literature.[14] I propose their division into the categories of proposals, rationalizations, threats, and commitments, to be illustrated by quotations from interviews and recorded negotiations.

Proposals are offers of settlement, but they are more as well. They are intended as clues to the expectations of the proposer, and as indications of what further proposals may be expected. They must be interpreted in the light of the stage of negotiations and in the light of what proposals are already on the table:

> The initial bargaining proposal is an information-seeking device. During the early states of negotiation, each party, in addition to giving information about (and concealing) his preferences, is attempting to discover the true prefer-

14. See Stevens, *op. cit.;* Iklé, *op. cit.*

ences of his opponent. In part, the negotiator will infer
these preferences from his opponent's bargaining position.
He will also infer these from his opponent's reaction to his
own bargaining position.[15]

Thus, the initial offer and demand in a bodily injury negotiation
are seldom meant to be accepted by the other party. They are
rather made almost entirely for their communicative value. The
initial demand of $25,000, for example, is a way of saying, "I
think this is a serious case, which deserves a settlement in the
thousands and not in the hundreds of dollars." A following offer
of $2,000 would be a way of communicating agreement on the
more general principle, whereas an offer of $400 would most
likely be meant and construed as a disagreement. The communicative function of proposals is also evident in the meanings
attached to changes in them through the course of negotiation.
An attorney reducing his demand from $25,000 to $15,000 and
then to $14,500 is saying something different from one whose
third proposal is $10,000.

The communicative function of proposals is amusingly illustrated in the following exchange, in which the lawyer was tacitly
informed that his demand had been too low. His embarrassment
was evident, yet he was prevented by Rule 3 above from re-
tracting his offer, once made.

> *Lawyer*: Well, I talked with Mrs. Jones, and she felt that
> around $600 would be all right. That would take into con-
> sideration some future minor doctor bills, etc. Since I'm not
> taking a fee and am being honest, that's the actual figure.
> *Adjuster*: Golly, you don't think I can bring you down
> some? You know, that's what I'm supposed to do.
> *Lawyer*: Well, I had considered starting at $750, but after
> talking with my friend at lunch I decided to be direct.
> I figured if you were at $310, that $600 would be the figure
> so why should we waste our time?
> *Adjuster*: Well, I think that's a reasonable figure. That's
> why I'm not trying to bring bring you down. Since I can't
> bring you down I guess I can make out the check.

15. Stevens, *op. cit.*, p. 63.

Lawyer: Well, isn't the settlement usually figured at three times the specials? [Specials are $310.]
Adjusters: No! That's a folk tale. Each case has to be figured differently.
Lawyer: I see. Well, let me check with my client as to the $600 before you make out the check.

Rationalizations are tactics intended to legitimize proposals in the eyes of the opponent. The discussions that my students and I observed were most frequently focused around rationalizations. Each party was attempting to convince the other that general, mutually shared principles justified the contentions indicated by his proposals. Perhaps the principal issue in the majority of negotiations was whether the case ought to be considered routine or serious. The following example is excerpted from one such discussion:

> *Adjuster*: We are looking at a hell of a lot of damages here for what may be a bruised hip as opposed, say, to a broken hip. . . .
> *Lawyer*: She of course did not have a broken bone, but yet did complain quite bitterly, and she did everything short of surgery—that she would not go through. . . . Although you seem to feel that this $1000 in specials is a bit too high for what you are calling a bruise, as far as I'm concerned, my knowledge of this woman which is extensive—I've known her for many, many, many years, goes way, way, way back—from my own personal knowledge, this woman is not a complainer—just exactly the contrary. . . . As a comparison I've got an accident case where there is a broken hip and a rather severely broken hip in three or four places, if I remember rightly. That woman has healed up completely and she had no residuals, nothing, with the breaks. And here we have one where there are no breaks and yet she still has residuals and I believe her sincerely when she says, "It hurts; it bothers me." I don't call it a mere bruise. . . .
> *Adjuster*: . . . I think about the only thing we have is a demonstration of tenderness and pain upon palpitation

which seems to be compatible with the type of injury she has described.

The import of this distinction is that cases defined as routine are acknowledged by both sides to warrant a relatively small settlement, the amount arrived at implicitly through the use of a formula muliplier of the medical bills. Having obtained the concession that a case was routine, an adjuster would then argue, as in the case just cited, "How do the majority of people do this? In a rear-end accident they take the specials and multiply by four."

On the other hand, a case defined as serious would be further discussed in terms of previous settlements or of jury awards in similar cases, as well as the specific injuries and impairments, the peculiar characteristics of the parties, and other particulars relevant to the expected value in litigation.

The simplicity and clarity of the payoffs in the claims studied curtailed potential discussion of the value of various outcomes to the parties—a dollar given to the claimant was a dollar taken from the insurance company. However, there was considerable discussion of the potential costs involved in failure to agree, each side stressing the costs of the other. For instance:

> We're only a thousand dollars apart. [To litigate you would have to] bring in four doctors and pay an arbitrator.

It is at this point that the issue of delay becomes a bargaining tool. Delay can be a threat when it is under the control of a party who proposes to use it deliberately, but some degree of delay is inevitable in the event of no agreement, and it will be cited to rationalize a proposal. It is more effective as an argument by the company, which is less harmed by delay, than as an argument by the claimant:

> *Lawyer*: My client is greedy.
> *Adjuster*: He'll be cured when he finds he has to wait five years. . . . We have thousands of cases in suit. This is just one case additional. We have no aggravation. This is all part of our premium.

The threat is an attempt to change the opponent's expectations concerning the party's reactions to his choices. The party conveys the information that if the opponent chooses a particular course of action, the party will react in a way prejudicial to him. Variations upon this are the promise—a negative threat—and the warning—in which the undesirable consequences of the opponent's choice will come not from the party, but from a third person or an impersonal source, such as nature.

The principal threat used in bodily injury claims negotiations is to go to trial, thus forcing processing costs upon the threatened party. The threatener must obviously bear these costs as well, raising the problem of making the threat believable. This can be accomplished by the insurance company through rationalizations of the type appearing in the quotation just cited. The claimant's threat generally has to be supported by commitment tactics, which are explained below.

As mentioned previously, delay can also be threatened. Again, the consequences of this threat are clearly more harmful to the claimant than to the insurance company, and the latter can use the threat more effectively:

> Now right here you can do one of two things. You can settle with me right now, and I'm going to consider this as three times your medical, or if you don't want to accept this you have a right to go further: seek what you may, wait a lot longer, have a lot of harassment, a lot of wonderment, a lot of complications, witnesses will die, people will move, and eventually you might get more. . . .

If the above-mentioned threats are more useful to the insurance company than to the claimant, the claimant has unique access to the threat to manipulate the apparent loss by "building" the claim. The company's threat to take the case to trial may be met with:

> You know what the specials will be by that time! . . . You must understand that I cannot let a case like this lie fallow for five years. Then I would look stupid before the judge.

One adjuster's advice to a hypothetical claimant would be:

> I think I'd tell the fellow that I plan to want to see a neuro-
> logical associate in here, and get some tests done, and
> you're going to get yourself X-rayed from head to foot,
> and so forth. There are a couple of doctors in town—you
> hate to throw in their names—and of course, if you knew
> them you'd be going to one of them.

The threat to "build" specials is effective to the extent that
the claimant is not tied to a definitive version of costs. It is most
useful to the claimant who has refused a statement to the adjuster, or whose statement recites, "I was injured but I have
unknown injuries at this time."

An unusual example of a powerful threat by an adjuster
capitalized on the special circumstances of the claimant. This is
an unusual case, but it seems to be a good example of a tactic
that could be very powerful in negotiation, yet useless in
litigation:

> I tried to talk to a woman who was a colored gal on Public
> Assistance. . . . She had about 19 kids and no husband,
> and there I had something else to talk about because I
> threatened the attorney, threatened her, with the fact that:
> "You know where your recovery is going? Right to the
> Commonwealth! To offset my taxes. . . . I am serious. Let's
> not talk about the City and State, etc. Let's just get these
> things wrapped up here. Look at the specials. . . ." And
> this is the way we closed that claim because I had a good
> file and . . . they would just as soon the State not know
> about the thing.

The commitment for negotiation purposes is a backing of a
proposal, rationalization or threat by making a pledge to it of
resources, reputation, or principle. In brief, commitment establishes credibility by making it more difficult to abandon a negotiation position. It works because both the committing party
and his opponent know that the former has more to lose by a
concession because of the commitment, and thus both know that
he will not yield as easily.

Commitment to a proposal tends to turn the negotiation "game" into take-it-or-leave-it. The party seeks to limit the opponent's choice to agreement on the terms proposed or no agreement rather than the three-fold choice permitting further negotiation. This commitment will be used, for instance, when the party believes that his offer is regarded by the opponent as acceptable but not optimum. The commitment, if successful, constrains the opponent to accept a proposal that may barely exceed his resistance point. The committing party may thus obtain agreement at his target.

Commitment to a rationalization converts the latter into a principle. This was observed with respect to the formula multiplier in certain cases. The "going rate" might be resisted by the claimant on the grounds that the case was not a routine one; this would be encountered by a commitment to the formula, with an explanation such as, "this case is not flesh and blood. It's paper! Its value is based on a market value to a bureaucracy."

Commitment to a threat makes it more credible, insuring that the threatener will fulfill his threat even though it would otherwise be patently to his disadvantage, as in the case of the threat to "blow us both up." The threat to go to trial often requires a commitment, particularly for the claimant; filing suit papers, taking depositions, and other more or less costly pre-trial procedures are assumed not only for their manifest purposes, but because they demonstrate commitment.

The commitment is potentially a very powerful negotiation technique, but it possesses very powerful disadvantages. Among these is the fact that at times it will be necessary to withdraw from a commitment, particularly when the commitment is to a threat that is detrimental to the interests of the threatener, when the threat has failed to secure the action it was intended to elicit. To withdraw involves a loss, not only to the principle that was committed, but to the total bargaining reputation of the negotiator. Moreover, a strong commitment exacerbates this problem, but a weak commitment is less effective in obtaining the desired action from the opponent. Another problem in the liberal use of commitment is that it poisons the atmosphere of negotiation through suggesting hostility and bad faith.[16] More-over, commitment tactics involve the risk of simultaneous com-mitment of the parties to incompatible positions, which is likely not only to ruin the chances of agreement, but to force the parties to incur the additional costs of fulfilling threats that cause mutual harm or to suffer the weakening of bargaining reputations consequent on abandoning commitments.

The commitments observed in bodily injury claims negotiation tended to be weak and therefore easily abandoned, but of only marginal effectiveness in negotiation. The commitments most frequently observed consisted of invoking dependence on clients or supervisors who were alleged to be uncooperative or irra-tional. The following recitals are typical:

> Oh, very many times you call an attorney to offer $1,000 and he wants you to wait until he calls his client. He calls the client and he can't accept it because the client wants him to get $1,200. Normally, an attorney who has the case under control knows how much he can settle the case for when the case is ready for settlement. He doesn't have to call his client because if you have the case under control you can tell your client, "That is the best I can do; I recommend you to settle it," and normally the client will go along with you.

> I had a case that he started at $7,500 on, and I was sticking at $1,500, and [Home Office] was screaming to settle it. I met him on a Friday afternoon and said, "Let's settle this case." He said, "I'm going on vacation and I need some money." I said, "Well, I offered you $1,500. . . . I discussed it with our attorney and he said, 'If you pay a nickel over $2,000 I'll kill you.'" He said, "And what will you settle it for?" I said $2,000 and the next 15 minutes he said, "I'll take it," on the street by the parking meter.

---

16. Stevens suggests that for this reason commitment to a fixed position is less often used in labor negotiations than in international relations.

Pure Bargaining in Bodily Injury Claims Negotiation

It was mentioned above that the formation of a settlement range is a necessary condition for a negotiated agreement, but that it is not sufficient. A settlement must be not for a range of amounts, but for a specific sum. This presents the problem of pure bargaining. In Schelling's words:

> There is some range of alternative outcomes in which any point is better for both sides than no agreement at all. To insist on any such point is pure bargaining, since one *would* take less rather than reach no agreement at all, and since one always *can* recede if retreat proves necessary to agreement. Yet if both parties are aware of the limits to this range, *any* outcome is a point from which at least one party would have been willing to retreat and the other knows it! There is no resting place.[17]

The formation of a settlement range is thus no guarantee of an eventual settlement. For instance, an adjuster may know that his opponent would be willing to settle for as little as $1,000, and the opponent may know that the adjuster would be willing to pay as much as $1,500, and both may know that their knowledge is shared by the other side. This situation presents a large range of potential agreement, but paradoxically, it may result in no agreement whatsoever. Each side will try to insist that the bargain be set at its own target, knowing that the other side would prefer settlement at that point to trial, and one possible outcome of the situation is the trial that no one prefers. To reach a bargain, the parties require a point from which they cannot reasonably be expected to depart and from which they cannot reasonably expect the other to depart. Firm commitment by one party could provide such a point, but as noted before, not only is commitment a dangerous tactic, but the commitments available in bodily injury claims negotiation tend to be relatively weak and ineffective. In the absence of effective commitments,

17. Thomas C. Schelling, *The Strategy of Conflict* (Oxford University Press, 1963), p. 22.

there appears here as elsewhere reliance on points of "intrinsic magnetism":

> If we then ask what it is that can bring their expectations into convergence and bring the negotiation to a close, we might propose that it is the intrinsic magnetism of particular outcomes, especially those that enjoy prominence, uniqueness, simplicity, precedent, or some rationale that makes them qualitatively differentiable from the continuum of possible alternatives.[18]

Points of "intrinsic magnetism" are provided in the situation at hand by formulas and round numbers, among other things.

The use of round numbers and of simple formulas is not peculiar to bodily injury claims negotiation, but is found in a wide variety of bargaining situations:

> In bargains that involve numerical magnitudes, for example, there seems to be a strong magnetism in mathematical simplicity. A trivial illustration is the tendency for the outcomes to be expressed in "round numbers;" . . . More impressive, perhaps, is the remarkable frequency with which long negotiation over complicated quantitative formulas or *ad hoc* shares in some costs or benefits converge ultimately on something as crudely simple as equal shares, shares proportionate to some common magnitude (gross national product, population, foreign-exchange deficit, and so forth), or the shares agreed on in some previous but logically irrelevant negotiation.[19]

18. Schelling, *op. cit.*, p. 70. Similar principles are involved in the discussion of the figure-and-ground problem in *Gestalt* psychology. See, for instance, Wolfgang Kohler, *Gestalt Psychology* (Liveright, 1947), especially Chapter VI.

19. Schelling, *op. cit.*, p. 67. An amusing example from the study is the following anecdote:

> I had a case today I settled for $900. The guy's name was Mamorella, which has nine letters. I said, "I will pay $100 for each letter in your name." So he thought that was cute and I was just joking around, but the case was worth the money. But he wanted $1,200. And I said I couldn't pay that unless he changed his name. So he knows he couldn't do that so he accepted the money.

Dependence on formulas is virtually always denied in the abstract by both adjusters and attorneys, as explained in Chapter 3. In practice, formulas are used very often, not only for evaluation but also for purposes of negotiation. Where a range of possible agreement points exists, and there is a need for singling out one of them, the artificial and conventional formula is one of the few means available and suitable. There is frequent reference to it in my observations. Two instances are:

> Do I understand your demand would be the specials and half of that for pain and suffering?

> Well, of course, if you are going to take a look at the specials with the idea of multiplying them out to arrive at what you think the case is worth, I suppose you could.

The rule is not applied blindly. In order to get a point within the existing range of settlement, recoveries from collateral sources such as sick pay and Blue Cross may or may not be included; lost wages may or not be included; certain medical expenses, such as X-ray diagnosis, may be excluded; and the multiplier may be two, three, four, five, or more. There is in fact nothing logical about the formula methods, and their apparent basis in legal considerations (special damages) is merely nominal. Their major and crucial value is as a way to point the parties to a bargain, where a bargain is possible but danger exists that it may not be reached, and the situation is otherwise devoid of guidelines.

Round numbers also loom large as foci for potential agreement. Again, there is little to be said for them in logic or in law, yet they seem to be inevitable in the absence of other guides. The following set of offers and counter offers from one negotiation illustrates the role of round numbers in negotiation. The particular claim entailed property damage estimated at $138, in addition to the bodily injury.

1. Offer by adjuster of $500 for the bodily injury claim plus $138 for property damage. The $500 is a round number within the contract zone already established for this case.

2. Demand by lawyer for $888. This odd figure is the sum of adjuster's $500 basic offer, plus the property damage, plus half the $500 for the attorney's fee. Lawyer wants to "put $500 in her pocket."

3. Adjuster offers to "split it"—$838, composed of $700 for client and attorney plus the property damage.

4. Lawyer demands $850 to "round it off."

5. Adjuster agrees to $850.

Note in this example the use of round numbers: $500, one half (for fee), $700, and $850. Three different arguments are used to justify the offers and demands: clean numbers, allocation of payment to various sources, and splitting the difference. These are no more based in law or logic than is asking for three times the specials. No considerations of equity or justice point to clean numbers as a basis for settlement, to the rightness of the midpoint between offer and demand or, as in the example above, to a settlement that can be divided into simple fractions according to cause of action on the one hand, and recipient on the other. They are used because attention to equity or justice at this point in negotiation would get the parties nowhere. They are used because there is no alternative. For all the disavowal of these methods on both sides, they are inevitable.[20]

---

20. Among the Acme cases for which some payment was made, 28 percent settled at an exact unit multiple of one hundred dollars. Erving Goffman comments, in a private communication:

> To accept a settlement proposed by the other is to expose oneself not merely to "easily" missing a better deal, and hence being a fool, but also to being dictated to, told what is to happen. . . . An object then is to accept a solution which won't discredit one's status as a person with dignity who can't be pushed around, a person whose word means something. A round number allows the accepter to act as if he is being gracious, unconstrained by details and particular sums, willing to do things with a little dash. The offer of a round number is then by way of being a tactful move, a set up for the accepter's use of the move to prove desirable things about himself and get him out of a bind.

Failure of Negotiation

In automobile bodily injury claims, the savings to both parties of a negotiated settlement over litigation, coupled with the separate advantages of informality to one or both parties, make litigation seem a very unsatisfactory resolution. True, only a small minority of claims proceed to judgment, but the considerations of this chapter raise the question of why any claims at all are tried. Certainly, hindsight after trial would indicate a wide range of figures within which both parties would have been better off had they settled. This range would be, at a minimum, the judgment figure plus and minus the processing costs of the parties. Why, then, do some claims resist settlement and go to trial?

The commonsense answer to this question is that in some proportion of cases the parties are inherently at odds concerning the expected value of the claim in litigation. We may term this situation one of manifest disagreement. Each side believes that the outcome of litigation, reduced by processing costs, will be more favorable than the other party's best offer. In retrospect it can be said that at least one of the parties must have been seriously wrong in his estimation. An honest difference in opinion concerning expected value in litigation would have to exceed the combined processing costs of the parties in order to necessitate trial. Differences in expectations of this magnitude are more likely to occur as the size of the claim increases and processing costs become smaller relative to the amount at stake. Therefore, insofar as manifest disagreement is a factor in the failure of negotiation, trials should be more common in larger cases. This study and others have found that proportionately more large cases than small cases do in fact go to trial, consistent with the hypothesis that trial reflects manifest disagreement in negotiation.[21]

However, though failure of negotiation may sometimes be due to manifest disagreement, it would seem that this situation should be relatively uncommon among experienced and realistic

21. See Chapter 5 below; also Conard *et al., op. cit.,* pp. 181–185.

negotiators. Moreover, manifest disagreement is unlikely to cause full-scale trials for small amounts of money, yet these do occur. Based on studies of labor-management negotiations, Carl M. Stevens suggests three other sources of negotiation failure that may occur despite the fact that there exists a settlement range— a range of potential agreement which both sides would prefer to no agreement.[22] Stevens' analysis applies to the failure of negotiation in bodily injury claims as follows.

Negotiation can fail, paradoxically, when there is a manifest large area of agreement. In this case, both parties know that there exists a range of values that both they and the other would prefer to no agreement. Each side may in fact make an offer that he knows the other would prefer to no agreement. These offers, however, may not be accepted because each side is waiting for the other to accept an offer more favorable to himself. If a deadline is imposed, for example by the filing of suit papers, the case may go to trial rather than be settled. Although my data do not permit an estimate of the frequency of this situation in bodily injury negotiation, it would seem to be a reasonable explanation of the trial of many of the small cases that do fall into litigation. More frequently, of course, the dilemma is solved, through commitments and through proposals characterized by the "intrinsic magnetism" discussed above.

Another possible cause of failure of negotiation is the undiscovered area of agreement. In this case there does exist a range of values that the parties would prefer to no agreement, but the parties do not know this fact. Were the parties to make proposals close to their resistance points the contract zone would become manifest, but they do not make these proposals for one or more of the following reasons: First, they may fear that a concession would be interpreted as a sign of weakness, causing the opponent to expect even more. Second, they may believe it necessary to save some concession for later stages in bargaining, such as negotiating during trial. Third, they may fear that their best offer may concede more than is necessary to obtain agree-

22. Carl M. Stevens, "Collective Bargaining: Theory and Practice," unpublished manuscript, 1967.

ment, thus "throwing away" money.[23] Since weakness is always a reasonable interpretation of a concession, and bargaining does continue even after trial is commenced, and it is indeed difficult to make a concession that exactly meets the opponent's minimum demands, this reasoning seems to be a convincing explanation for some proportion of bodily injury trials.

In this situation, as in the previous one, a mediator may be able to secure agreement where the unaided parties cannot. In the first situation, the mediator's suggestions may solve the problem of pure bargaining by providing a unique and obvious solution. In the second situation, the mediator may be able to perceive the existence of an area of agreement through privileged communication with the parties. His mere announcement that the parties could agree does not guarantee agreement, but makes it more likely because the contract zone is manifest.

A third possible cause of failure of negotiation is incompatible commitments. The parties would in fact prefer to yield rather than to go to trial, but because of commitments the price of yielding has been increased in terms of resources or reputation. If a way were found to disavow the commitments, there would be a possibility of settlement. Commitments, particularly strong and credible ones, appear to be rare in bodily injury claims negotiation. Thus, this problem is probably rarely a cause of litigation in the case at hand, but it cannot be ruled out altogether. One of the most efficient methods of resolving this problem where it occurs in labor negotiations is to change the negotiator. Such a change occurs in bodily injury claims negotiation when suit is filed and the company obtains representation by a defense attorney. The same result can be accomplished by referring the claim to the claims manager or to the home office. Likewise, the attorney may call in a trial specialist, not so much to prepare the case for trial as to permit negotiation without the burden of previously undertaken commitments. The large number of cases that are settled at the stage of pre-trial may be partly explained by this shift in representation, in addition to

23. In labor negotiations this possibility is termed "leaving a nickel on the table."

such factors as more realistic appraisal and professional camara-
derie which may distinguish attorneys from adjusters.

Negotiation may appear to fail in some proportion of cases
where trial is in fact desired by one or both parties, not because
the other's offer was insufficient, but to gain certain advantages
intrinsic to litigation that are irrelevant to the parties' interest
in most cases. One such advantage of trial is to make the law
explicit. In the occasional case where a legal point may not be
clear, a party may wish to litigate in order to determine the
formal rule for future cases. Trial also offers the opportunity to
fulfill a commitment or to build a bargaining reputation. Such
litigation is more concerned with the negotiation of future cases
than with the disposition of the case being litigated. Another
advantage of litigation may be to protect the adjuster and the
local field office staff from criticism by home office supervisors.
Particularly in very large cases, it may be difficult to defend a
particular settlement on the file, but there can be no argument
about paying a judgment imposed by a court. Finally, it may be
that some badly financed, marginal insurance companies use
litigation in order to obtain additional delay for its own sake. I
doubt that a very large percentage of all cases brought to trial
by the companies I studied were litigated for these reasons, but
all except the last may well account for some trials, particularly
in the rare cases potentially involving tens of thousands of
dollars.

Negotiation with the Unrepresented Claimant

To this point I have been discussing negotiation between adjusters and either attorneys or sophisticated claimants. Now I
wish to turn to the situation in which the adjuster confronts an
unrepresented and unsophisticated claimant. This is in fact the
most common type of insurance claims situation. The vast majority of claims for property damage liability only are unrepresented, as are virtually all claims by insureds in such matters as
collision damage and the fire and related perils coverages of the
homeowner's policy. With respect to bodily injury liability, the
Michigan study shows that the victim is generally unrepresented

in claims where the economic loss is $1,000 or less,[24] and it would seem to be a fair guess that most unrepresented claimants are poor negotiators. Raw data collected for the study emphatically support this guess. Taking all claims together, the average unrepresented claimant receives a settlement of about $250. Claimants represented by lawyers who practice by themselves (who are, according to the literature, the least talented on the average) receive an average recovery of about $1,500. When the claimant is represented by a firm, the average recovery rises to around $2,225, and when a member of the negligence specialist group, the American Trial Lawyers Association,[25] represents a claim, the average recovery is almost $5,000. Examination of the data in the next chapter will show that part of this effect is doubtless the result of the lawyers' selectivity concerning the claimants that they represent. Those claimants with minor injuries are less likely to obtain representation than claimants having experienced major injuries. Nevertheless, on the whole, similar claims receive far higher payments when represented than when handled by the claimant directly. The magnitude of the difference far exceeds that admitted by adjusters when they discuss their evaluation of represented claims, as in Chapter 3.

The unrepresented claimant is not necessarily easy to deal with. In the words of an adjuster:

> Strange as it may seem, the types of claimants that give you more trouble are those that you might say are less educated. . . . They aren't realistic. Frankly, I would sooner deal with a person who, shall we say, has a better than average job, has been around a little bit, that is, in the sense of being in today's world, who knows who the Secretary of State is, and so forth, and a person you can sit down with—in other words, let's say a person on my own social level. I would sooner deal with a person like that— I think I'd have better success with him—than a person who, shall we say, is at the bottom rung, the bottom of the

24. Conard *et al.*, *op. cit.*, p. 226.
25. Formerly NACCA, National Association of Claimants' Counsel of America.

ladder, and who sees this as a once-in-a-lifetime opportunity and who will be unrealistic, not only in dollars-and-
cents figures, but also from even discussing the accident in
the first place. And also in his entire outlook, various
persons like that will want to be given partial settlement,
which we can't do. They want to settle this phase of the
claim today and this one tomorrow, and they'll want advance money; I don't know what that is, but one fellow
wanted advance money, he understood that all insurance
companies did that, he wanted a flat sum of money to be
advanced to him, to sort of tide him over during the term
of his claim. I don't know where these people get their
ideas, but it's like you have to beat them over the head, so
to speak, to even get through to them what you're there for
in the first place. This is even before you get into settlement, which is another job.

But if dealing with an unrepresented claimant is often more
difficult than dealing with an attorney, the settlements are generally cheaper. I believe that a good part of the discrepancy
between the amounts received by represented and unrepresented
claimants stems from the deficiency of the latter in negotiation
skills. Either the "game" of negotiation is played very badly or
it is replaced by a different game substituted by the adjuster. I
shall mention a few common approaches used by adjusters in
this situation.

One manner of dealing with the unrepresented claimant is for
the adjuster to ask the claimant to document his losses. The
specific items are added up, after which the adjuster asks, "Is
there anything else?" If nothing more is mentioned, the total is
offered, usually by the adjuster's commencing to fill out a draft
and a release, offering the latter to sign along with the draft.[26]
In formal terms, the sum thus arrived at is the total of special
damages, less collateral source benefits. Even cases with rather
questionable liability can support payment of special damages
in the companies I studied. That clear liability can support a

---

26. A draft is the instrument of payment, similar to a check, which is
used in paying insurance claims.

good deal more is not generally mentioned, and many claimants settle for much less on this basis than the company would be prepared to pay.[27]

Frequently, the somewhat knowledgeable claimant will challenge an offer of special damages only. He will refuse to sign the release tendered in the described manner, or he will ask, when presented with the total, "How about something for myself?" On occasion, the terms of art, "pain and suffering," will occur. In a clear liability case, the adjuster will not resist an additional payment. He will usually ask the claimant how much he wants. If the amount is well within what the claim can support (i.e., within the reserve or specific authorization by the supervisor), the demand is usually accepted on the spot. The unsophisticated claimant is quite likely to demand a good deal less than the company would be willing to pay, even if he knows his right to recovery of general damages. However, the claimant frequently asks too much, in which case the adjuster can so inform him and present a counter-offer.

Another approach is akin to Boulwareism: the adjuster evaluates the claim and makes a single offer, often bolstered by a commitment such as the statement that this is his professional evaluation or that it is the most that his supervisors will allow him to pay. The offer is generally at a level that strikes the adjuster as fair, meaning at least the amount of special damages in most situations, and "something more" in serious injury cases. It is more than he would offer if he expected to entertain a counter-offer, but less than the amount he would be willing to pay rather than having the case go to trial. If the claimant should seek an attorney, the adjuster can easily abandon the commitment and offer considerably more in the way of settlement.

These techniques hardly qualify for the designation of negotiation. Indeed, they may be thought of as replacing negotiation when dealing with a party who is unable to play the "game." The unrepresented claimant has a less precise idea of the ulti-

27. The frequency of special damages as a basis for payment is indicated by the fact that, of the 1,250 Acme cases in which payment was made and special damages were known and were greater than zero, 269 or 22 per cent were settled at exactly special damages.

mate value of his possible recovery, and thus is less able to make appropriate demands. His demands may be too low as well as too high. He is ignorant of the accepted principles according to which his demands can be rationalized. He does not know which, if any, threats may be effective in the situation, and he is incapable of making deliberate commitments to support these threats. The theory of negotiation tells us that a person who attempts to negotiate with these handicaps runs a strong chance of accepting an unusually low settlement or, on the other hand, of forcing the opponent to drop out, possibly ending in a trial detrimental to both parties.[28]

Denial

In the considerable proportion of claims that are closed without payment, a somewhat different problem is presented for negotiation. Many of these claims, of course, are not seriously pressed. A file is opened when an insured reports an accident with a potential injury or serious property damage, and the adjuster will visit the potential claimant, but the claimant may readily agree not to hold the insured responsible for the accident, or it may be possible to quiet the bodily injury claim, for example of a passenger in the insured car, by paying the medical bills from a first-party medical payments coverage. On other occasions, though, the claimant thoroughly expects payment, but the adjuster will decide on the basis of apparent lack of liability to deny the claim. This is generally done only in claims where the objective damages and the claimant's attitude suggest that the claim will not be put into litigation. However, denial of a seriously pressed claim produces not only a loss of expected dollar recovery, but also a loss of face for the claimant. If the adjuster is to deny the claim with confidence that it will not be reopened,

28. Paradoxically, an irrational and unyielding claimant may be able to get a very favorable settlement, if his demand happens to be acceptable to the company. The claimant's irrationality may make his unyielding stance credible. The company knows that it will have to deal with an attorney and perhaps endure trial if the demand is not met.

he must win the claimant's acquiescence to the justice of no pay-ment. Unless the claimant feels that the denial was fair, he may attempt to secure representation and thus at a minimum create trouble and expense for the company, and at a maximum, with a skillfully manipulated picture of liability and damages, the revived claim may terminate in an expensive judgment.

An unflattering parallel to this situation can be found in the criminal con-game, in which the victim is duped by the criminal who poses as a friend.[29] In the con-game as in the denied claim, one of the participants not only loses financially, but is also made to look foolish. This loss of face must be rationalized away. The adjuster's principal technique is a lecture on the negligence law, in which he takes the position of a sympathetic but help-less actor trapped by the directives of a technical and heartless law. For example, an Acme adjuster explained his denial tech-nique on a homeowner's liability claim as follows:

> If you are dealing with a contemporary, so to speak, or a person better than I am, a professional of some sort, then of course you have to be very blunt: you simply tell him the facts and that's the end of it, and if they don't under-stand then you tell them there must be something wrong with their hearing. But if you are dealing with a person who might really have trouble understanding the law from the legal aspect of the thing then you try and take the time out necessary to explaining it in detail—exactly what the social guest law is, and in many cases the social guest law is difficult to understand and people think they owe a great deal of care to guests in their homes. The law is just the opposite. . . . Maybe sometimes if you sit down and explain the law not only to the claimant in detail but also to the insured in detail—and even times I've expressed an opinion and advised them to call our attorneys to double-check what I've said. If that isn't satisfactory, I tell them to call a friend of theirs who might be an attorney . . . to double-

29. Erving Goffman, "On Cooling the Mark Out: Some Aspects of Adop-tation to Failure," *Psychiatry* 15:451, 1952.

> check whether this fellow [the adjuster] is giving them a line, you know, and usually that works. . . . Usually that will satisfy 80 or 90 per cent of the claimants.

The adjuster, like the con-man, must allow the loser to depart gracefully without facing the implications of his economic loss for his self-esteem. Perhaps the most effective technique is to "leave the file open":

> Don't slam the door in his face. Don't say it is final. They're saving face, too, and will say, "I'll see if I can locate that witness," and you never hear from them again.

The adjuster just quoted followed his own advice in the following telephone conversation:

> The question is whether our insured would be legally liable. Our conclusion is no. . . . I realize your position but I'm trying to tell you what our position is. . . . We'll have your file open and I'll be glad to review the facts and discuss it again with you. You're not signing a release and this is not final. . . . I don't like to say I can't pay you. You have reason to be concerned. The case will remain open. We'll reconsider it.

The adjuster then explained it to me:

> I tried to deny as nicely as possible and softened it by saying I would reconsider. I'll go back again and say, "No, I'm sorry." I told her the truth the first time, but she didn't want to hear it. I was getting to the point that everything I said was wrong, and she was getting annoyed. It worked like a charm.

Internal Negotiation

The adjuster is the man in the middle, balancing demands from numerous directions. This chapter has focused on negotiation with the claimant or the plaintiff's attorney, but it should be noted that demands from other directions must also be negotiated. The most important of these come from inside the company, from the first-level supervisor, who must in some way endorse every significant settlement made by adjusters in the three companies studied. Paradoxically, the need for supervisory endorsement appeared more frequently at Acme, where the claims men had authority to write a draft for any amount, than at Great Plains or Mid-West, where the adjuster's authority to write a draft without specific approval of a supervisor was limited to a dollar amount that varied according to the length of service.[30] The paradox is explained by the fact that at Acme all claims handled by adjusters were individually evaluated by the supervisors for the purpose of setting a reserve, and the adjuster was generally expected to settle for no more than the reserve figure. At Mid-West and Great Plains, the supervisor concerned himself routinely only with claims exceeding the settlement authority of the particular adjuster.

The problems to be solved and the rules and tactics used in negotiating approval of a supervisor for a desired reserve or settlement authority are similar to those involved in negotiation with a claimant. Vis-à-vis the supervisor, the adjuster plays the role of the plaintiff's attorney, attempting to secure the most liberal evaluation possible. It is true that there is some bargaining power for the adjuster when dealing with the claimant if his ability to agree to a large sum is limited,[31] but the adjuster much prefers a generous authority from which he can attempt a saving. This is because the adjuster faces the "Sentry's Dilemma" with respect to his supervisor.[32] If he successfully settles on the basis of his authorization, he has done his job in a normal manner. If he settles for considerably less than the authorization, he may be commended, but the saving may be attributed

30. These companies also limited the authority of first-level supervisors. Settlements above a certain amount had to be cleared at higher levels.

31. In that situation the settlement authority offers a credible basis for a commitment.

32. The Sentry's Dilemma is a game theory choice where one alternative is heavily loaded. The sentry hearing a suspicious sound must decide whether to shoot. If he shoots and the source turns out to have been a friend, this is unfortunate. If he shoots and an enemy falls, this is good. If he fails to shoot and it is a friend, this is fortunate. But if he fails to shoot and the sound indicates an enemy the consequence is catastrophic. The solution to the problem is always to shoot.

to an over-generous authorization, rather than to the skill of the adjuster. In contrast, settlement of a claim for an amount exceeding the authorization or reserve is extremely troublesome, and is avoided whenever possible.

The following account of a negotiation between an adjuster and his supervisor to obtain settlement authority illustrates internal negotiation:

> *Supervisor*: This is not a $9,000 claim [as the attorney represents it].
> *Adjuster*: Give me something to work with and I'll try to settle for around $1,200. [Suggests $1,250.]
> *Supervisor*: No more than $1,200.
> *Adjuster*: [The attorney] is in such a position with his client that he can't settle. Let's go in with a figure saying, "He's your problem and this is a fair figure, representing what the claim is worth."
> *Supervisor*: There's nothing wrong with the claimant. The arthritic condition was traced to childhood by the company physician, and there is some corroboration by the plaintiff's physician.
> *Adjuster*: Give me $1,200. I'll go in and dump it on him and leave him with it.
> *Supervisor*: He saw the doctor in January and didn't do anything else until August.
> *Adjuster*: Want me to tell [the attorney] to go to Hell?
> *Supervisor*: No, it's for settlement. We rear-ended him.[33]

33. The tactics here are familiar. The adjuster made an error in mentioning $1,200 too early, where $1,250 would have been five times the medical specials and therefore defensible by the prevailing formula. His major argument relays to the supervisor the plaintiff's attorney's commitment to the claimant. In response, the supervisor seems to rationalize a denial. The adjuster suggests using a commitment tactic on the attorney, and tacitly warns the supervisor that the attorney's own commitment will force the case to trial if the supervisor denies. The supervisor thereafter authorized the $1,200 in settlement authority.

Recapitulation

Negotiation is not a phase, but rather an aspect, of the settlement process. It reflects on other aspects, evaluation and investigation, and in turn is affected by them. Most important, it has an effect on the outcome of a claim independent of the type of accident and the injuries experienced.

The negotiation of bodily injury claims is a far less costly and less formal alternative to adjudication. It can be understood as a kind of game, with its own rules and tactics, the goal being at least partly cooperative, obtaining settlement out of court, and partly competitive, as the parties are adversary. Bodily injury negotiation is a relatively simple class of negotiations, lacking the elegance of labor and international negotiations, but perhaps its study as begun here may yield insights that are applicable very generally.

It was found that negotiation of bodily injury claims by "professionals" conformed to four rules and used four classes of tactics. The "game" was frequently successful, claims being closed without litigation better than 19 times out of 20. However, a not inconsiderable absolute number of claims do go to trial, sometimes apparently because of peculiarities of the negotiation situation itself.

The unrepresented claimant appears to be a poor negotiator. At least, the outcomes on the whole are less favorable to him than they are to the represented claimant, and observation on interactions between adjusters and unrepresented claimants suggests that the "game" being played in this situation is attenuated and is simpler than the one played with the represented claimant. It may be on the whole less profitable for the claimant, but it is prevented by the ethical standards of the adjusters (in the companies I studied) from being unfair or exploitative, at least as viewed by these adjusters. Other concerned people will have to compare the outcomes with their own standards. Therefore, in the following chapter I shall attempt to depict the broad pattern of bodily injury claims settlements, as seen in a representative sample of the files of the Acme Insurance Company.

5. Recovery

AUTOMOBILE LIABILITY INSURANCE currently pays $1.5 billion annually to victims of traffic accidents.[1] These payments are made on the basis of claims grounded in the formal law of negligence but, as the previous chapters of this book have demonstrated, the distribution of these funds is made in large part through a mechanism generally ignored by the formal law: the negotiated settlement. The reasoning of the previous chapters suggests that settlements are influenced by the personalities of the negotiators, the organizational structure within which they operate, and the normative structure of negotiation. Therefore, it is expected that the pattern of outcomes of negotiated settlemen will exhibit differences from the outcomes predicted by the formal law, and that the differences will be not random, but systematic. This chapter will describe the pattern of payments

1. Estimate based on figures cited in Alfred F. Conard, James N. Morgan, Robert W. Pratt, Jr., Charles W. Voltz, and Robert Bombaugh, *Automobile Accident Costs and Payments: Studies in the Economics of Injury Reparation* (University of Michigan Press, 1964), Table 1-2, pp. 48–49.

actually obtained according to the files of the Acme Insurance Company. The deviations from formal expectations will be demonstrated, and will be explained in part as consequences of the factors discussed above.

The Data

The data to be examined in this chapter come principally from 2,216 claims drawn from files closed by the Acme Insurance Company in March and April of 1962. Before presenting the analysis of these files, I would like to recapitulate the methodology employed, and to elaborate on some of the notable features of these data.

Ideally, analysis of a system as complex as automobile liability insurance, with perhaps as many as 1,000 companies involved, would employ data from a large number of companies chosen to be statistically representative of the universe of American insurance companies. This study was for practical reasons limited to the files of the Acme Insurance Company. Strictly speaking, the results presented below can be generalized only to companies with equivalent procedures. As noted in Chapter 1, several factors suggest that Acme is not atypical of insurance companies more generally, and thus that the results of this study have a broader validity. I place the greatest weight on the subjectively impressive similarities between the interviews with Acme adjusters and those obtained at Great Plains and Mid-West. The latter companies have a substantially different corporate structure and mix of business, yet it would be difficult when reviewing an interview protocol to guess which company employed the adjuster being interviewed. In contrast, it would be relatively easy to guess whether the adjuster worked in a metropolitan or a provincial office, or how experienced he was. Another factor supporting Acme's typicality is the similarity among the several companies in many routine procedures: setting reserves or otherwise evaluating cases, taking statements, and the like. Additional evidence comes from the opinion of many attorneys who negotiate with a wide range of companies that the differences between the major companies are slight. On the whole, Acme was rated as "realistic" and "easy to work with" in all the areas I studied.

On the other hand, Acme is a distinctive company, with some traits that the critical reader may wish to keep in mind. The very cooperativeness with which it approached the study is an indication of the unusual faith of its executives that analysis of its behavior would not be prejudicial to itself or to the insurance industry. Although each of the following traits is common in the insurance industry, the combination may be peculiar to Acme: a relatively modest proportion of automobile business in its total portfolio, the use of the American Agency System of independent agents (rather than direct writing), stock-company rather than mutual corporate structure, a relative concentration of business in the Eastern United States, employment of unspecialized house adjusters, and the grant of theoretically full authority to these adjusters. To the best of my knowledge, and in the eyes of most of the attorneys I know, these characteristics exercise relatively minor influence on the claims practices under consideration. In sum, I offer the generalizations below in the belief that they are characteristic not only of Acme, but of most reputable companies writing insurance to protect the American motorist.[2]

The sample of files on which this chapter is based was drawn at random from all closed files received by the Home Office of Acme during March and April of 1962. The representative nature of the files may have been somewhat compromised by this procedure, since the various geographical areas of company operation were not necessarily represented in proportion to their general level of activity.[3]

2. Companies specializing in high-risk insurance are reputed to be considerably different in their practices. See *The Insurance Industry* (Hearings before the Subcommittee on Antitrust and Monopoly of the Committee on the Judiciary, U.S. Senate, 89th Congress, 1965), Part 12: High-Risk Automobile Insurance. An illuminating document in this report is the South Carolina Insurance Department analysis of Chesapeake Insurance Co. liability insurance claims, at p. 7115.

3. This is suggested by the fact that statistics based on the company's total experience in 1964 show a somewhat lower proportion of cases closed with payment—56 per cent, as against 66 per cent in the sample—and a lower mean payment in paid cases—$921, as against $1,106. One possible explanation is an overrepresentation of metropolitan claims offices in the sample.

The files from which I sampled were those assigned to adjusters and therefore, by company rule, involving either substantial property damage or apparent bodily injury. Those files that involved property damage only and no bodily injury were discarded from the sample. Payment on the remaining files could be made on one or more of three bases: bodily injury liability, medical payments, or property damage liability (if bodily injury was also involved). The study directly concerned only those payments made on the basis of bodily injury liability.[4]

Two principal variables to be explained in the following analysis are payment and time-lapse or delay from the time of the accident to final disposition. The overwhelming majority of the cases were disposed of by settlement before trial—2,123 of the 2,216. The remaining 93 cases went to trial, some of these being settled during the course of trial. Most of the analyses concern all cases, but it should be understood that the vast bulk of dispositions were in the nature of negotiated settlements (including cases closed without payment). A separate analysis is presented concerning differences between cases that settled before trial and those that went to trial.

The data in the files appeared in two different formats, which exerted a profound effect on the adequacy of the data. In the first, the data appeared on standard forms that were to be found in all or nearly all files. Two of the most important forms were the Reserve Notice and the Closing Advice, filed after 90 days and on closing the file, respectively. From these could be obtained such information as the dates of occurrence of the accident and of payment or denial of the claim, the amount paid, the location of the accident, names of the claimants, and certain

4. In the course of the analysis there arose the suspicion that some payments made on the basis of medical payments coverage may have become confused with bodily injury liability payments, in the course of transcribing the files. It was not possible to recheck the coding at that point because, by agreement with Acme, the files had been destroyed. The extent of this bias, if any, is thus not known, but, since medical payments are generally small and are available only to the occupants of the insured car, the bias has been accepted. However, where the possibility of such bias may be disturbing to the results, separate analyses confined to claimants outside the insured car have been performed. The results of these analyses suggest that the general level of bias is negligible.

other basic information. For most claims of considerable size, several other forms were also found with regularity. Pending File Reports were required every six months, and claims remaining unpaid for at least that length of time would have in their files at least one such form, on which some more detailed information was found: for example, the adjuster's opinion of liability, injuries sustained, and additional facts about the accident. In a similar status were forms that were not always present, but that were entered whenever certain contingencies arose. Examples are the Reserve Change Advice, which was included whenever a reserve change was necessary, and which had space for remarks explaining the change; the Suit Record, entered when notice of suit was received; copies of drafts in payment of the claim and in payment of direct outside services such as medical examinations and legal representation; and the Reopening Advice, filed when a dormant claim (usually previously denied) was reopened. Statements, defense medical reports, and similar documents were also included in the files on a routine basis, where these had been obtained.

Of a rather different nature, but of great importance, were "memos" from the adjuster to his supervisor and from supervisors, managers, and others, to the adjuster. Acme had a standard form, which appeared in many files, consisting of nothing but lined paper identified as to the case, and on this (and scratch pads, backs of envelopes, menus, and various other informal media) appeared much interesting information about the file, which was coded for the study when available. Matters such as the race of the claimant and the defendant, the quality of the lawyer, and the adjuster's opinion of the "witness value" of parties were for the most part available only in this informal manner. However, unlike the items appearing on the standard forms, these were not routinely available. The content of the memos was quite variable and, even more important, the memos varied in number and amount of information depending on the complexity of the claim. A claim that was quickly settled—usually a simple one with clear liability and small injuries—would yield a thin and uninformative file, whereas a difficult case would yield a fat file, replete with information.

A consequence of this situation that encumbers the following analysis is that less is known about small cases than about big ones. It renders invalid or impossible several comparisons that I had scheduled on the basis of information from the interviews. An example is the test I proposed of the hypothesis that Negroes, being less sophisticated negotiators, would receive smaller awards than whites. Analysis of files of claimants identified as Negroes failed to support the hypothesis, which I had offered with great confidence; in fact, the data indicated that Negroes receive more for their claims than whites. Not only is this finding in conflict with a theoretical approach that is supported by many other comparisons, but it is inconsistent with the finding that Negroes as defendants pay considerably less. (Negro defendants drive disproportionately in areas where Negro plaintiffs are likely to be found.) I believe that the disconfirmation of the hypothesis results from the fact that the routine forms allow no room for identifying race. This information is given only in the memos. Since the memos are found mainly in the bigger cases, it is only Negroes with complex claims whose race is identified. Evidence for this interpretation comes from the fact that reasonable estimates of the proportion of all drivers and thus of all claimants who might be Negro far exceed the number of Negroes identified in the files. I have tried to warn the reader where this artifact seems to be a possible contaminant of the analyses given below.

For both the major dependent variables, the measure routinely used is the mean. This leads to another problem in interpretation of the analyses. Claims settlements are not normally distributed; the distribution is skewed, with the majority of payments at zero or near to it, and some few in the neighborhood of $100,000. In this situation, the mean, though significant, can be an unstable statistic. The addition of one settlement for $20,000 to a small group of settlements averaging $100 can change the findings markedly.[5] In the light of this danger, and the fact that resources did not permit analysis of a larger number of cases, I

5. The median might have been a more stable statistic, but the available computer facility was unable to supply a routine computation of median values.

have tried to keep the numerical bases of comparisons large by the use of simple divisions such as dichotomies. However, this device was insufficient to prevent the possibility of occasional misleading results, and particular caution must be taken in evaluating means based on small numbers of cases such as 20 or 30.

In sum, the sample analyzed was randomly drawn from the universe of claims files received by the home office of a major insurance company during a limited period in 1962. Statistical generalizability is limited to the practices of Acme offices reporting at that time. I do not believe these practices to be importantly different from those of other reputable companies in the recent past. However, certain analyses are hampered by defects in the data. The most important of these in my opinion are the instability of the mean where the underlying distribution is skewed, and the differential availability of certain kinds of data as this is associated with claims size and complexity. To overcome these defects I have omitted certain analyses and based others on a division of the data that might appear less refined than would otherwise be desirable. I have also tried to circumscribe with qualifications any conclusions that strike me as questionable for methodological reasons. On the other hand, where consistent results of a respectable magnitude occur in the direction predicted by theory, I believe they should be accepted as genuine unless more convincing evidence is offered to the contrary.

Recovery Over-All

The average payment made for the 2,216 claims sampled was $733. However, a large proportion of the claims were closed with no payment at all; these constituted 34 per cent of the sample. The mean payment on claims for which any payment was made equalled $1,106. Although these figures might suggest that most claims dealt with fairly serious losses, this impression is misleading. It results from the fact that the distribution of payments is highly skewed. Many claims are paid in trivial amounts: 33 per cent of all paid claims received $100 or less, and 67 per cent received $500 or less. On the other hand, 3 per cent received more than $5,000, and payments as high as $100,000 were found.

The formal tort law prescribes that liability claims payments are to be made as a result of negligence on the part of the insured, and management policy at Acme strongly supported negligence as the *sine qua non* of payment. The policy was pervasive throughout the supervisory structure and, as shown in Chapter 2, it was supported by the personal attitudes of the adjusting staff. Accordingly, I predicted with great confidence that there would be a positive relationship between the amount of payment and the degree of apparent liability shown in the file. Two different tests support the projected relationship.

The first and most straightforward test compares the adjuster's opinion of liability as expressed in the first Pending File Report with the number of claims paid and the average amount paid per claim. The claims were rated as being of liability, no liability, or questionable liability. Of the 486 claims judged to entail liability, 444 (91 per cent) were paid, with an average payment of $2,103; of the 232 claims judged to entail no liability, only 78 (34 per cent) were paid, and these received the much smaller sum of $386 per paid claim; of the 168 claims judged questionable, 134 (80 per cent) were paid an average of $1,942. A weakness of this measure is that claims closed before 180 days had elapsed contained no rating of liability, and this rating was missing in a fair proportion of the longer-running cases because of missing forms and forms lacking the necessary data. Thus, the relationship and the figures are based on only 886 cases of the more than 2,200 cases in the sample.

A more encompassing but less direct measure of liability is the judgment of the coders for this study, based on the diagram or description of the accident as contained in the file. Coders were instructed to ascribe apparent liability according to an accident typology derived from the interviews.[6] Thus, all rear-end collisions with the insured behind were categorized as cases of apparent liability; where the insured was in the front car, they were categorized as apparent nonliability. One-car accidents were categorized as involving apparent liability (for claimant passengers), as were intersection accidents where the insured was faced with a stop sign, etc. Other types of accidents, such as those involving an uncontrolled intersection, were characterized as questionable. This procedure led to a categorization whereby 1,444 claims were judged to involve apparent liability, 567 were judged to involve apparent non-liability, and 205 were

6. See Chapter 3, pp. 102–104.

basically questionable or could not be resolved because of insufficient information. Although there is room for error in this simple categorization, it is based on the entire sample of 2,216 cases, and, as demonstrated in Table 3.2, the measure correlated well with the more direct measure of the adjuster's opinion.

This measure of apparent liability also shows a strong relationship with payment outcome. Of the cases judged to involve liability, 76 per cent were paid, at an average of $1,254 each; of the cases judged to involve no liability, 38 per cent were paid, at an average of $493; of the questionable cases, 73 per cent were paid an average of $902.

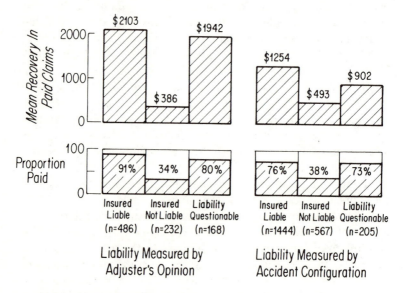

Figure 5.1 Recovery and Liability

The relationship between recovery and liability, approximated by these two different measures, is diagrammed in Figure 5.1. It is clear from this figure that there is strong evidence in support of the hypothesis that payment is related to liability. Both the proportion of claims paid and the average payment were related to apparent liability in the Acme files. This relationship is legitimated in the formal law, and in the policy of the company and the attitudes of the adjusters, and the result is surprising only in the proportion of apparent nonliability cases that receive some payment, although this is considerably smaller than the proportion of payments made in cases of apparent liability.[7] For the purpose of this study, the relationship is not so much important in its own right as it is in statistically controlling other comparisons concerning variables that are not within the compass of the formal law.

A second fundamental correlate of payment is also derived from the formal law. This is losses. According to the formal law, payment by one whose negligence causes injury to another is to compensate the victim for the losses which were caused by that negligence. I proposed with confidence that greater losses would be associated with higher payments on bodily injury liability claims. Figure 5.2 shows strong support for this hypothesis, where

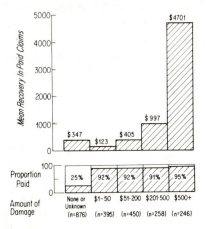

Figure 5.2 Recovery and Loss, Measured by Special Damages

*Despite the curvilinearity of the results, the data in the top graph conform statistically to an expected ranking that increases from top to bottom. The test used is the Jonckheere Distribution-free K-sample Test against an ordered alternative. This test pits the null hypothesis that the samples are randomly drawn from the same population against the alternative hypothesis that the samples conform to an expected ranking. The probability of these figures appearing if the null hypothesis were valid is less than .02. The data were also submitted to an analysis of variance using unweighted means, in which this effect was shown to be significant at the .01 level. References: A. R. Jonckheere, "A Distribution-free K-sample Test Against Ordered Alternatives, *Biometrika* 41:133, 1954; Jerome L. Myers, *Fundamentals of Experimental Design* (Allyn & Bacon, 1966), pp. 104–111.

7. I have checked these relationships for claimants outside the insured car to be sure that these payments were not merely first-party medical payments that had become confused with liability payments. The pattern is identical in these tabulations.

the measure of loss is total special damages as computed from the file. The index adds medical expenses, lost wages, and occasional additional costs such as nursing care or physical therapy, and with one exception shows a direct correlation with the average payment. (Note also in Figure 5.2 that payment is made in at least 9 out of 10 claims where any measurable loss has been incurred; the proportion of claimants recovering something does not increase with the amount of loss.) Another approach relates the average payment to the type of injury sustained. The injuries were categorized as (1) non-existent or unknown; (2) totally subjective, with no external signs of harm; (3) visible, but unimportant, such as scratches and bruises; (4) minor injuries, leaving no residual conditions; (5) moderate or severe injuries; and (6) fatal injuries. The relationship to payment is seen in Figure 5.3. In general, the shape of the relationship is similar to that in Figure 5.2, but there are two important irregularities. First, it is seen that the most

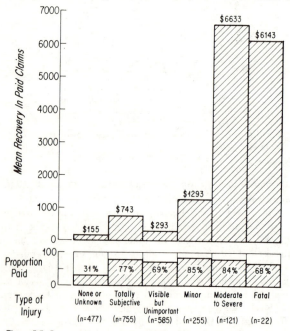

Figure 5.3 Recovery and Loss, Measured by Apparent Injury

° Despite considerable curvilinearity, the data are shown to conform to a predicted ranking from top to bottom to a degree well beyond chance expectations. Both the Jonckheere test and the analysis of variance show the probability of these results under the conditions of the null hypothesis to be less than .01. For references, see Table 5.1.

severe, i.e., fatal, injuries are not compensated quite as highly as the previously listed category. This may be understandable in terms of the formal law, which grants reparations for the pain and suffering and residual impairments of the living, but not for death *per se.* Indeed, the recovery for death may be limited to a specified maximum by a wrongful death statute. Of more interest is the fact that payments for totally subjective injuries are higher than those for injuries that are visible but unimportant. In other words, an injury that is impossible or at least highly difficult to prove may be a source of a considerably higher payment than is one that is readily proved and difficult to deny, but that is equally easy to demonstrate as being trivial. It seems reasonable to assume that the advantage appears in the negotiation process, by enhancing the ability of the claimant to increase or threaten to increase the monetary measure of damages and by making it more difficult for the adjuster to commit himself to a particular evaluation of the case.[8]

Again, with the exception of the unexpected advantage of the claimant with totally subjective damages, the results of testing the relationship between damages and claims outcomes are unsurprising.[9] They are predicted by the formal law and are inherent in company policy. As with liability, the principal significance of damages for this study is that they must be statistically controlled in looking for other relationships.

Control of liability and damages has been attempted in evaluating many of the relationships to be discussed further in this chapter. The control consists of dichotomizing all cases according to both apparent liability and apparent injury, resulting in a four-fold division, as follows:

1. Liability likely; injury moderate, serious or fatal. There were 94 such cases, of which 82 received some settlement from the insurance company.

2. Liability likely; injury minor or unknown. There were

8. This interpretation implies that the represented claimant would be more likely to obtain the advantage mentioned than would the unrepresented claimant. The relevant data appear below in Figure 5.5, p. 193, and support the interpretation.

9. Higher settlements with more serious injuries or greater economic loss are consistently reported in the literature. See, for instance, Conard *et. al., op. cit.,* Figure 6–16, p. 201, and Allen M. Linden, *The Report of the Osgood Hall Study on Compensation for Victims of Automobile Accidents* (privately printed, 1965), Chapter IV, p. 18. However, both studies report that the higher settlements in larger cases constitute a lower percentage of the loss experienced.

1,350 of these cases, more than half of the total files. Of these, 1,021 received some settlement.

3. Liability unlikely; injury moderate, serious or fatal. There were only 49 cases in this category, of which 35 received some settlement.

4. Liability unlikely; injury minor or unknown. There were 723 such cases, of which 331 received some settlement.[10]

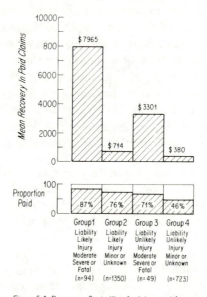

Figure 5.4 Recovery, Controlling for Injury and Apparent Liability

*It was predicted that the recovery of cases in Group 1 would exceed that in Group 2. Group 3 would exceed Group 4, Group 1 would exceed Group 3, and Group 2 would exceed Group 4. All these predictions are confirmed at the .01 level by the Jonckheere test. For references, see Figure 5.1

10. It was unfortunate for the purposes of the following analyses that the categories contained very unequal numbers of cases. Group 3 was particularly short on cases, rendering several proposed analyses either weak or impossible. A different conceptualization of injuries would have remedied the problem by defining more cases as serious, but the categories as presented rest on theoretical grounds: the line between minor and moderate injuries seems to correspond roughly to the dividing line between routine and serious cases, as the participants view the matter.

The distribution of payments for the cases within this four-fold categorization is shown in Figure 5.4. As expected, the payments were highest in Group 1, lowest in Group 4, and intermediate in the remaining categories. This categorization controls in part for the two formally most important correlates and justifications of claims outcomes. It is, however, to the variation that remains within these categories that I wish to turn now. With liability and injury under some degree of control, I will explore some other factors, most of them outside the purview of the formal law, that affect the outcomes of claims within the limits set by these powerful and recognized criteria. For it is here that the pressures and procedures of human institutions transform a system of abstract rules, modifying it so that it may be rendered workable.

Characteristics of the Parties

Part of the conventional wisdom of the legal profession is the idea that recoveries, either litigated or settled, are affected by the socioeconomic characteristics of the parties. Age, sex, minority status, and similar attributes of litigants are believed to affect the determinations of juries, for the extralegal reasons of sympathy and prejudice. These beliefs are often put forward in negotiation in support of raising or lowering the proposed settlement in a parallel manner. Several such factors are specified in guides to attorneys and adjusters on settlement,[11] and some empirical research relevant to these matters appears—for tried cases only—in the Jury Verdict Reports.[12]

These ideas concerning the effect of certain socioeconomic variables on settlement were adopted as hypotheses for this study, and I extracted as much relevant material as the data sources permitted. Unfortunately, apart from age and sex, very little information on these hypotheses was available in the routine cases, and on the whole I believe the attempt to investigate these matters provided little illumination. Not only were the differences generally small, as compared with other factors investigated in this study, but there is also reason to believe that some of the factors mentioned are partially correlated with the major explanatory variables of liability and damages, and it was not always possible to isolate the interrelated variables.

11. See Chapter 3, footnote 17.
12. *Personal Injury Valuation Handbooks* (Colorado Edition, Jury Verdict Research, Inc.)

differences generally small, as compared with other factors investigated in this study, but there is also reason to believe that some of the factors mentioned are partially correlated with the major explanatory variables of liability and damages, and it was not always possible to isolate the interrelated variables.

As an example, the sex of the claimant was examined for a possible relationship with recovery. The Jury Verdict Reports had investigated this matter, and found no systematic effect of the plaintiff's sex on jury verdicts.[13] The present study found a similar state of affairs in settlements. Although there were some over-all differences—women recovered slightly more often (70 per cent of claims *vs.* 64 per cent for men) but received somewhat less in the average paid claim ($956 *vs.* $1,228)[14]—these differences disappeared when liability and injury were controlled.

The Jury Verdict Reports show differences in recovery by age of the claimant. Children and teenagers to age 16 are there reported to do less well before a jury than do adults, and although the aged receive awards in fewer cases, the awards they receive are no lower than those of other adults.[15] The Acme data indicate differences in the same direction for children and teenagers for all recoveries, including settlements. The mean compensation in paid claims for adults was $1,386; for claimants under age 14, the mean was $1,216, and for those from 15 to 20 it was $992.[16] Opposed to the Jury Verdict Reports finding is the fact that in the Acme files the elderly, over 65, had an average recovery of $1,954—considerably more than other adults[17] —and they did not differ importantly in the proportion of cases in which they recovered. It may be that old people have an advantage in settlement that they do not have in trial; for

13. *Personal Injury Valuation Handbooks* 5:2025, 1964.
14. The percentage differences, but not the dollar differences, are significant at the .05 level. ($Z = 2.86$ and 1.11 respectively).
15. *Personal Injury Valuation Handbooks* 5:3026, 1964; 5:3102, 1965; 5:2050, 1964.
16. However, the differences are not sufficient; $Z = 0.13$ and 1.42 respectively. Nor were the differences in proportions of claims paid significant.
17. However, this difference was not significant ($Z = 0.44$).

instance, their claims may be perceived by adjusters as being more "dangerous" than the claims of younger people.[18]

Perhaps the most interesting hypothesis furnished by the Jury Verdict Reports concerns the recovery of Negroes. In the trials studied, members of "minority groups" recovered no less often than did other people, but their awards averaged 15 per cent less.[19] In contrast, those Acme claimants known to be Negro not only recovered slightly more often than other people, but their average award was more than 50 per cent higher.[20] As explained above, it is probable that this finding is an artifact of the availability of data; race was identified only in the adjusters' memos, and these were more likely to be available in the more serious cases. An important reason to doubt the validity of the finding concerning Negro plaintiffs appears when one looks at the experience of Negro defendants. Knowledge of the fact that an insured was a Negro also depends on the existence of a memo, and thus is more frequent in more serious cases, yet cases with Negro insureds on the average were settled for less than half the amount of cases with white insureds. Note, however, that 76 per cent of people claiming against a Negro insured recovered, as against 66 per cent of all claimants. In sum, the picture concerning race is clouded by insufficient data, and the image that does come through suggests that the effect of race on settlements is not a simple one.

Many people interviewed in the study suggested that residents of large cities recover more than small-town and country people for similar injuries, and this impression has been supported in previous literature.[21] The impression was verified in the Acme files. The average settlement of rural residents is exceeded by that of small-town people, which is exceeded by that of residents of small cities, which in turn is exceeded by that of the

18. See the section on danger value, pp. 199–204.
19. *Personal Injury Valuation Handbooks* 5:2076, 1964.
20. The average recovery for all claimants identified as Negro was $1189, compared with $733 for the entire sample. Claims with Negro *defendants*, however, were paid an average of only $347.
21. See Linden, *op. cit.*, Chapter IV, p. 14. However, city-dwellers report proportionately more small accidents: Conard *et al.*, *op. cit.*, pp. 169–170.

residents of large cities.[22] However, the proportion recovering shows little variation, and the figures for represented claimants show a rather different pattern.

In passing, it is interesting to look at the recovery of claimants who, according to the record, had made previous claims for automobile bodily injuries. This information is obtained by the insurance company by checking the names of current claimants with the Index Bureau, which serves the bulk of the insurance industry in this matter.[23] Notification that a person has made a previous claim puts the adjuster on guard by raising the suspicion that past injuries may be claimed to be a result of the present mishap, or the possibility that the claimant may be habitual or dishonest. This information notwithstanding, the claims of the 87 people who had a record with the Index Bureau were more frequently paid (74 per cent *vs.* 66 per cent) and at a higher amount ($1,387 *vs.* $1,093).[24] Perhaps one reason why claimants with an Index Bureau record did not fare worse is that more of them were represented (40 per cent) than of the claimants with a clear record (27 per cent).[25]

Since the insured plays a smaller role in settlement than does the claimant, it was expected that his characteristics would be less of a factor than those of the claimant. The analysis here was again hampered by insufficient data. The only interesting finding concerning the characteristics of the insured was that when the driver was covered as an employee of an insured, cases were almost twice as expensive as when the driver was insured in his own right.[26] This finding is perhaps explained by the feeling of adjusters that cases involving large corporations

22. See Table 5.3, p. 186. Combining represented and unrepresented cases, and comparing SMSA cases with the remainder, the difference is statistically significant at the .01 level (Z = 8.55).

23. The Index Bureau is described in Chapter 3, p. 93.

24. The advantage of those with Index Bureau records is not statistically significant. For the proportion, $Z = 1.46$; for the mean difference, $t = 0.75$. However, it is clear that those with Bureau records are not disadvantaged.

25. The data were not sufficient to test this explanation.

26. The average payment in paid claims where the defendants were employees was $1535, compared with $980 for others. However, the difference failed to reach statistical significance: $t = 1.45$.

and transport companies are more dangerous than most before a jury and therefore require higher settlements.

Representation

Representation was found to be the most important single factor accounting for payment, apart from liability and damages. Although it is formally irrelevant to the worth of a claim, and is denied or minimized in discussion by most insurance company executives and by many adjusters, the presence of a lawyer is none the less a major influence on the outcome of bodily injury claims.

An advantage to the attorney in terms of gross recovery was predicted because of the fact that claims men generally evaluate a represented claim more highly than an unrepresented one.[27] However, the amount of advantage that a represented claim bears was unexpected. A first glimpse of the effect of representation is provided by Figure 5.5, which shows the average recovery of represented claimants to be from 4 to 12 times as high as that of the unrepresented

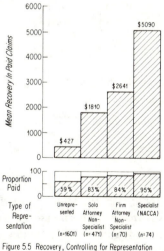

Figure 5.5 Recovery, Controlling for Representation

* The differential in mean recovery between unrepresented cases and all represented cases combined is significant at the .01 level, for all cases and for paid cases only.

claimants.[28] Although some of this apparent advantage is spurious—
related to the kind of claims that attorneys agree to represent—the fact
remains that at every level of damages and liability, the outcome in a
represented case is likely to be more favorable to the claimant than that
in an unrepresented case. This fact is documented in Table 5.1 which
shows the recovery in represented and unrepresented claims with a

*Table 5.1. Recovery and representation with control for apparent
liability and injury*

	Liability likely, injury moderate, severe or fatal	Liability likely, injury minor or unknown	Liability unlikely, injury moderate, severe or fatal	Liability unlikely, injury minor or unknown
Per cent represented	60	29	53	20
Per cent recovering:				
unrepresented cases	79 ⎫ °	69 ⎫ °	61 ⎫ †	42 ⎫ °
represented cases	93 ⎭	92 ⎭	81 ⎭	62 ⎭
Mean recovery in paid cases:				
unrepresented	$1,652 ⎫ °	$329 ⎫ °	$5,769 ⎫ †	$235 ⎫ °
represented	$11,608 ⎭	$1,438 ⎭	$1,655 ⎭	$763 ⎭
Total cases with information available	94	1,350	49	723

° Difference significant at the $p < .05$ level.
† Not statistically significant.

simultaneous control for liability and injury. The judgment concerning
liability and injury was made for each case by coders, who looked
mainly at the accident configuration to determine apparent liability,
and at medical reports and statements to determine injury.[29] The table
shows that in every liability-injury category the *proportion* of

28. The magnitude of the differences renders statistical tests unnecessary.
29. See Chapter 3, pp. 116–122.

claimants recovering some award is considerably higher when the claimants are represented. The advantage of the represented claimant in terms of chance of recovery is not obliterated by unlikely liability. Table 5.1 also shows considerable advantage in terms of *average* settlement for all paid claims in all categories except the one embracing unfavorable liability and serious injury. This exception is explained by the instability of the mean because of the small number of paid cases (14) and the presence in this group of two extrordinary settlements, one for $61,000 and one for $11,000. The median shows a difference in the expected direction—a recovery of $1,125 for the represented and of $500 for the unrepresented.

The above-mentioned findings suggest that there is some value accorded to claims merely because of representation.[30] This situation is understable, less in the light of the attorney's knowledge of the formal law than in the light of his negotiation power. Were knowledge of formal law the key to the attorney's advantage, one might expect the advantage to weaken proportionately as the case became weaker in formal law but the fact is that the attorney has as great an advantage over the unrepresented claimant in cases where liability is weak and injury is insignificant as in cases where liability is clear and injury is significant. Negotiation power, on the other hand, is present throughout the range of liability and injury combinations. The attorney, as compared with the unrepresented claimant, understands the rules of negotiation; he knows that payment will be made on a danger or nuisance value basis in nearly any bona fide claim, provided that the insurance company believes that the claims will be pressed, and the attorney can credibly threaten to take any claim to court. He may

30. The suggestion is strongly supported in the literature. See Conard *et al.*, *op. cit.*, Figure 6–7, p. 189; Linden, *op. cit.*, Chapter IV, p. 27; Clarence Morris and James C. N. Paul, "The Financial Impact of Automobile Accidents," *University of Pennsylvania Law Review* 110:913, 1962; Mark H. Franklin, Robert H. Chanin, and Irving Mark, "Accidents, Money and the Law: A Study of the Economics of Personal Injury Litigation," *Columbia Law Review* 61:1, 1961.

also credibly threaten to accumulate testimony favorable to liability and to magnify the appearance of an injury. Moreover, an attorney in accepting a case has the advantage of a tacit commitment: both he and the insurance adjuster know that his (the attorney's) business and reputation would be threatened by a trivial settlement or a denial. This knowledge lends additional credibility to the attorney's threats, and makes his threats and rationalizations more effective tools in securing a higher settlement for any given claim.

To this point I have been concerned with the effects of representation on recovery. To continue, I would like to consider some prior correlates or causes of representation. Superficial consideration of the attorney's interest in a bodily injury claim suggests that the contingent fee among other factors would strongly favor representation of more serious cases. The top line of Table 5.1 verifies that representation is in fact much more likely in cases with at least moderate injuries.[31] On the other hand, superficial considerations would also suggest that attorneys would tend to restrict representation to claims with favorable liability, yet the top line of Table 5.1 shows that unfavorable liability exerts but a small influence on the proportion of cases represented. In other words, the size of the claim is much more important in determining representation than is apparent formal liability. This state of affairs may be explained by the fact that represented cases tend to receive substantial settlements even when formal liability is doubtful. The third line of Table 5.1 attests to this fact. It is particularly interesting to note that when injuries are moderate or serious there is very little reduction due to unfavorable liability in the high proportion of represented claims on which some payment is made.

Two additional correlates of representation verify impressions received in the interviews. First, Table 5.2 presents the relation-

31. See also Conard *et. al., op. cit.,* pp. 226–227; Linden, *op. cit.,* Chapter V, p. 15. Although part of the correlation may be explained as manipulation of the facts concerning a given claim by the attorney, I believe that the bulk of the association is due to the inclination of claimants with higher losses to seek representation and to the greater willingness of attorneys to accept claims with larger losses and thus potentially larger recoveries.

ship between representation and recovery controlling for the size of the city, and indicates that representation is generally related to the urbanization of the jurisdiction.[32] The proportion of claims represented in the large central cities is double that in small cities or in the countryside, and this in turn can probably be explained by the relative sophistication and wariness of the city-dwellers. On the other hand, the proportion of represented cases that recover does not fluctuate much in this instance, and the average settlement in paid cases actually declines with increasing urbanization. This apparent paradox is most likely explained by the inclusion of larger numbers of small cases and cases of tenuous liability in the total mix accepted by the urban lawyers. The small town and country lawyers probably deal with a more selected group of cases. The higher payments on unrepresented claims in the urbanized jurisdictions are in accord with general

Table 5.2 Recovery and representation with control for size of city

| | City size SMSA° more than 1,000,000 | | | | |
	Central	Ring	SMSA less than 1,000,000	Other urban	Rural
Per cent represented	38	33	21	16	19
Per cent recovering:					
unrepresented	61	58	60	58	57
represented	81	90	87	· 90	85
Mean recovery in paid cases:					
unrepresented	$576	$344	$405	$386	$326
represented	$1,422	$2,452	$2,609	$4,891	$2,697
Total cases with information available	698	383	576	268	130

° Standard Metropolitan Statistical Area.

32. Statistical significance is reported in footnote 22, above.

expectations concerning the effect of the city size on claims; however, the effect is not as drastic or as uniform as one might have thought prior to viewing the data.

A second suggestion in the interviews was that Jewish claimants, along with certain other nationality groups, were particularly likely to be represented. Analysis of the files confirmed this suggestion; claimants with Jewish surnames were found far more likely to be represented than others (59 per cent *vs.* 26 per cent for other whites). The probability of their receiving any award, however, was somewhat lower (77 per cent *vs.* 84 per cent, respectively).[33] The explanation for the lower recovery of represented Jewish claimants is probably identical to that for the relationship with urbanization—the larger number of Jewish claims represented must have included some less meritorious claims.

Additional analyses were attempted to explore the relationships between representation and other characteristics of the claimant. No differences were found in representation by age or sex of the claimant, and an attempt to investigate race was abandoned because of the unsatisfactory state of the data concerning Negroes.

In sum, representation is unequally distributed in the population of claims: large claims, claims with apparent liability, claims of metropolitan residents, and claims of Jews are instances of categories where representation is relatively high. Although groups with high proportions of represented cases may experience a somewhat smaller proportion of paid claims, the level of payments in represented claims is considerably higher than in unrepresented claims, even though the official policy of the company and the formal law are both to the contrary. This fact is most likely explained in large part by the superior negotiating ability of an attorney as compared with the usual unrepresented claimant.

33. The use of last names to identify Jews is a very imprecise technique, but it was the only one available for these data. The status of the findings with regard to Jews is merely suggestive.

Recovery without Liability: Danger Value

All claims made under bodily injury liability policies are based on formal law, which requires proof that the insured was negligent—that he failed in his duty to others to exercise reasonable care as a driver. Moreover, in 44 of the 50 states, the law requires that the claimant himself be free of the taint of negligence. In these states, a claimant who contributed significantly to the accident in which he was injured has no right to any recovery at all.

Critical scientific studies of traffic accidents suggest that a literal application of these rules would result in very few recoveries. Routine accidents involve ordinary drivers making ordinary mistakes; the behavior that causes accidents is usually no more "unreasonable" than that which results in a safe journey. The fact is that ordinary men with ordinary capacities are not always a match for the combination of vehicles and highways that contemporary automobile transportation demands. Moreover, in two-car accidents, it is seldom the case that one driver has not contributed substantially to the accident.[34]

However, the rules of the law of negligence are not in fact literally applied, even at the level of the courts.[35] Even less are they applied at the level of the law in action. Perhaps the best evidence for this proposition is the proportion of claims that are

34. See *Selected Reports from Case Studies of Traffic Accidents* (Northwestern University Traffic Institute, 1960); Arthur D. Little, Inc., *The State of the Art of Traffic Safety: A Critical Review of the Technical Information on Factors affecting Traffic Safety* (Automobile Manufacturers Association, 1966); Murray Blumenthal, "Dimensions of the Traffic Safety Problem," *Papers of the Automotive Engineering Congress of the Society of Automotive Engineers*, No. 670011 (1967). The latter quotes a U.S. Department of Commerce analysis of road safety as follows:

> Drivers are being asked to make judgments that they cannot make well: to make decisions faster than humanly possible, and to make changes in direction and speed more accurately than they possibly can.

Blumenthal also notes the persistence of accidents among professional drivers at the General Motors Proving Grounds, despite their superior training, supervision, and carefully engineered highways, as evidence of the inevitability of accidents under the conditions of current technology.

35. See Chapter 6, pp. 233–243.

in fact paid. Recall that Acme opens a file for all accidents that appear serious unless there is a very strong indication of no liability in the first notice (e.g., the insured was parked). Recovery occurred in 66 per cent of the claims studied, and in 58 per cent of all claims made by parties outside the insured car.[36] For comparison, consider that if the insureds were negligent, strictly speaking, in as many as three quarters of all reported accidents, and if the claimants were free of significant negligence in half of these, one would expect liability payments to be justified in only about 38 per cent of all claims.

The suspicion that payment is made in the absence of clear liability is supported by more than gross estimates. In this section I shall marshal evidence from the interviews of adjusters to the effect that such payment is knowingly made, and shall support the interviews with further analyses of the data. That these payments are made not only despite the formal law, but also despite the expressed policy of company management, can be explained by reference to the informal pressures operating in settlement negotiation.

It was noted previously that adjusters and attorneys use different principles of evaluation, depending on whether they classify the claim as routine or serious. This distinction is carried over into negotiation, and one of the major issues in claims handling concerns into which of these categories a particular claim is to be classified. The distinction also regulates the matter at hand. The occasion and reasons for payment in the absence of liability differ depending on the size of the damages. Where the objective loss has been serious, I shall speak of "danger value," words considered legitimate at Acme. Where the claim is routine, I shall speak of "nuisance value," a term much less in favor but apt and descriptive.

Danger value is legitimized at Acme, although not for the amount that is often paid in cases that seem to fit the description. Acme's training materials put the matter of danger value thus:

36. Parties not in the insured car are ineligible for medical payments benefits, and payments to them must be on a liability basis. See footnote 4.

Our [claim policy] is a very simple one: to operate on a merit basis, paying every dollar we owe no matter how great or small the amount involved and to deny liability in those cases in which we are of the firm conviction that no liability attaches to our insured . . .

As is true of all rules, there are exceptions to this one. Experience has clearly demonstrated that in fatal cases, as well as in those involving extremely serious injuries, juries are prone to be swayed by sympathy, completely ignoring the evidence and the law as charged by the court. Rather than expose ourselves to large though unwarranted verdicts, we endeavor to dispose of such claims by paying what we call a "danger value," usually ranging from $500 to $750, which is ordinarily adequate to cover the funeral or hospital or medical expenses. This practice is followed universally in disposing of claims arising out of automobile accidents, because a question of fact may be developed almost without exception, actual witnesses to the event seldom being in complete accord as to all the circumstances surrounding the occurrence. In other liability cases we are dealing for the most part with fixed objects and with conditions about which there can be no dispute. Here we refuse to pay even a danger value.[37]

A letter from a top claims official at Acme explains the source of the danger value rule:

The reason the danger value rule was established over 25 years ago, no longer exists. In the 1930–40 period a large percentage of the population was without accident-sickness or death benefits insurance, and when accidents occurred and the case was considered to be one of no liability no money was available to pay the medical expenses, so the doctors and hospitals would direct the injured party to an attorney in an effort to collect their fees. By paying "danger

---

37. Education Department, Acme Insurance Company, *Readings in Property and Casualty Insurance* (privately printed, 1965), p. C&L 2.

value" it was believed a great deal of pressure was removed from the claimant and no litigation would result . . . .

> We use the rule now mostly where there are serious injuries, such as will produce a jury verdict for the claimant due to jury sympathy. . . . We now actually consider it as a "compromise" as exposure to a jury is dangerous.

According to the Acme adjuster's manual, danger value payments may be made when injuries are so serious that a likely jury verdict upon a finding of liability would be $7,500 or greater. The amount assigned to danger value reflects the company's assumption that a successful suit, while not impossible, would be unlikely, but that without any payment many claimants would attempt suit, the defense of which would always be an expense to the company.

What is explicitly recognized in Acme's danger value is tacitly recognized in the handling of large cases by all the companies studied. Most seriously injured people are expected to have a fair chance of securing representation and filing suit in the event their claims are denied. A considerable amount of expense will be borne by the company even if motions to dismiss at trial are successful. Moreover, judges as well as juries may be sympathetic, and most adjusters know of several cases in which what appeared to be a no-liability claim won an award of five or six figures. Thus, a settlement of a claim in this category represents a very likely saving of hundreds of dollars in processing costs, as well as an occasional saving of thousands of dollars in judgments. All this is specifically acknowledged by adjusters. For instance:

> I'm thinking of a case of a thirty-five year old retarded man. . . . Even though he ran the red light, and I have witnesses, I think the jury will become so emotional about this that this is a special circumstance. This is a case where in fact I should deny it, but I don't intend to. I intend to pay this person. It's dangerous insofar as the insurance company is concerned.

Statistics from the Acme files support the assertion that some payment is made in the vast majority of cases in which damages are high, regardless of the liability situation. Indirect proof comes from Figure 5.2, where it was shown, for example, that among the 246 cases with damages in excess of $500, 233 or 95 per cent recovered something. A different computation, based on Figure 5.4, shows that there were 49 cases in all where injuries were judged to be moderate or worse, yet where liability was at best questionable. Of this group, 71 per cent received some payment.[38] This is a considerably better recovery rate than that of all claimants, and is not so very much less than the 87 per cent who recovered with similar injuries but favorable liability. Recomputation to exclude possible medical payments awards showed an even higher payment rate for this group—80 per cent. It is, then, only the exceptional claimant with serious injuries who recovers nothing from the insurance company.[39] The law in action would seem to embody danger value.[40]

In the light of considerations of potential cost, the payment of danger value would seem to be rational. Failure to settle large claims where liability was unfavorable to the claimant would be likely to result in many suits, some of which would be successful. Direct and indirect processing costs would be paid by the company, and isolated judgments for the plaintiff might be for considerable amounts. The level of payment actually made in these cases would seem to represent a saving over total costs under a more resistant policy, but this judgment is, of course, speculative.[41] Buttressing the rationality of these payments is the

38. The average payment in paid cases was $3,000, much less than the average $8,000 received in the 94 cases with similar injuries and favorable liability, but considerably more than the $500 to $750 officially payable as danger value.

39. Further analysis of this category, as well as of the category of claims with liability but no payment, would be desirable. These analyses were not pursued here because of the small number of cases and the condition of the data in the files.

40. Although the claims philosophy and evidence are those of Acme, similar philosophies and outcomes are reported to obtain generally. See Jerry S. Rosenbloom, *Automobile Liability Claims: Insurance Company Philosophies and Practices* (Richard D. Irwin, 1968), pp. 100–101.

41. Top claims officials of Acme believe that savings are accomplished by danger value payments. One of them speculates, in a private communication, that 20 claims closed at $1,000 each in danger value payments may avoid one $25,000 judgment.

intangible gain by the insurer in the form of greater good will and public esteem when it would seem to be acting generously.

Recovery without Liability: Nuisance Value

There is no policy at Acme comparable to danger value that could legitimate making payments in routine claims where liability was unfavorable to the claimant. On the contrary, the making of any payment in such circumstances is vehemently denied, and adjusters are unwilling to apply the term "nuisance value" to any payments they make. Witness the following statement:

> As long as I have been working here I have always hated the term, "nuisance claim." Really we don't pay nuisance value claims, and I never have. Maybe I have, but I won't admit it's a nuisance claim. . . . I'll give you an example: we went to Small Claims Court and it cost us $90 through our attorneys on a $27 claim. . . . I took two days off from work; the first trial was postponed due to lack of information. We went back and judgment was for the defendant in our favor. We could have paid the claim but the insured wasn't negligent.

This is common rhetoric in the companies I studied,[42] although its apparent irrationality in the context of a profit-oriented enterprise may be a first clue to the state of reality. Businesses are rarely run primarily on matters of principle. Claims of this sort are in fact very frequently paid, and nuisance value would seem to be a very descriptive term for the reasons why they are paid.

42. Rosenbloom contends that insurance companies are "almost without exception" opposed to paying nuisance value (*op. cit.*, p. 102). But note the following directions from training manual of one fairly important company:

> When a man says his neck hurts and that he's going to a doctor and build it up unless he gets a settlement, it may be best to give him something over his [property damage], twenty-five, fifty, even maybe a hundred dollars, depending on his appearance—how likely it appears that he can make it convincing if he tries.

Moreover, a textbook advises nuisance settlements if the claim is not false, fraudulent or groundless. See Victor C. Gorton, *Auto Claim Practice* (Rough Notes, 1963).

Two supervisors at Acme elaborate the above clue:

> We use a danger value, we use an infant value, but we don't consider a nuisance value—but sometimes, from an economical standpoint, you may pay a claim: it might pay you to pay $25, $50, maybe even several hundred dollars to settle a claim that is highly questionable [rather] than be faced with $750 in legal expenses to defend that case. . . . Well, to me it is nuisance value, but the Company says we don't have nuisance value, so to be out of trouble with the Company just say it is economical. . . . But this has to be very questionable liability. If it's no liability and a matter of principle is involved, I say [deny it].

> If you have any chance at all—the way I look at it—any chance at all of losing, it's better to settle this now for $50 than to see a file about four inches thick five years from now, and about $1,500 paid to our attorneys, and then go to court. You still stand a good chance of losing—not a good chance, but you stand a possible chance of losing the thing.

In fact, the same considerations mentioned above concerning the rationality of danger value would seem to warrant smaller payments for routine claims. Prosser, who alleges that nuisance payments are common, justifies them as follows:

> This is good business, since it retains the good will of both the plaintiff and the defendant, who may buy more insurance, and it helps the reputation of the company as a liberal payer of claims. It is also the cheapest way out in any case in which the "nuisance value" of the suit, which means the probable cost of investigation, preparation and trial, together with the off chance that the plaintiff might after all be able to prove his case, exceeds the amount paid. For obvious reasons, the claims so settled are almost invariably the smaller ones.[43]

43. William L. Prosser, *Torts* (Foundation Press, 1964), p. 570. The false last sentence testifies to the law professor's need for empirical research.

However, the question of payment is decided by claims men, and not by the company in some grand sense, nor even very effectively by top executives. In order to understand more completely why nuisance (as well as danger) produces payment in violation of official policy it is necessary to consider the problem of payment as the adjuster experiences it in his day-to-day rounds. From this perspective, the problems of handling an individual file become part of handling a total workload. The perspective is illustrated in this quotation from an adjuster working largely in the property line:

> When someone is pressuring for settlement . . . let me give you an example: You've got 85 to 90 cases—and many in this office have that many—I'm not speaking just of myself. . . . I drive about 2,500 miles a month. . . . Have you ever stopped to figure out how much time you spend just in an automobile? This is possibly two weeks. . . . Then you have a day in the office each week, so this leaves you at the most ten days to get out and make personal contact and to look at all the losses, this many losses, and take care of them. Now, then, an insured will have some sort of a loss, let's say a small fire loss, a kitchen fire loss, where you get smoke damage and maybe some curtains and some formica burned, and you just can't get to it in a fast enough time. They call the broker and the broker calls here and everybody starts running around all upset and you've got pressure. The first thing you do to get the pressure off of you is to adjust this thing with the broker, and you are going to give away money by doing this. I know I have done it and everybody else has done it, just because you have pressure and you don't have time to get it off of you in a hurry. . . . This costs the Company a fantastic amount of money.

The same pressures operating here, causing a property damage adjuster to pay amounts demanded by a broker for unverified damage, are operative in the bodily injury field. As previously noted, the heaviest pressures of supervision on the adjuster are the result of open files. Pending cases are highly visible in the aggregate; failure to close them subjects supervisors to complaints from claimants and their attorneys—both directly, and indirectly through letters to the home office, and to branch office managers. Moreover, open cases demand more investigation: thus, large numbers of pending files result in more work per file. From this perspective, the fact that payment in cases of doubtful liability may in the long run save the Company money is seen as a rationalization for the most effective technique of relieving short-range pressure on the adjuster. That the rationalization is objectively valid may partly account for the tolerance of nuisance payments on the supervisory levels, but in my experience the most direct cause of these payments is the pressure felt by adjusters to limit the numbers of pending files:

> I pay small claims that perhaps won't warrant it, and I shouldn't have paid when the case is questionable and there is no liability, and I should have denied. I have paid them to get rid of them. The thing is you sometimes get an overload. . . . Let's put it this way: . . . Mrs. Smith had a $15 bill. I don't want to go to Mrs. Smith and get a statement and then have to go to the Market and get another statement. I'll pay her [$15] and then go home.

How is this pattern, which I shall show to be rather general, allowed to prevail despite strong official opposition from top management? A ready answer is that the same pressures felt by adjusters are felt to some extent by first-level supervisors with respect to local management. The very small cases to which the nuisance value concept applies are not supervised directly above this first level. Tolerance of this deviance by first-level supervisors protects it from direct encounters with higher-level officialdom. A second and more general condition that preserves ability to pay claims with doubtful liability is the control that the adjuster exerts over the file. The appearance of liability can be manipulated to significant degree in the manner in which the statement is recorded, or in the memoranda and diagrams prepared by the adjuster. The following handling was prescribed for the case of "Mrs. Smith," just cited:

> I won't exactly lie in the file, but you butter up with a little here and a little there. You don't say that our Market was responsible and you don't say there was no liability.

The fact of payment of nuisance claims can be seen in the Acme files. In cases of minor or trivial injury and liability questionable or unfavorable for the claimant, payment was received by 42 per cent of the unrepresented claimants, and 62 per cent of the represented. Taking only cases where medical payments would not be available, 48 per cent of these claimants were paid. Mean payments were, as expected, small, but not neglible: they averaged $235 and $763 for unrepresented and represented cases, respectively. An extreme case is provided by the 111 cases in which the claimants drove into the insureds from the rear, and the claimants were not eligible for medical payments. Even here, 39 claimants managed to recover something, albeit the mean payment was $236. In sum, there is strong support for the interpretation offered by this adjuster, working with Mid-West:

> We never justify a payment of a nuisance claim. We're not supposed to make any payment. This is Company policy. We're not to make any payment. You never pay nuisance claims. But in fact the adjuster, because of this vagueness and the incompleteness of the investigation and different allegations, will find ways of justifying a payment of a nuisance claim. But he will never refer to it as that. There is a tremendous amount of nuisance claims today that are paid.

One might ask why, in the light of the apparent rationality of paying on small claims with doubtful liability, and in the light of the fact that somewhere near half of these claims seem to be paid, the managements of all the companies studied deny the legitimacy of these payments and declare sincerely that they do not make them. Consideration of the nature of negotiation provides an answer to this question. The statistics just submitted can be reversed: in particular, over half of the small claims based on tenuous liability are closed without payment. The same is true for more than a quarter of those claimants who suffer moderate or severe injuries with doubtful liability. Perhaps those claims that are successfully denied represent clearer instances of non-liability, but I have shown that even in the apparently clear-cut case of rear-end collisions, some claims are being paid. A simpler and more reasonable interpretation, supported by the differences in recovery between represented and unrepresented claimants, is that many unpaid claimants are less persistent. They are willing to take the company's denial with less of an argument than those who are paid. Added to these claimants are those whose inflexible demands exceed the adjuster's standards for nuisance payments. Most of the adjusters I studied would agree to a $50 demand to close *any* claim they believed would otherwise be seriously pressed, but few of them would pay more than a few hundred dollars in a case they believed was one of nuisance rather than liability.

Perhaps the most persuasive justification for an official philosophy that denies nuisance value although such payments are routinely being made is that the philosophy furnishes negotiation power to deny claims in marginal cases. The company's official stand is predicated upon principle: upon duties to policyholders, to stockholders or the members of mutual companies, and to the integrity of the law. The principle provides a rationalization for denial and is also available to strengthen a commitment to deny. At the same time, in those cases where the claimant impresses the adjuster as being unlikely to abandon his claim the ability to make covert nuisance payments results in the termination of large numbers of claims at less than processing costs.

In other words, the rational company ought to aim at a reputation for not paying nuisance value, while simultaneously utilizing nuisance payments to quiet claims that are not deterred by its reputation. The fact that policy is made by higher management, but claims are paid by adjusters, permits the companies studied to pursue these apparently conflicting goals with some degree of success.[44] Many insurance managements express distress over what they feel is a low image of their industry among the public.[45] Perhaps the silver lining to this cloud is that an image of the insurance industry that includes resistance to claims may create some bargaining power to counteract the very strong pressures that on a day-to-day basis favor payment of marginal and dubious claims.

Before leaving the matter of recovery in the absence of liability, I would like to note the comparison between recoveries in states following the contributory negligence rule and in the six states which, at the time of the study, had replaced the contributory negligence rule with comparative negligence. Under the latter rule, negligence on the part of the plaintiff merely reduces his recovery rather than eliminating it. The comparative negligence rule is favored by many representatives of the plaintiffs' bar and by many social critics, who believe that it results in more generous overall payments to claimants. For the same reason the new rule has generally been opposed by representatives of the insurance industry. For example:

> The effect of such a change in the law would be that a much higher percentage of negligence cases would go to

44. The problem of obtaining a reputation for resisting nuisance payments is, of course, most serious vis-à-vis members of the plaintiffs' bar but, as the following adjuster explains, even here little may be lost by nuisance payments:

> By nuisance value we mean it is a situation where the injury is not the important thing, except that the question of liability as to whether the injured party was contributorily negligent. In this situation some of these claims do have a nuisance value, and if you were to settle them for what you feel might be defense costs you would do it. However, every once in a while you work on the basis of the principle: Do you want to go ahead and continue paying these claims to eliminate them, or do you want to try and attempt to discourage them? And the only remark I can make about the latter alternative is the fact that there is not any publicity as to whether you discouraged it or not, and really it might have some effect upon that particular attorney, but if it goes through counsel elsewhere it is the same thing over again.

45. See, for instance, Insurance Information Institute, "The Public Appraises the Property and Casualty Insurance Industry," pamphlet, 1961; and "Trends in Public Appraisal of the Property and Casualty Insurance Business," pamphlet, 1964.

juries in which the only problem for the jury would be to determine the amount to be awarded to the plaintiff.[46]

Rosenberg reports that in Arkansas following the adoption of the comparative negligence rule lawyers and judges were of the opinion that plaintiffs won the liability question more often, but that there was no change in the size of the verdicts.[47]

The facts appearing in the Acme files are presented in Table 5.3, which indicates that, controlling for liability and injury, the proportion of claimants recovering in the comparative negligence states is not higher than that in contributory negligence states. Although the average recovery in paid cases is somewhat higher in the comparative negligence states, the difference is not significant.[48] It is not possible to press this analysis further with the number of cases available, and differences in region, urbanization, and other factors between the two groups of states hinder interpretation of these findings. However, the comparative negligence rule is not shown to produce necessarily higher settlements than the contributory negligence rule. Moreover, the comparative rule appears to offer a time savings in settling doubtful liability cases, which may benefit all parties to the negotiation.

Discounts

The previous sections suggest that in some circumstances the insurance company is at a disadvantage in negotiation relative to its position in the formal law. However, the pressures affecting the insurance company are also felt by the claimant, and there is a wide range of circumstances in which it would seem

46. Marcus L. Plaut, "Damages for Pain and Suffering," *Ohio State Law Journal* 19:200, 1958, p. 210. However, insurance industry opposition to the comparative negligence rule is not universal. Note the developments cited in Chapter 6, pp. 257–267.

47. Maurice Rosenberg, "Comparative Negligence in Arkansas: A 'Before and After' Survey," *Arkansas Law Review* 36: 457, 1964.

48. The differences are entirely due to represented cases, which recover an average of $5,493 in comparative negligence states. The average recovery in unrepresented claims is $422 and $428 in comparative negligence and contributory negligence jurisdictions, respectively.

Table 5.3. Recovery by negligence rule, controlling for apparent liability and injury

Liability-injury category	Comparative negligence states				Contributory negligence states			
	Number of cases	Per cent recovering	Mean recovery in paid cases	Mean time lapse in days	Number of cases	Per cent recovering	Mean recovery in paid cases	Mean time lapse in days
1. Liability likely; injury moderate, serious, or fatal	7	°	°	°	87	86	$6,208	546
2. Liability likely; injury minor or unknown	72	68	$410	337	1,278	76	$548†	342
3. Liability unlikely; injury moderate, serious, or fatal	2	°	°	°	47	72	$2,431	625
4. Liability unlikely; injury minor or unknown	36	42	$229	188	687	46	$171†	374

° Base too low for computation.
† Differences from comparative negligence states were computed and were found not to be significant at the .05 level.

that the claimant is at a disadvantage in negotiation. In these circumstances, settlement is likely to be more favorable to the insurance company than litigation might be. The difference between the settlement figure and the expected value in litigation can be termed a discount.. Although the files provide no data with which to test this assertion,[49] its reasonableness can be argued.

A first source of the adjuster's advantage is his superior access to commitment. If either negotiating party can successfully commit himself to an offer within the settlement range, this action will dictate the terms of the bargain.[50] Specifically, if the adjuster can commit himself to an offer of the expected value in litigation less the plaintiff's prospective processing costs, he can obtain a discount corresponding to the amount of these costs. The claimant would achieve nothing by litigating, because his expected gain would be cancelled by the cost of that gain. Theoretically, the claimant could attempt the same tactic, but his ability to commit himself is not as great. The insurance company, as an organization, can afford to devote resources to the defense of principle, and both claimant and adjuster know this. With the possible exception of the successful specialized negligence attorney, the claimant and his representative have no comparable resources to devote to principle, and again this is mutually known. Thus it would seem reasonable that were the parties to agree on an expected value in litigation, settlement would discount the claimant's processing costs.

A good example of this situation appears in those situations where the company is clearly liable for the policy limits. For instance, were special damages to be several thousand dollars and liability clear, and if a policy limited to $10,000 were involved, settlement would very likely be for an amount in the neighborhood of $9,500. Here, the expected value in litigation would be the policy limits, since a judgment in excess of this amount would be confidently predicted by both sides, yet the assets of the insurance company could be called on to provide at most

49. One would have to compare actual settlements with estimates of value in litigation. The latter is not routinely given in the Acme files.
50. See Chapter 4, pp. 156–158.

$10,000. However, processing costs would have to be incurred in order to get the judgment. Because these are avoided in settlement, the insurance company can successfully demand a discount, regardless of how high a judgment might be expected.[51] Both attorneys and adjusters reported this phenomenon at the policy limits, and it is reasonable to expect that it operates throughout the entire range of settlements.

A second advantage for the adjuster is his relative indifference to the uncertainty of litigation, brought about for two reasons: the adjuster as negotiator does not have a personal stake in the outcome comparable to that of both the claimant and his attorney, and furthermore, the insurance company as a whole in defending large numbers of claims is unaffected by uncertainty with respect to any one claim.

The claimant contemplating settlement or litigation is faced with a calculus of probabilities. Settlement offers a known award with certainty whereas litigation offers an unknown award with an unknown probability, although both the award and probability may be estimated by the experienced attorney. In other words, litigation involves not only additional processing costs from the claimant's viewpoint; it also involves a gamble that may be totally lost. By taking many such gambles in litigating large numbers of cases, the insurance company is able to regard the choice between the certainty and the gamble with indifference. In the words of another analyst:

> Generally speaking there will often be asymmetry between the parties, insofar as the suit is a regular, calculable element in business operations for one of them, and a unique event for the other. It means that the former will be . . . much less deterred by the likelihood of losing individual cases, providing he can transfer the loss to a group of customers or clients.[52]

51. See Schueler *v.* Phoenix Assur. Co. of New York, D.C. Mich., 223 F. Supp. 643 (1966).

52. Vilhelm Aubert, "Courts and Conflict Resolution," *Journal of Conflict Resolution* 11:40, 1967, p. 45.

The insurance negotiator therefore expects the claimant to yield a discount for the certain payment:

> We should always try to fix the fair settlement value from the standpoint of what a judge or jury would award. This does not mean that the defendant should pay in settlement the full sum that he feels would constitute the jury's verdict. He should force proper reductions from that sum by taking advantages of the considerations that the outcome of a lawsuit is always uncertain and that the defendant has some opportunities of emerging victorious.[53]

Moreover, this expectation is shared by the claimant's side of the bar:

> I have always recommended to the injured person that a settlement of 75 to 80 per cent of the probable recovery should be accepted.[54]

In sum, because of the negotiating advantages of the insurance company, it is likely that in cases where liability favors the claimant, the company obtains a discount for settlement. However, it must be recalled that negotiating disadvantages also exist for the company. When liability is unfavorable to the claimant, the company must often pay a premium for settlement, as explained in the previous discussion of danger and nuisance values.

Suit and Trial

The meaning of filing suit in claims negotiation is ambiguous. On its face, this act may be seen as a sign of incipient failure of the negotiation: the attorney for the claimant prepares for an expected trial. Another interpretation is that filing suit is a move in the game of negotiation: it establishes the credibility of a

53. Fred H. Rees, *Claims Philosophy and Practice* (The Spectator, 1947), pp. 65–66.

54. Joseph Schneider, "Accident Litigation: The Common Man Sues," *Annals of the American Academy of Political and Social Science* 287:69, 1953, p. 74.

threat to go to trial, but relies on a long delay between the filing of suit and the setting of trial to produce a negotiated settlement.[55] This interpretation seems to me more satisfactory for the bulk of suit cases I observed. The filing of suit may also be required to preserve the legal basis for the claim and thus to continue negotiation when the statute of limitations threatens to bar the claim. Finally, it is the practice of some attorneys, particularly in urban areas with long delays in trial calendars, to file suit as a routine matter, regardless of their confidence that a settlement will take place. The last-mentioned procedure is also reputed to be encouraged by those contingent fee agreements that provide a higher share for the attorney in sued cases.

The bringing of a case to trial is a less ambiguous indication of failure of negotiation. Even though many cases brought to trial may settle during the course of trial, major processing costs are assumed by both parties. Since a principal benefit of the negotiated settlement is the mutual avoidance of these costs, a conclusion of at least partial failure of negotiation is unavoidable. In this section I will present data concerning recovery in tried cases as compared with those settled prior to trial and will suggest some reasons why these failed to be settled out of court. There were too few cases brought to trial to make distinctions among them, and I am treating together those cases that settled during trial (23 per cent), those that went to verdict (72 per cent), and those that were appealed (5 per cent).

Table 5.4 presents a summary picture of proportions of cases entering the successively more advanced stages of the legal process, and indicates the recoveries in each condition. The columns control for known economic loss, and the groups of rows represent the stages of the legal process. I have previously shown that representation increases the value of a claim as measured by its recovery,[56] so the results in the section of Table 5.4 dealing with representation come as

55. Wallace E. Sedgewick, in "Accident Litigation: The Insurance Carrier Defends," *Annals of the American Academy of Political and Social Science* 287:75, 1953, refers to the "rapidly increasing custom of plaintiff's counsel to file suit immediately"—due to court congestion and the advisability of an early report of tangible progress to the client. See also Franklin *et al., op. cit.*

56. See pp. 193–196.

Table 5.4. Recovery according to representation, suit and trial, controlling for special damages

		Special damages			
	None or unknown	$1–$50	$51–$200	$201–$500	$501+
Total cases	867	395	450	258	246
per cent recovering	25	92	92	91	95
mean payment, paid cases	$87	$123	$374	$911	$4,453
Represented cases	75	67	186	135	152
per cent of total	8.7	17.0	41.3	52.3	61.8
per cent recovering	41	90	90	89	93
mean payment, paid cases	$579	$247	$546	$1,166	$5,916
Suit cases	39	40	104	72	122
per cent of total	4.5	10.1	23.1	27.9	49.6
per cent of represented	52	60	56	53	80
per cent recovering	41	83	85	85	90
mean payment, paid cases	$632	$265	$564	$1,258	$6,736
Trial cases	13	6	20	20	34
per cent of total	1.5	1.5	4.4	7.8	13.8
per cent of represented	17	9	11	15	22
per cent of suit	33	15	19	28	28
per cent recovering	15	17	35	55	71
mean payment, paid cases	$1,172	$8*	$449	$1,289	$4,655

* Based on fewer than 10 cases.

no surprise. More interesting is the effect of suit. Insofar as suit is merely a negotiation tactic or a routine procedure, it may be expected to have relatively little effect on value as compared with representation alone. Insofar as suit is a sign of a failing negotiation, sued cases should be denied more frequently than other represented cases, the fraction largely corresponding to cases that the company is determined to resist. The data of Table 5.4 seem to support both interpretations to some degree. There is a slight diminution from all represented cases to sued cases in the proportion of claims paid, and a relatively small increase in the amount paid per claim in all columns but the first.

The expected effect of trial on recovery is a more complicated matter, as trial can occur for several different reasons, each of which leads to a different predicated pattern of recoveries. The existing literature testifies to a relationship between trial and the size of loss or damages, without much explanation of this relationship.[57] The theory of negotiation indicates that with higher damages there is greater opportunity for errors in estimating value in litigation to lead to manifest disagreement. For the reasons discussed in Chapter 4, I think manifest disagreement based on errors in estimating value in litigation rarely occurs in bodily injury negotiations where the claim is represented by an attorney. However, the interviews suggest that there may be a group of cases in which a perverse type of utility calculation produces manifest disagreement. Ordinarily, the parties prefer negotiation partly because of its certain recovery, and the claimant usually prefers the certain recovery even more than the insurance company, thus yielding a discount from the expected value in litigation. In some cases, however, the certain payment comes to appear trivial, and the gamble is preferred. The best example of this occurs when the prospective settlement would be largely or entirely taken by liens from hospitals or welfare departments. Here, the claimant may receive nothing from a negotiated settlement after the liens have been satisfied. The following is an example:

57. The relationship is implied in Conard *et al.*, *op. cit.*, at pp. 241–242. See also Linden, *op. cit.*, Table V-4, p. V-23.

I have a claim right now where the pedestrian is alcoholic —a bum, no money. He went into the hospital first as a charity patient. He and his attorney are asking for a huge amount of money. There's a question of liability: it's a pedestrian case, and he was crossing in the middle of the block, so this is a question as to whether we would owe the claim. This guy has everything to gain and nothing to lose [from trial]. We did offer a compromise, so to speak, which would have paid his medical bills and given him a few hundred bucks. He don't care if the medical bills are going to be paid or not. It's not out of his pocket. If he goes to court and gets a big verdict, he has a lot of money to buy some more bottles. If he loses the case, say he didn't hit it big, you know, he still don't have to pay the medical bills, and he never will be in a position to pay them, so he has everything to gain and nothing to lose by going to court and trying to gamble to get a large verdict. If he gets the right jury, he may hit it lucky. If we get the right jury and they follow previous cases and go according to the statutes and laws, we should win the case.

Perhaps more common is the case where liability is so unfavorable to the claimant that a reasonable compromise offer from the insurance company would be defined as trivial or next to nothing. An attorney may be persuaded to try the case on the assumption that an occasional large fee may carry the expenses of litigating several cases that fail to recover. Tried cases of this type should be characterized by large damages but should lead to a high proportion of lost cases and a very modest amount of recovery on the whole.

The weaknesses of the commitment tactic may lead to another group of trials. An attorney develops a commitment to a claim the moment he agrees to represent it. His reputation will suffer for claims denied or settled for trivial figures, and he will probably experience a financial loss in handling such claims. More over, he cannot accept an offer that nets the claimant less than the adjuster's last offer before representation. Yet a claim that an attorney agrees to represent may prove to be a poor one on grounds of either liability or damages as the case develops. The attorney may be unable to accumulate the papers—bills, depositions, etc.—that render the claim significant in the eyes of the claims man and his supervisors. As one adjuster said:

> We don't pay inconvenience—we can't! If there are no specials, no doctor bills, no matter how good an argument I make nobody will approve paying on the claim.

Furthermore, if specials are trivial, only a trivial settlement can be expected. And occasionally an adjuster has unwisely exhausted his negotiation margin with an unrepresented claimant:

> You get in this position once in a while, where you give an individual too high a figure and I have done this and I've been trapped, I guess you'd call it. . . . I lost my negotiation area because it went to the attorney. The attorney can't take that figure because he can't justify his fee, so where are you? You're on your way to trial, 'cause you've given what you've got.

In these circumstances, the commitment alone may be sufficient to lead to trial, despite the fact that the attorney stands to lose even more with a low verdict than with a low settlement. The attorney's determination to take a claim to trial must be made credible so that his future threats may be more believable. Such action may be rational in the long run, if not the short run. Cases of this type may be relatively small in the amount of damages sustained, and contribute to a different segment of the spectrum of tried cases than those discussed previously.

A rather different potential source of trials springs from organizational considerations. Very serious claims are supervised not only at the local level, but also at the regional or even home office levels of a company. It is not only the adjuster has to justify his evaluation to his supervisor, but the supervisor in turn must justify a joint evaluation to one or more higher executives. The understandable tendency in this situation is to be very conservative in evaluation. Moreover, where much is at stake, assumption of processing costs inherent in trial is easier, because these costs become trivial compared to the potential verdict. Trial in this case may serve a bureaucratic function. A supervisor may recriminate with his subordinate if he disagrees with the reasonableness of the latter's negotiated settlement. He cannot disagree with a subordinate's payment of a judgment ordered by a court. In this situation, trial may be a way of preserving the bureaucratic structure of the insurance company. Witness the following case: [58]

> You probably get a little bit of fear of the organization, you know, in paying a high figure on a case whether it's liability or not. We were hit with a case not too long ago, a high paying case on this _____ Hospital. . . . We were hit with two-and-a-quarter—$225,000. Now this was dead liability. There was no question about liability, no question about it. Nobody would go out on a limb and pay $150,000 to get off. Nobody would put their name on a check. . . . It looks much better if a jury comes in. . . . What I'm looking for, in essence, is someone to place this responsibility on, other than myself. . . . I don't want to bear this responsibility of paying a big settlement in a serious case.

Cases of this type would also be expected among claims that are complicated, regardless of how large they may be. A complicated case makes negotiation more difficult. An example would be the multi-car collision, where agreements have to be reached among a large number of parties. Such cases may be expected over the entire range of values of damages, and should lead to a fairly low number of recoveries since there are other parties who may possibly be held for the damages in each case. Organizational convenience may again be involved here: the time and effort of a complex negotiation may require more resources than a trial:

58. Observations of intercompany arbitration of property damage cases found that some companies were routinely submitting large numbers of claims, many of them apparently worthless. It was the opinion of many participants in the arbitration that these claims were submitted to avoid the local office's responsibility for settling them. Since the cost of arbitration was trivial—a $5 filing fee—freedom from responsibility could be bought cheaply in these claims, and some adjusting staffs seemed to feel it worth the price.

Collisions in which there are several cars involved [go to trial]. Everyone is pushing the blame on the rear car. Maybe four cars are involved, each passing the buck to the one in back of him. Normally, they go into litigation because nobody wants to take the responsibility.

The variety of factors that may explain trial is reflected in the confusing picture presented at the bottom of Table 5.4. The fact that more cases with higher damages are tried is in accord with expectations based on the view of trial as a gamble with high stakes and low probability, and also with expectations based on the view of trial as externalizing the problems of a bureaucracy. That some cases with very low damages are tried accords with the commitment hypothesis. The high recoveries in tried cases with large damages accord with the idea of externalizing organizational problems.

Table 5.5. Recovery in tried and untried cases, controlling for liability and injury

	Liability favorable to claimant, injury moderate or serious	Liability favorable to claimant, injury minor or unknown	Liability unfavorable to claimant, injury moderate or serious	Liability unfavorable to claimant, injury minor or unknown
Per cent tried	12.8	3.0	16.3	4.6
Per cent recovering				
untried cases	88	76 °	78	47 °
tried cases	83	63	38 ‡	21
Mean recovery in paid cases				
untried cases	$7,288	$660 °	$3,565	$380
tried cases	$12,847 ‡	$2,990	$483 ‡	$521 ‡
Total cases with information available	94	1,333	49	716

° Significant at the .05 level.
‡ Based on fewer than ten cases.

Some clarification of the situation is afforded by Table 5.5, which controls for liability and injury. Trial is seen to be most likely in cases with serious injury yet unfavorable liability. This is the situation where the lawyer's gamble would seem to be a fitting explanation. Trial is also relatively common where both liability and injury favor the claimant. Here, the externalizing of bureaucratic problems is the most fitting explanation, particularly in light of the high proportion and amount of awards. The low injury cases relatively seldom lead to trial, suggesting that commitment and the inability to provide acceptable documentation are relatively infrequent causes of trial, although when trial is undertaken the cases are successful to a surprising extent.

Table 5.6. Trial, recovery, and multiple defendants

	Number of defendants	
	Only one (N = 1,648)	*More than one* (N = 544)
Per cent tried	2.6	10.6
Per cent recovering:		
untried cases	74	48
tried cases	86	25

The complexity hypothesis is explored in Table 5.6, which lends confirmation. Cases with more than one defendant are tried four times as frequently as those with a single defendant, and the proportion recovering is lower, as expected.

In sum, the data are in accord with four hypotheses concerning the meaning of trial in automobile bodily injury claims. Some trials appear to represent a gamble where damages are severe, yet liability is unfavorable to the claimant, and in which a reasonable compromise would have to be defined as trivial by the claimant. Less frequently, others appear to be attempts to fulfill commitments originally made as negotiation maneuvers, but failing in their goal. Others seem to occur in order to place responsibility for expensive payments on an outside agent, thus avoiding threats to organizational personnel. Finally, trial seems at times to be a response to the inherent complexity of certain claims.

Delay

My major concern in studying the matter of recovery has been with monetary settlement, whether in terms of the proportion of claimants recovering anything or in terms of the mean recovery in paid cases. However, from the social critic's perspective, the timing of an award may be as important as its amount. An award received five years after an injury may be less adequate than an award half as large, promptly paid. The variable of delay is also relevant to the theory of negotiation: ability to affect the timing of an agreement may create negotiation power. In this section I will summarize what the analysis of Acme files has shown concerning delay, or the time from the accident to the settlement.

The time from the occurrence of an accident until the definitive settlement of a claim arising from the accident averages around 400 days, or slightly more than a year. The distribution is, of course, skewed. Of the 2,216 claims studied, 593, or more than a quarter, settled within three months, and 1,083, or nearly half, settled within six months. In contrast, 225, or ten per cent, took three years or longer to settle.[59] In the light of the fact that some delay is virtually inevitable in the process of reporting an accident, setting up a file, contacting the insured and the claimant, and making a routine investigation, it would seem that the run-of-the-mill claim is settled as expeditiously as can be expected, given the requirements of the formal law and bureaucratic procedures. On the other hand, a sizeable minority of claims experience delay well in excess of anything that reasonable procedures might be expected to entail, and it is here that investigation is needed. Relying on the analysis reported so far in this chapter, it is likely that attention ought most

59. Similar results are reported generally. See Conard *et al.*, *op. cit.*, pp. 221–223; Linden, *op. cit.*, Chapter V, p. 4.

properly to focus on the roles of apparent injury, liability, representation, and stage of the legal process.

Delay might well be expected to be greater with more serious and costly injuries. The settlement of a claim is required by law to be a one-time agreement covering both past and future damages.[60] Where injuries are serious, it is often the case that considerable time must lapse before the extent of the damage is known, and no reasonable settlement can be made in the interim. The claimant will not accept a low offer knowing of the possibility of permanent injury, and the insurance company will not meet a high demand in light of the possibility of significant recovery. Another reason to expect more delay with more expensive injuries is that a more complete investigation is required of the liability aspect of the claim. Hospital and medical reports will be gathered, the company will make its own medical examination, statements will be taken from all witnesses, etc. The file will not support a large payment without a complete investigation, which can be time-consuming. Yet another reason to expect delay in large claims comes from consideration of the bargaining process. Delay is in fact a negotiating tool that seems to be rarely used in routine claims because of the previously discussed pressures for relieving the case load; however, it is sometimes consciously used in large claims, particularly when representation is involved. Often it is used to exert pressure on the attorney to cooperate in the company's investigation, as by authorizing defense medical examinations. It is also sometimes used purely as a rationalization for a small offer, or as a threat against a large demand. The use of delay as a negotiating tool in the companies studied would seem to be selective. In the words of a high official in the claims department of Acme, in a private communication:

> I consider delay an appropriate tactic when there are no other means of resolving claims lacking in merit or involving unreasonable demands. It is a tactic applied in individual cases, not an over-all strategy or policy.

60. An exception is found in advance payments plans. See Chapter 6, pp. 260–263.

Table 5.11. Delay by degree of injury

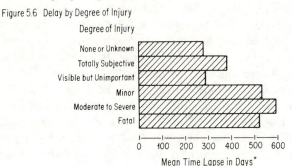

Figure 5.6 Delay by Degree of Injury

* Despite curvilinearity, data conform to a predicted ranking from top to bottom. The Jonckheere test indicates the probability of the results under the conditions of the null hypothesis to be less than .05; the analysis of variance shows a probability of less than .01. For references, see Table 5.1.

Figure 5.6 displays a test of the hypothesis that delay is related to more serious injury. On the whole, the hypothesis is supported.[61] A minor exception occurs in the case of fatal accidents, which take slightly less time to dispose of than do accidents involving moderate or severe injury. Fatalities are, in fact, less complicated as legal problems, and less expensive, and the apparent exception is probably best interpreted as a disparity between seriousness in the medical and legal senses. The more striking and significant exception is the category of totally subjective injury. It may be remembered that this category also formed an exception to the association of payment with degree of injury. My interpretation of both these discrepancies is that this category represents the principal bone of contention in settlement negotiations. Totally subjective injuries are those in which the symptom of pain may be present, but in which there are no objective medical correlates. The law allows recovery for pain, and these claims arise on that basis; however, the oppor-

61. Similar findings are reported in the Michigan and Osgoode Hall studies; see references in footnote 59. See also Maurice Rosenberg and Michael I. Sovern, "Delay and the Dynamics of Personal Injury Litigation," *Columbia Law Review* 59:1115, 1959.

tunity for exaggeration and for sheer fraud seems very broad in this category.[62] In consequence, the adjuster is strongly tempted to minimize or deny these cases, whereas indignant claimants—and their attorneys—find reason to insist on payment. These cases constitute more than a quarter of all claims, and the issue is not one to be ignored. The relatively long delay in settling these claims, as against claims that have visible but unimportant objective symptoms, probably reflects a battle of principle between the parties. Complicating the matter for the adjuster is the similar perspective of the supervisory structure concerning a file that is skimpy on medical evidence, which makes it more difficult to justify any payment that may be made.

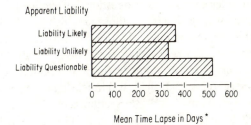

Figure 5.7 Delay by Apparent Liability

Mean Time Lapse in Days *

° The differences between "liability questionable" and other categories are significant at the .05 level. The difference between "liability likely" and "liability unlikely" is not significant.

With respect to liability, delay ought to be least where liability is clear-cut, whether favorable or unfavorable, and most where liability is questionable, for in the latter case more investigation is required, and the negotiation will bear the additional burden of compromising a claim, even if both sides were to agree on a value under the condition of clear liability. Figure 5.7 confirms this hypothesis, using the criterion of apparent liability coded from the description of the accident. A

62. The insurance company's distaste for the whiplash injury is profound, and with some justification. For two years after Acme opened offices in France, it experienced only two whiplashes, out of 300 claims made. In the United States, this is the single most common complaint justifying a claim.

Table 5.13. Delay according to control at intersection

Figure 5.8 Delay According to Control at Intersection

Location of Accident

0	100	200	300	400	500

Mean Time Lapse in Days *

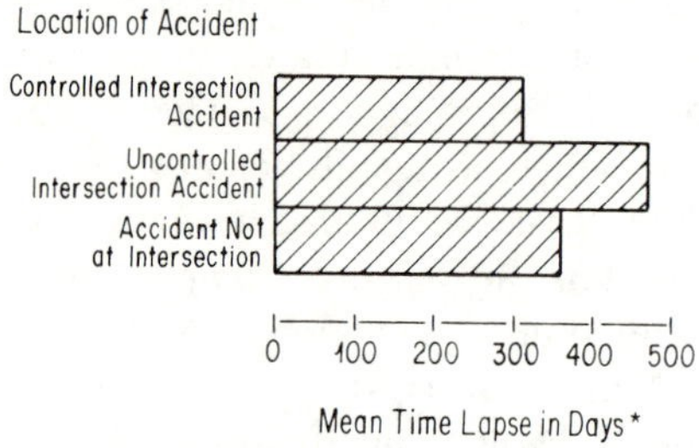

° All differences are significant at the .05 level.

similar correlation appears in a tabulation based on the adjuster's opinion of liability. Cases of questionable liability take on the order of half again as long to settle as those in which liability is clear, whether favorable or unfavorable. Figure 5.8 provides additional indirect confirmation, since intersection accidents are relatively easy to analyze from the liability standpoint, as this is interpreted by adjusters, when the intersection is controlled by a traffic light or by stop or yield signs. In contrast, uncontrolled intersection accidents are among the most difficult to analyze. Compared with all other accidents, controlled intersection accidents take 15 per cent less time to settle, whereas uncontrolled intersection accidents take a third more time.

Finally, representation increases delay very impressively. Documentation is provided in Figure 5.9.[63] Interestingly enough, the presumably most competent and specialized NACCA attorneys took less time on the average to settle their claims than did other firm or solo attorneys. Figures on the time lapse by stage of the legal process, contained in Figure 5.10, suggest that delay is mainly a function of

---

63. Conard *et al* note that suit cases take a relatively long time to settle (*op. cit.*, pp. 243–244). The possibility that representation by itself may be responsible for this delay, though consistent with their findings, is not recognized. In this instance, Linden seems to be more perceptive (*op. cit.*, Chapter V, p. 7).

Table 5.14. Delay by type of representation

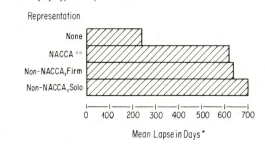

Figure 5.9 Delay by Type of Representation

° The differential in mean delay between unrepresented cases and all represented cases is significant at the .01 level.
† National Association of Claimants' Counsel of America, now American Trial Lawyers Association.

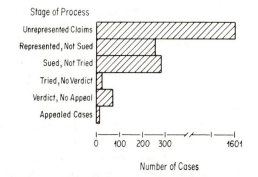

Figure 5.10 Delay by Stage of the Legal Process

representation, pure and simple, with relatively little increase due to formal steps beyond filing suit. It would seem that such reasons as the time involved in securing representation, the time for the attorney's investigation, perhaps a more deliberate use by the insurance company of delay in bargaining with an attorney as against an unrepresented claimant, and some degree of selectivity (the attorney accepting proportionately more claims with high damages) may go further to explaining the additional delay with representation than does the commonly cited problem of overcrowded courts.

Recovery in Action

The analysis of the Acme files shows that although settlement negotiations produce a considerable percentage of claims denied or closed without payment, the bulk of claims are paid, and the mean or average payment is substantial—on the order of a thousand dollars. In conformity with the formal law, payment is related both to apparent liability and to the degree of injury or economic loss. Controlling for these matters, some evidence is found for a relationship of payment to various characteristics of the parties. Representation, which is not acknowledged as a legitimate factor either in the formal law or the claims philosophy of the insurance companies, is none the less an important factor in increasing recovery.

Among claims generally, and particularly among represented claims, many appear to be paid in the absence of clear liability of the insured. This finding is contrary to the prescriptions of both the formal law and Acme's management, but evidence from the interviews and from the analysis of the files proves the existence of danger payments when losses are large and of nuisance payments when losses are small. This finding is predictable and comprehensible on the basis of negotiation theory. Danger and nuisance values are rational outcomes of the conditions of negotiation, just as are the company's denials of their existence.

The opposite side of the danger value coin is discounts. Although the files provide no direct test, the interviews and observations suggest an advantage for the insurance company in negotiating large settlements, based on the company's relative indifference to trial as against settlement, on the lack of personal interest in the outcome on the part of the negotiator, and on the company's greater access to the commitment tactic.

Contrary to conventional wisdom, trial is found not to be superior to settlement from the claimant's standpoint. A relatively high proportion of tried cases recover nothing, and the average recovery in tried cases that do recover is not consistently higher than recovery in represented cases generally. Among the reasons for trial are posited the claimant's gamble in a case with serious loss but unfavorable liability, the need to fulfill commited bargaining threats, the externalization of the responsibility for payment of large claims, and the relative inability of settlement procedures to handle complex cases.

Routine claims are settled within a reasonable amount of time, the median lapse from accident to closing the file being approximately six months. In contrast, some claims take years to settle. Associated with unusual delay are large losses, questionable liability, and representation. Although delay may be used as a negotiation tool, much of the delay actually experienced in handling automobile liability claims would seem to be inherent in the nature of good-faith negotiation under the law of negligence. The fact that tried cases take little longer to terminate than do all sued cases suggests that it is not so much congestion in the courts that accounts for delay, as it is the time-consuming procedures involved in investigation and negotiation.

6. Implications

THE MAJOR THESIS of this book is that legal relationships cannot be understood as a product of the formal law alone, but must be understood in terms of the interplay between the formal law and aspects of the situation in which the law is applied. The determination of legal rights is in the vast majority of cases undertaken by means of informal procedures, the character of which substantively changes the rights thus processed. Moreover, the changes are not random. Informality does not mean lack of structure. Informal procedures exhibit regularities that result from the goals and purposes of the people involved, and from sociologically comprehensible pressures and strains upon them.

The regularities induced from the observation of the day-to-day working out of legal relationships constitute the law in action. It is these regularities that have to be taken into account by the ordinary man and his attorney when the question of rights and duties becomes concrete. I propose that the legal critic and the social analyst ought to share this perspective.

In this chapter I shall review the settlement process in automobile bodily injury claims, pointing to the structured differences between the law in action and the formal law in this area of legal rights, and suggesting sociological explanations for the differences observed. This review will lead into a discussion of the current critical debate over the inadequacies of the tort law in this area. Much of this debate has ignored the distinction between the formal law and the law in action. Many of the criticisms and suggestions for change seem to be premised on formal concepts that do not reflect what happens in the real world of day-to-day events. I believe that the debate might be less bitter, and certainly more realistic, were the parties to discuss the real world rather than the world of doctrine.

My understanding of the law in action, along with my experience in the study of automobile accidents, leads me to take a position in the debate over the proper role of the tort law and automobile insurance in today's car-owning society. In closing, I will explain and attempt to justify this position: that reform is needed to bring the law and insurance system into harmony with new ideas concerning the needs that it can and ought to fulfill.

The Tort Law in Action

In the insured claim, it is the adjuster's task to evaluate the case according to the criteria of formal law, and to negotiate a settlement that will be justified in the light of these criteria and avoid the expensive formal procedure of courtroom trial.

The formal law of torts specifies that someone injured in an automobile accident may recover from a driver if he can show, by the preponderance of evidence, that the driver violated his duty to conduct the vehicle in the manner of an ordinarily prudent person. The driver, however, need pay nothing if he in turn can show by the preponderance of evidence that the claimant also violated a similar duty. Various qualifications apply, depending on the jurisdiction. For example, a governmental or charitable organization may be excused from paying claims, or a husband may not be able to recover from his wife, or a guest from his host. In some exceptional states payment may be reduced rather than eliminated where the claimant's negligent behavior has contributed to the accident. The formal law prescribes a recovery sufficient to make the claimant "whole," repaying in cash for everything he has lost in the accident (regardless of whether or not some other source such as health insurance or sick leave has also compensated for the accident-related losses), and for pain, suffering and inconvenience in addition to more tangible losses.

The formal criteria might lead to the expectation that relatively few people injured in an automobile accident would receive reparation. Most drivers may be thought to be ordinarily prudent people, and even where one is not, formal law embodies the difficulty of affirmative proof of unreasonable behavior. Moreover, to the extent that numbers of negligent drivers are on the highway, an equivalent number of negligent claimants might be expected, who ought to recover nothing. On these assumptions one would expect most claimants to be denied completely, the balance recovering something more than their economic losses. In contrast, the actual picture of recoveries shows that most people injured in traffic accidents are paid, and those who are seriously injured are paid in the large majority of cases. The amount of recoveries fits the formal model only for small claims; where injuries are serious, most claimants fail to recover even their out-of-pocket losses.[1]

The reason the distribution predicted by knowledge of the formal law does not fit the observed distribution of claims settlements is that other factors influence the settlement process. Some of these have been described in this book. Among them are the attitudes and values of the involved personnel, organizational pressures, and negotiation pressures. They exert a direct

---

1. See Alfred F. Conard, James N. Morgan, Robert W. Pratt, Jr., Charles E. Voltz, and Robert L. Bombaugh, *Automobile Accident Costs and Payments: Studies in the Economics of Injury Reparation* (University of Michigan Press, 1964), pp. 181–236.

effect on the enormous majority of bodily claims. As Fleming James indicates:

> The settlement practices of insurance companies constitute another factor which has a great impact on the actual operation of tort law today. The vast majority of accident claims never get into any stage of litigation; only an infinitesimal proportion of them ever come to trial. The "law" that directly governs the disposition of most tort claims, then, consists in these practices. The legal rules affect most cases only to the extent that they are reflected in the process of settlement.[2]

The personalities—attitudes and opinions—of the personnel are perhaps the least significant of the factors mentioned. Generally speaking, adjusters approach their work with conventional business values. Other things equal, they will seek low, conservative settlements, although a sense of fairness makes them disinclined to settle for less than net out-of-pocket losses in a case that is deemed to warrant any settlement at all. The goal of paying no more and no less than these tangible losses is often achieved in routine cases settled directly with the claimant. This is a settlement that many adjusters would characterize as ideal. However, many settlements are made for amounts quite different from the ideal, reflecting pressures and constraints of the employee role and the negotiating situation. Personal dispositions may affect the style with which an adjuster responds to external demands, but they seem to be relatively unimportant in determining the outcome of claims.

Organizational pressure would seem to be a more important factor than personality in affecting the outcome of claims. Pressures from the supervisory structure can even lead adjusters to violate some of the most important company rules, such as those forbidding nuisance payments. Perhaps unexpectedly, the most insistent of organizational pressures is not to keep payments low, but to close files quickly. The closing of files represents for adjusters something of the same kind of central goal as the attain-

2. Fleming James, Jr., "Accident Liability Reconsidered: The Impact of Insurance," *Yale Law Journal* 57:549, 1948, at p. 566.

ment of good grades represents for the college student, or number of placements for an employment counselor, or a high clearance rate for policemen.[3] As explained in Chapter 2 and elsewhere, the chief effect of this pressure on the behavior of claims men is to increase the number and raise the level of payments. This effect is unexpected and unrecognized by many claims department executives, who are insulated from the front lines by organizational distance, but it is understandable as a means to alleviate specific and recurring pressures experienced by adjusters from their supervisors. The pressure to close files quickly also causes adjusters to simplify their procedures of investigation, as well as their thinking in evaluation. Although the textbooks and manuals propose elaborate and time-consuming routines, the case load prescribes short cuts and approximations. There is a strong parallel here with the behavior of police detectives noted by Skolnick, who deliberately overlook many reported crimes and accept numbers of admittedly false confessions in order to raise the rate of crimes cleared by arrest. Skolnick comments:

> The behavior of the detectives involved should not be seen as an instance of corruption or even of inefficiency. On the contrary, their actions are to be interpreted as an unanticipated consequence of their superiors' development of a method for controlling their efficiency. The response of the detective to the clearance rate is easily understandable. It stems from a sociological tendency manifesting itself in all work organizations: the worker always tries to perform *according to his most concrete and specific understanding of the control system.* That is, in general, workers try to please those supervising *routine activities.*[4]

Another important factor affecting settlement outcomes, par-

3. See Howard S. Becker, Blanche Geer, and Everett Hughes, *Making the Grade: The Academic Side of College Life* (John Wiley, 1968); Peter M. Blau, *The Dynamics of Bureaucracy* (University of Chicago Press, 1955); and Jerome H. Skolnick, *Justice Without Trial* (John Wiley, 1966); on students, employment counselors, and policemen, respectively.

4. Skolnick, *op. cit.*, pp. 179–180.

ticularly with represented claimants, is the medium of negotiation. Negotiation is a social process with a strong implicit rule structure and a repertory of tactics different from those available in litigation. In the case at hand, the most effective tactics threaten recourse to the expense of formal trial, and these threats can be nailed down with commitments. Bodily injury claims negotiators are in roughly the same position as negotiators for two nations disputing a border city, where all involved know that each party can obliterate a major interior city of the other. In such a situation there is strong pressure for compromise, as opposed to an all-or-none disposition. It does not matter much that the formal law prescribes the latter.

As a consequence of these and other pressures, the tort law in action is differentiated from the formal law by its greater simplicity, liberality, and inequity. The concepts of the formal tort law are quite complex: definitions of both damages and negligence suggest the need for case-by-case consideration. The rule of contributory negligence as a bar to recovery makes the formal law appear close-fisted, though it may be lavish in the recovery that it grants a "blameless" victim of a "negligent" driver. Above all, the formal tort law—like the bulk of Anglo-American law—is equitable in its insistence that cases similar in facts be treated in a similar fashion. The law in action departs from the formal law on these three main dimensions.

In order to process successfully vast numbers of cases, organizations tend to take on the characteristics of "bureaucracy" in the sociological sense of the term: operation on the basis of rules, government by a clear hierarchy, the maintenance of files, etc. Such an organizational form produces competence and efficiency in applying general rules to particular cases, but it is not well suited to making complex and individualized decisions. One form of response of bureaucracies to such demands involves a type of breakdown. There will be long delays, hewing to complicated and minute procedures, and a confusion of means with ends.[5] A common and perhaps more constructive response

5. See Robert K. Merton, "Bureaucratic Structure and Personality," in Robert K. Merton, *Social Theory and Social Structure* (Free Press, 1957), pp. 195–206.

is to simplify the task.[6] This was the tack taken by the claims men I studied.[7] Phone calls and letters replaced personal visits; only a few witnesses, rather than all possible, would be interviewed; and the law of negligence was made to lean heavily on the much simpler traffic law.

Traffic laws are simple rules, deliberately so because their purpose is to provide a universal and comprehensible set of guidelines for safe and efficient transportation. Negligence law is complex, its purpose being to decide after the fact whether a driver was unreasonably careless.[8] However, all levels of the insurance company claims department will accept the former rules as generally adequate for the latter purpose. The underlying reason for this is the difficulty if not impossibility of investigating and defending a more complex decision concerning negligence in the context of a mass operation. In the routine case, the stakes are not high enough to warrant the effort, and the effort is not made. The information that a given insured violated a specific traffic law and was subsequently involved in an accident will suffice to allocate fault. No attempt is made to analyze why this took place or how. The legal concepts of

6. See Joseph Bensman and Israel Gerver, "Crime and Punishment in the Factory: The Function of Deviance in Maintaining the Social System," *American Sociological Review* 28:588, 1963.

7. Such simplification is here not without a formally legitimate basis, for the law of many states finds a very strong presumption of negligence in the violation of a traffic law. The strongest statement of this is the doctrine of negligence *per se,* such as prevails in New York, in which the violation of the safety rule is literally defined as negligence, but this doctrine is qualified by many others.

8. The incongruity between the purpose of traffic law and negligence law is stressed by Judge Edward C. Fisher in a plea for total abandonment of the negligence *per se* linkage:

> Traffic laws can have but one legitimate purpose, and that is to establish standard rules of procedure to be followed by motorists in the operation of their vehicles so as to promote the safe and orderly flow of traffic. . . . The fine distinctions and technicalities of the law of negligence have their place in the determination of civil liability arising from the use of automobiles, but do not apply in criminal prosecutions for violation of the law. . . . To forcibly weld together the two incongruous purposes and elements is to produce a mutilated hybrid of no particular value in any direction. [Edward C. Fisher, *Vehicle Traffic Law* (Northwestern University Traffic Institute, 1961), pp. 34, 58.]

negligence and fault in action contain no more substance than the simple and mechanical procedures noted here provide.

The law of damages is also simplified in action. Although the measurement of special damages appears rather straightforward even in formal doctrine, some further simplification occurs in action when, for instance, life table calculations are used to compute future earnings. More important, the measurement of pain, suffering, and inconvenience is thoroughly routinized in the ordinary claim. The adjuster generally pays little attention to the claimant's privately experienced discomforts and agonies; I do not recall ever having read recitals of these matters in the statements, which are the key documents in the settlement process and in which all matters considered relevant to the disposition of a claim are recorded. The calculation of general damages is for the most part a matter of multiplying the medical bills by a tacitly but generally accepted arbitrary constant. This practice is justified by claims men on the theory that pain and suffering are very likely to be a function of the amount of medical treatment experienced. There is of course a grain of truth in this theory, but it also contains several sources of error. Types of injury vary considerably in the degree of pain and suffering, the necessity for treatment, and the fees charged for treatment; and the correlations between these elements are low. I believe that the more important reason for the use of the formula is again that all levels of the claims department find it acceptable in justifying payment over and beyond special damages. The formula provides a conventional measurement for phenomena that are so difficult to evaluate as to be almost unmeasurable. It provides a rule by which a rule-oriented organization can proceed, though the rule is never formalized. This simplification also meets the comparable needs of plaintiffs' attorneys and is acceptable to them as well. Because of the mutual acceptability of the formula, attorneys will try to capitalize on it by adding to the use and cost of medical treatment, a procedure known as "building" the file, and adjusters will argue concerning the reasonableness of many items that purport to be medical expenses and thus part of the base to which the formula is applied. The procedure is still far less complicated—and less sensitive—than that envisaged in the formal law. Thus again it appears that, relative to the formal law, the law in action is simple and mechanical. Although more individual consideration occurs in larger cases, the principle of simplification governs to a great degree the entire range of settled claims.

The tort law in action is more liberal than the formal law. The formal law of negligence appears to be very stingy from the victim's point of view; this appearance is not surprising considering the law's development as a means of relieving nineteenth-century industry of charges imposed for accidental injuries by the earlier strict liability doctrine.[9] The doctrine of contributory negligence is of course the main block to recovery in the formal tort law, and it is this doctrine that is most strongly attenuated in action.

The principal evidence of this attenuation is in the large number of claims on which some payment is made. Insurance company procedures create a file for nearly every accident victim involved with an insured car. Any reasonable estimate of the number of cases in which the insured is not negligent plus the number in which the claimant is contributorily negligent suggests that well under half of all claims deserve payment by formal standards. It is pointed out in Chapter 5 that contrary to formal expectations the majority of claims are paid, and where serious injuries are involved virtually all claimants recover something from someone else's liability insurance. Similar findings have been reported in other studies.[10] It is true that in larger claims particularly, the payments may not equal the economic loss experienced, but they may still exceed the level of payment required by the formal law with its rule of contributory negligence.

In small claims, a fair number of denials are successfully made. The adjuster rationalizes his actions on the basis of formal law and the company is shielded from reprisals by high processing costs for the claimant relative to the amount at stake. The ad-

9. See, for example, Albert A. Ehrenzweig, *Negligence Without Fault* (University of California Press, 1951).

10. See Conard *et al., loc. cit.*, and the studies cited in footnote 17 below.

juster closes his files by denial when he feels the formal law warrants this and also that the claimant will take his case no farther. When he believes that the formal law favors the claimant, and thus finds himself ethically obliged, or when he believes the claimant is determined to press the claim, a payment can be made of considerable magnitude relative to the economic loss involved, although collateral sources—e.g., Blue Cross and sick pay—are usually deducted from negotiated settlements.

In claims based on large losses, the claimant's threat to litigate becomes more credible, and denial thus becomes more difficult. However, the adjuster uses the uncertainty of the formal process as a tool to secure a discount from the full formal value of the claim. Although processing costs may be disregarded, most claimants seem to prefer a definite settlement for a lower amount of money to the gamble of trial for a higher amount of money. The company—like a casino, which is able to translate a large number of gambles into mathematical certainty—is indifferent between these outcomes and can demand a concession for the definite settlement.

The claimant determined to press a claim that would most likely be thrown out of court and the company determined to obtain a discount on a claim that would most likely prevail are unforeseen in the formal law, but it is in predicaments like this that the law in action develops. The result may correspond to no theory of formal law, but it is none the less comprehensible. The resultant law in action, on the whole, is more liberal than is the formal law. More claims are paid, particularly where the loss is serious, than might be predicted on the basis of the latter. However, the ratio of payment to loss declines as the size of the loss increases.

The tort law in action may also be termed inequitable. It is responsive to a wide variety of influences that are not defined as legitimate by common standards of equity. The interviews and observations I conducted convinced me that the negotiated settlement rewards the sophisticated claimant and penalizes the inexperienced, the naive, the simple, and the indifferent. Translating these terms into social statuses, I believe that the settlement produces relatively more for the affluent, the educated, the

white, and the city-dweller.[11] It penalizes the poor, the unedu-
cated, the Negro, and the countryman. It is also responsive to
such matters as the appearances and personalities of the parties
and witnesses to the accident. Above all, it rewards the man
with an attorney, despite the adjuster's honestly held belief that
the unrepresented claimant will fare as well. Apart from the dis-
crimination embodied in allowing recovery of different levels of
lost income, these differences are unjustified in formal law, yet
their effect on negotiated settlements is considerable.

Although this research was based for the most part on experience in a single, narrow, area of the law, I believe that the
distinctions noted here between the formal law and the law in
action may be more generally applicable. Wherever law or any
other body of rules is applied on a day-to-day basis by a bureaucracy, pressures similar to those observed here may be expected
to be present and to produce similar results. Simplification is
the essence of mass procedures, and one would expect to find a
deemphasis upon sensitivity, individualization, and subtlety in
such situations, regardless of the complexity of the philosophy
underlying the procedure. Where every man has his day in
court, where each is judged according to his ability, where the
whole man is being treated, an examination of the machinery
in action can be predicted to yield evidence of routinization,
categorization, and regimentation. Liberality or something akin
to it may also be expected when rules are applied by a bureaucracy, depending on the extent to which sheer volume is empha-
sized by the processor. The bureaucratic employee under these
circumstances seeks a trouble-free and expeditious resolution of
disputes, and this may lead more frequently than previously
thought to a liberal treatment of the case. Finally, inequity in
the sense of applying formally inapplicable criteria is also likely
to mark a wide variety of situations in which bureaucracies apply
rules. Cases that are alike according to the formal rules may
be for many reasons dissimilar when regarded as material to be
processed. Factors ranging from the bureaucrat's idiosyncratic

11. Although some of these expected differences could not be shown
with the Acme files, I believe the data were particularly deficient with
respect to these matters.

whim to strong and systematic organizational pressures may be expected to affect both the process and the outcome wherever the formal law or other rule is put into action.

Tort Recovery as Compensation

For the past 40 years, critics have raised the question of how well victims of traffic accidents are compensated by automobile insurance. The question itself might appear paradoxical, since the bulk of insurance coverage contained in the automobile insurance package is found in the liability policy, which was never intended directly to serve the needs of claimants. The purpose of the liability policy—as viewed by virtually all insurance personnel—is to protect the policyholder. One of the hazards to which an individual's assets may be exposed is claims from others whom he has injured through his negligent conduct. Just as a man may protect the assets in his home through fire insurance, he may protect his total assets through liability insurance. The proper test of the adequacy of the latter, according to this viewpoint, is whether insureds are protected when claims are in fact made. I am not aware that this matter has ever been systematically investigated, but there seems to be little concern on the part of critics that a person with reasonably high limits of liability insurance in a prudently managed company is poorly served in this respect.

Liability insurance, then, covers liability. Accidental injury may or may not involve liability; in any event, it is a separately insurable hazard, and insurance against injury in virtually any type of accident is easily purchased on the market. A small accident policy paying medical expenses of the driver and passengers in an insured car is a common part of the total package of insurance routinely sold to automobile owners. Accidental injury is also covered in health insurance plans such as Blue Cross and Blue Shield, and a variety of policies specifically concerned with accidental injuries are also available. The proper test of accident insurance is whether adequate benefits are being paid to all such insureds who are injured in accidents. Again, there has been little critical clamor in this matter.

If both accident insurance and liability insurance seem on the whole to be adequately protecting those who purchase the appropriate policies, why do the critics persist in judging liability insurance by accident compensation standards that are manifestly inapplicable? Two principal reasons are evident. First, many of the millions of people injured in automobile accidents every year are not covered by accident insurance. Moreover, accident insurance seldom covers all economic losses experienced by these victims.[12] Second, liability insurance constitutes a pool of funds to which nearly all users of automobiles contribute. The size of this pool is very large.[13] The vast bulk of automobile victims potentially have access to it, regardless of their own insurance, if liability can be proved, and the allowable damages can compensate for all economic losses and for pain and suffering in addition. If the question of liability could be overcome, automobile liability insurance could virtually guarantee adequate compensation for all aspects of loss on the part of victims of automobile accidents. Furthermore, the payment of all victims from such a fund would be in accord with the thesis that motoring inevitably produces accidents, that these are a true economic cost of motoring, and that those who profit from this enterprise ought to pay all the costs that it entails.[14]

The opportunity to use liability funds for compensation purposes has long been recognized informally and even formally in the tort law. Perhaps the best example of formal recognition is the doctrine of *respondeat superior* by which an innocent employer is held responsible for the negligent acts of his employees when these are done in the course of the job. Although several reasons are offered for this apparently odd doctrine, the

12. Conard *et al.* report that all non-tort sources of reparation together repaid only about a quarter of the economic losses experienced by the victims of automobile accidents. Private loss insurance paid 38 per cent of the total recoveries (*op. cit.*, p. 63).

13. The premiums for automobile bodily injury liability insurance amount to more than $4,000,000,000 per year. See Insurance Information Institute, *Insurance Facts 1968*, p. 16.

14. See, for example, Ehrenzweig, *op. cit.*, and Guido Calabresi, "Views and Overviews," in Robert E. Keeton, Jeffrey O'Connell. and John H. McCord (eds.), *Crisis in Car Insurance* (University of Illinois Press, 1968), pp. 240–259.

most persuasive is that the employer could pay for the damage, whereas the typical employee (as conceived by judges at the time of the evolution of this doctrine) could not.[15]

There is in fact a long history of developments in the tort law that make it easier for the injured party to prove fault on the part of the defendant and thus to recover. Fleming James summarizes this history as follows:

> Except for Workmen's Compensation and an occasional other forward looking statute, the main assault on the citadel of fault has not been a frontal attack but rather a boring from within. The main trends have been concerned with the enlargement of duties, the liberalization of standards of proof; the increasing concern of society to provide a financially responsible defendant and the erosion of contributory negligence, imputation of negligence to the plaintiff, and other doctrines which impede recovery.[16]

As many critics have suggested, the development of liability insurance accelerated these developments, for courts and legislatures realized that payment of damages was done not by another individual, whose rights had to be balanced against those of the injured, but by a financial pool to which each participant had contributed a relatively small sum. Liability insurance could be seen as creating assets rather than protecting them.

The formal law of negligence is an increasingly liberal law. Perhaps the greatest formal liberalization of the law in recent times has been the replacement of the contributory negligence doctrine by that of comparative negligence, which has been accomplished by statute in six states. However, even in comparative negligence states, the fundamental rule remains that of negligence, and it denies access to the pool of liability insurance funds to people whose injuries cannot be related to the fault of some other insured party.

15. See John G. Fleming, *The Law of Torts* (Law Book Company of Australasia, 1961), pp. 322–323.
16. Fleming James, "Accident Liability: Some Wartime Developments," *Yale Law Journal* 55:365, 1946, p. 374.

246 : *Settled Out of Court*

Judged by the criteria of compensation, the automobile liability insurance system does seem rather inadequate. The Keeton
and O'Connell critique points to five of the major deficiencies.[17]

> First, measured as a way of compensating for personal in-
> juries suffered on the roadways, the system we have falls
> grievously short. Some injured persons receive no compen-
> sation. Others receive far less than their economic losses. . . .

Several studies are relied on by Keeton and O'Connell in support of these assertions. The Michigan Study, for instance, found
fewer than half of all the injured received any compensation
from tort. A bare half recovered in the Philadelphia-area study
of Morris and Paul. Higher proportions were found to recover
in the study of the Columbia Project for Effective Justice and
the James and Law study in Connecticut, but these dealt with
represented claimants and insured defendants, respectively. The
empirical research does show, however, that payment was relatively common in cases with larger losses, and this picture is
confirmed in the present study with Acme data.

Given the difference in ostensible goals between liability
insurance and compensation, I think that the empirical data
require a different emphasis from that most often given. I am
most impressed by the extent to which the liability insurance
system has come to resemble a compensation system. It would
not be very much of an exaggeration to say that when serious
injuries have been sustained, at least in metropolitan jurisdic-

17. These quotations are taken from Robert E. Keeton and Jeffrey
O'Connell, *Basic Protection for the Traffic Victim: A Blueprint for Re-
forming Automobile Insurance* (Little, Brown, 1965), pp. 34–67. Among
the literature they consider are the following works: Columbia University
Council for Research in the Social Sciences, *Report by the Committee to
Study Compensation for Automobile Accidents* (1932); Mark H. Franklin,
Robert H. Chanin, and Irving Mark, "Accidents, Money and the Law: A
Study of the Economics of Personal Injury Litigation," *Columbia Law
Review* 61:1, 1961; Maurice Rosenberg and Michael I. Sovern, "Delay and
the Dynamics of Personal Injury Litigation," *Columbia Law Review*
59:1115, 1959; Fleming James and Stuart Law, "Compensation for Auto
Accident Victims: A Story of Too Little and Too Late," *Connecticut Bar
Journal* 26:70, 1952; Conard *et al.*, *op. cit.*; and Clarence Morris and James
C. N. Paul, "The Financial Impact of Automobile Accidents," *University of
Pennsylvania Law Review* 110:913, 1962.

tions, automobile liability insurance companies are making payments without regard to liability (though the latter may be reflected in the size of the payments). Flat denials are very largely confined to trivial losses, and although the system might not be paying on the average as much as the tort law says ought to be paid to innocent victims of negligent drivers, liability insurance is still paying more than half of total victim recoveries from all sources, far more than any variety of accident insurance is currently yielding.[18] The liability insurance system as it actually operates is very likely better when judged by the standards of compensation than when judged by the standards of formal negligence law.

Keeton and O'Connell continue:

"Second, the present system is cumbersome and slow. . . ."

The present study confirms previous research on the matter: although the majority of claims are settled within a few months, some of them—particularly the serious ones—drag on for years. Much of the delay is understandable in the light of the necessity to investigate, evaluate, and negotiate claims. The demand of the formal law that settlement cover all damages for once and forever is an important independent source of delay, as no claimant ought to sign a release of liability until he is fairly sure of the extent of his damages, and these may take some time to ascertain fully. Although the amount of delay seems excessive for the needs to which a compensation system is directed, perhaps cases are settled somewhat too expeditiously for the needs to which a liability system is directed. At least, the possibility of undue haste is suggested by the efforts of adjusters to close claims quickly.

> Third, the present system is loaded with unfairness. Some get too much—even many times their losses—especially for minor injuries. . . . Others among the injured, as we have just suggested, get nothing or too little, and most often it is the neediest (those most seriously injured) who get the lowest percentage of compensation for their losses. . . .

18. Conard *et al., op. cit.,* pp. 62–63.

Much of this "unfairness" is embodied in a formal law that asks questions totally unrelated to the goal of compensation. On top of this is the fact noted previously that the negligence law in action tends to inequities, penalizing and rewarding factors that have no status in the formal law.

> Fourth, the operation of the present system is excessively expensive. . . . Because of the role of fault in the present system, contests over the intricate details of accidents are routine. Often these contests are also exercises in futility, since all drivers must continually make split-second judgments and many accidents are caused by slight but understandable lapses occurring at unfortunate moments. . . .

This criticism is perhaps overstated. As Marryott has shown, when given typical claims files adjusters can generally agree on the question of liability.[19] Issue can well be taken with the meaningfulness of the judgments, as I will show later, but Keeton and O'Connell are wrong in their belief that claims men worry much about the intricate details of accidents. On the one hand, the expenditure of any significant amount of resources on determining fault may be unnecessary and intolerable in a scheme of compensation. On the other hand, for a scheme premised on liability, the mechanical and superficial analysis actually being performed by adjusters and lawyers seems very shoddy, and from this perspective the system ought to devote more resources to investigating liability—and to cost much more—than the present one.

> Fifth, the present system is marred by temptations to dishonesty that lure into their snares a stunning percentage of drivers and victims. . . .

This opinion of Keeton and O'Connell is unsupported by research. Opportunities for dishonesty certainly exist: the acknowledged existence of injuries that have no objective symptoms fur-

19. Franklin J. Marryott, "Mystery of Who's at Fault Easily Solved," *Trial* 3:41, 1967. See also his "Remarks," in Keeton, O'Connell, and McCord, *op. cit.*, pp. 27–35.

nishes a basis on which to present false and exaggerated claims, and many documented instances of fraudulent serious injury have been reported in the newspapers. However, it is not at all clear what percentage of drivers and victims are in fact thus tempted, nor that the percentage who are lured is "stunning." Furthermore, the intensity of the temptation would seem to have more to do with the amount of possibly booty than with the basis of the system in negligence law. Any system with benefits in excess of tangible losses might well be expected to suffer from the same degree of depredation as the present automobile liability system.

In sum, the current automobile liability insurance system can be viewed as functioning surprisingly like a compensation system, although judged by standards appropriate to the latter it contains many inequities and irrationalities and is intolerably slow and expensive. However, judged by its own formal standards it is remarkably improvident with its funds, as well as sloppy and inconsistent in its criteria for distribution. To a great degree these inadequacies are the result of strains on the liability system to play the role of a compensation system.

Tort Payment as Deterrence

The law of negligence prescribes payment not for all injured parties, but only for those who are innocently injured as a direct result of another person's negligent conduct. Among the several reasons that can be cited for this restriction, the most fundamental is that the law shares with its concern for the victim an equally important concern for deterrence of faulty behavior. The conventional view is expressed as follows by an insurance company attorney:

> The greatest single deterrent to the reckless disregard of the rights of others is the consequence of the act upon the wrongdoer. The fear of retribution, retaliation, and restitution has been a most determinative factor in keeping people on the "straight and narrow," whether the issue be one in-

volving morals or whether it be one involving the consequences of careless and reckless acts.[20]

The prevention of "careless and reckless" driving is a laudable
purpose, and its accomplishment may well warrant restrictions
on the compensation of victims, if such is necessary. Indeed,
pursuit of this goal may warrant attempts to strengthen the
negligence principle, to repair the breaches in the formal law,
and to create incentives for adjusters to follow the formal law
more closely. However, if we are to believe that the negligence
law does in fact deter careless driving, it must be shown that
the law contains sanctions that are in fact visited upon im-
proper driving behavior. Moreover, unless the driving we label
negligent is shown to cause accidents, its control is of no great
importance. These statements put the deterrence issue in the
form of empirical questions concerning which some evidence
is available.

Are accidents generally the result of negligent driving? Although knowledge concerning traffic accidents is still primitive,
most of what is known suggests a negative answer to the question. Careless or reckless driving certainly can and does cause
some accidents, but most accidents do not involve driving behavior that can be meaningfully described as faulty or deficient.
As claimed by T. Lawrence Jones, president of the American
Insurance Association, in presenting a plan for reforming the
current handling of automobile insurance:

> It must be remembered that the vast majority of crashes
> result not from wanton recklessness, as our critics' simplistic
> arguments would indicate, but rather from the momentary
> lapses or errors in judgment of ordinary people like you
> and me.[21]

Mr. Jones' position is supported very generally in the scien-

20. Gordon H. Snow, "Compensation and the Automobile," *Insurance Counsel Journal* 23:161, 1956, p. 165.
21. T. Lawrence Jones, " 'No-Fault' Auto Insurance: A Reply to the Critics," *Wall Street Journal*, December 24, 1968.

tific literature concerning accident causation.[22] It has my endorsement based on experience as the behavioral scientist in the most intensive study of traffic accidents ever conducted, the Case Studies of Traffic Accidents project at the Northwestern University Traffic Institute, which spent three years in the study of fewer than 100 accidents.[23] In the course of that study it became clear that run-of-the-mill accidents nearly all involve failure to see an approaching hazard and to predict its course accurately. However, in the context of these accidents such failure can rarely be considered faulty, in the sense of "unreasonably dangerous conduct by one who is free to choose a feasible safe way to carry on his legitimate activity." [24] As any adjuster could testify, the recurrent statement of the accident-involved driver is, "I didn't see him until too late." But hazards can come from many directions, and no driver can be looking everywhere at once. Successful prediction of the course of a moving car depends not only on accurate perception, but on the validity of a large number of conventional assumptions, for example, that a vehicle will proceed in the same lane at the same speed unless indications are to the contrary. These expectations are supported with a high degree of confirmation, and all drivers rely on them, yet occasionally they prove to be unfounded. When such failures occur in conjunction with other factors, including aspects of the road and the vehicles, accidents occur. To put the argument another way, a road network filled with cars driven only by the most skilled, reasonable, and prudent drivers will still generate accidents. Furthermore, if it is assumed that this hypothetical road network includes a representative share of high-speed roads, intersections, curves and turns, and hills

22. See footnote 34 in Chapter 5. This literature is reviewed from a logical perspective in Fleming James and John H. Dickinson, "Accident Proneness and Accident Law," *Harvard Law Review* 63:769, 1950.

23. See *Selected Reports from Case Studies of Traffic Accidents* (Northwestern University Traffic Institute, 1960). My personal conclusions are given in H. Laurence Ross, "Awareness of Collision Course in Traffic Accidents," *Traffic Safety Research Review* 5:12, 1961.

24. Oliver Wendell Holmes, *The Common Law* (Little, Brown, 1963), p. 94.

and bumps, it can be confidently predicted that the system will generate a certain percentage of serious injuries and of deaths without a single reckless or careless driver being on the road.

Yet many people believe that accidents are caused by "the nut behind the wheel," and they seem to be able to produce statistics in support of their contention. This belief may be explained in part by the fact that many operations within the tort law system itself have stretched the definition of negligence. The knowledge that a finding of negligence is necessary in order to get compensation to the victim has caused the courts to treat many common and ordinary driving practices as negligent. Such definitions control negotiated settlements, particularly in the serious cases where litigation is credibly threatened.[25] The legislative identification of negligence with the violation of traffic laws creates additional problems of analysis. As John Versace points out, "Safe driving is a personal thing and does not relate to moment by moment rigid adherence to minor traffic regulations." Versace cites a study conducted for the Public Health Service by the American Institutes for Research, which showed that the ordinary driver is a consistent law-violator. A motion picture camera revealed that 87 per cent of a sample did not stay in lane; 80 per cent changed lanes without signaling; 46 per cent turned without signaling; etc. However, this situation may be necessary for safe and efficient driving:

> Traffic would probably be paralyzed if drivers and police did not take a congenial laissez-faire approach to traffic regulations, and view them more as advisory than binding. It is probably just such flexibility and adaptability of the driver that allow him sometimes to stray innocently over

25. Keeton and O'Connell, *op. cit.*, put the case as follows, on pp. 248 and 253:

> The meaning of the negligence standard for particular fact situations in traffic cases is uncertain, and there has been a continuing tendency to brand as negligent more and more conduct that is neither avoidable not morally culpable. . . .
> A supercritical standard is frequently applied to a driver's conduct in order to characterize it as negligent and thus allow the victim to reach the insurance proceeds.

the hazard threshold into a collision, but which in most circumstances keep him safe and optimize the pursuit of his objectives. We call this skillful driving as long as nothing happens. However, those same maneuvers would be branded irresponsible and reckless if some unexpected occurrence were to cause a mishap.[26]

Even more misleading in relating negligence and accidents is the existence in most traffic codes of broad, catch-all prohibitions which permit police to cite at least one party in virtually any conceivable accident. "Failure to yield right-of-way" is a common example. Better yet is the following ordinance of the City of Denver:

> Every person operating a vehicle anywhere in the City and County of Denver shall . . . keep his vehicle under control so as not to endanger or collide with any person, structure, thing, vehicle, or other conveyance. Failure to observe the requirements of this section shall constitute careless driving and shall be unlawful.[27]

It can be seen that the act prohibited by Denver is the experiencing of an accident. Since the violation of a safety statute is *prima facie* evidence of negligence, a syllogism is created in which negligence is the logical consequence of an accident. In this way can it be proved to some people's satisfaction that accidents are caused by negligent driving!

The analytical viewpoint suggests, thus, that accidents are most likely not the result of deficient driving. Assuming for the sake of argument that there is still reason to try to deter the driving behavior that is labeled negligent, the question must be raised whether the current system in fact applies sanctions to the drivers whose behavior is thus labeled. As Fleming James, among many others, has pointed out, the tort judgment cannot reasonably be a deterrent to an insured defendant who pays

26. John Versace, "The Driver and Safety," in Eno Foundation for Highway Traffic Control, *Traffic Safety: A National Problem* (1966), pp. 25–46, at p. 31.

27. *Denver Municipal Code*, Section 512.2.

no part of the judgment.[28] Since the vast bulk of defendants are insured, they are susceptible in the main only to whatever deterrent effects may be inherent in the possibility of increased rates under a safe driver rating system—whereby insurance rates are increased as a function of the number of claims—and in the possibility of cancellation or nonrenewal of insurance if they experience what the company regards as an excessive number of claims. It seems unreasonable to posit a significant deterrent effect for these residual penalties in the insurance system as compared with the much more powerful sanctions of possible injury on the one hand, and criminal and administrative penalties leading to loss of license on the other. As Spencer Kimball says:

Fear of injury to oneself, habits of caution, concern for the trouble one might have if he is involved in an accident, even innocently, and simple human decency are all deterrents far more potent than potential liability for fault but only for fault. Moreover, the deterrent effect is greatly lessened by the relative infrequency of accidents—at least serious ones. Each person can say: "It can't (or won't) happen to me."

On the other side, potential liability based on fault can seldom be in the consciousness of the man in a hurry, the show-off, the person with a death-wish. Fault doctrines are deterrents so trivial that they can be safely ignored in any utilitarian evaluation.[29]

28. Fleming James, "Social Insurance and Tort Liability," *New York University Law Review* 27:537, 1952.
29. Spencer L. Kimball, "Automobile Accident Compensation Systems: Objectives and Perspectives," in Keeton, O'Connell, and McCord, *op. cit.*, pp. 10–26, at p. 14.

There is perhaps somewhat more substance to the assumption of a deterrent value in the rule of contributory negligence. The insured defendant, if he is judged at fault, loses nothing directly. The claimant, if he is judged at fault, may lose whatever he might otherwise have been paid, and this can be considerable. However, the degree of sanction bears no relationship to the degree of negligence displayed. The grossly negligent who has suffered a cut finger loses ten dollars of potential recovery. The barely negligent claimant who is paralyzed for life may lose hundreds of thousands.[30] The arbitrariness of the sanction violates all principles of scientific correction. However, the law in action is more merciful than the formal law, and even negligent claimants make recoveries that might be interpreted by some as rewards for their negligence.

In sum, insurance has in my opinion pretty much drawn the sting from tort law sanctions on the insured defendant, and the law in action has enormously moderated the effect of these sanctions on the claimant. The negligence system without insurance might conceivably be effective as a deterrent, but it would have to be judged grossly unfair because of a lack of proportion between the degree of fault and the degree of punishment. With insurance, I believe it is unreasonable to expect significant deterrent effects from the negligence system.

To be sure, not everyone is convinced by the evidence cited in the previous pages. However, the opposition seems to be grounded more in values than in evidence. Witness the following examples of utter nonsense from members of the legal and insurance communities:

> No doubt the fundamental argument for the tort system is that the abolition of court-jury litigation in automobile accident cases would put an end to the moral and legal responsibility of individuals who inflict bodily injuries on their fellows. The abolition of responsibility is contrary to our way of life, to morality, and especially does it come

---

30. A similar disparity occurs in safe-driver rating plans, where the increase in insurance rates is identical regardless of the degree of negligence exhibited by the insured.

with poor grace when in our time of widespread disorder we preach more individual responsibility. To embrace liability without fault would destroy the dignity of man.[31]

The denial of tort-liability is the denial of the principle that man is responsible for his action. To say that he is not responsible is to deny free will, for there can be no concept of guilt without moral choice. To deny free will is to embrace determinism, the doctrine that man's actions are caused by forces beyond his control. If determinism were true, man would not be able to decide whether an idea was true or false, including determinism. The denial of free will and the resultant tort-liability system is a self-refuting position. Only tort-liability is consistent with man's nature.[32]

On these grounds, insurance against liability may be deemed undesirable, as in this example:

The insuring of personal property for mysterious disappearance relieves a person of the responsibility for keeping track of his property. The insuring against bad debts relieves the merchant of the responsibility of a cash business. The insuring of one's legal liability relieves one of the responsibility for his failure to act as a prudent man.[33]

Such arguments are in my opinion more rhetoric than reason. If the evidence and reasoning of this chapter are accepted, it would appear that the irrationalities and inequities of the tort law and liability insurance system, as judged by compensation standards, cannot be justified as producing any demonstrable benefits in the way of deterrence of faulty behavior and the reduction of accidents.

31. Edward W. Kuhn, "A Defense of the Tort System," *Case and Comment* 73:15, 1968, at p. 19.

32. Keith Edwards, "Auto Insurance: Another Industry View," *Wall Street Journal*, November 19, 1968.

33. Paul W. Pretzel, "Adversary System Under No-Fault," *Insurance Adjuster*, April, 1969, pp. 56–58 at p. 56.

New Directions in Settlement

The research reported in the earlier chapters of this book was deliberately focused on standard and traditional methods of handling automobile liability claims. Among the hallmarks of traditional procedure is the one-time lump-sum settlement, exchanged for a written and binding release. This procedure is, of course, based on the requirements of the formal law. The insurance company through the adjuster takes a passive role concerning the handling of the injury, although some show of personal interest may be made in order to "control" the claimant and discourage recourse to an attorney. Most important, except for minor amounts that may be disbursed under medical payments insurance, payment may not be made without proof of liability in the case file.

The last several years have seen some innovations in claims handling by various companies. They are intended to make claims handling less complex, less adversary, more humane and —not least—less expensive. I did not observe these innovations in use, but they have been reported in interviews and in the literature. In this section I shall discuss some of the most important of these, and offer some speculations concerning the effects of the innovations on the law in action.

NO-RELEASE SETTLEMENTS

Perhaps the most stringently enforced rule in traditional claims handling is that no payment may be made unless the claimant signs a release. The release is a legal document that extinguishes the formal claim. It guarantees—in the absence of proof of fraud or duress or similar conditions—that the claimant cannot further sue for injuries suffered in the given accident. Files thus can be closed without a formal judgment in only one of two manners: by payment accompanied by a release, or by a denial.

Since the claims man's goal is to close files, he sometimes finds the choice between a release and denial to present a dilemma. A file will present a picture of clear liability and losses, but the claimant will not sign a release. This may occur even though the claimant accepts the adjuster's offer of settlement, because of his general suspicion and lack of trust with regard to signing documents. Of course it also occurs when the adjuster is unable to negotiate a satisfactory settlement. In such cases the claim is *pro forma* denied and the adjuster awaits either a notice of representation or the running of the statute of limitations, which will bar further action by the claimant. Many of these claims do return with representation, and claims personnel are unhappy about denying cases with clear liability and significant losses. The traditional procedure leaves them little alternative.

A solution to this dilemma has appeared in the form of no-release and walk-away settlements. As exemplified in the procedure of the Insurance Company of North America, a no-release settlement is used when the adjuster has tried and failed to obtain a release, although the claimant has agreed to a settlement figure. Payment may be made without a release "if good judgment and experience indicate that the claimant is dealing in good faith."

> Most claimants handled this way will not be heard from again. If the claim is revived or if an attorney appears, the claim should be readjusted only if the facts warrant it. If the reopening involves anything more serious than the mere payment of an additional bill, we normally would expect a release to be obtained. When making settlement without the benefit of a release, it must be clearly explained that we will reconsider the amount of settlement if injuries do develop or become more serious; that we will receive credit for payments made; and the claimant must be advised of the date of the Statute of Limitations before which claims must finally be made. This information can be imparted orally or, in questionable or doubtful cases, by means of a letter confirming the terms of the agreement.[34]

The walk-away settlement is the same technique applied to the situation in which an agreed settlement cannot be reached.

34. Insurance Company of North America, *Policyholders Service Representative's Guide to Contemporary Claims Service Techniques* (1969), pp. 2–3.

A draft is given to the claimant or his attorney in the amount that the adjuster considers is fair, and this is followed by a letter of confirmation. Company policy is not to consider a counter-offer in response to a walk-away settlement unless new facts or new evidence are presented.

From the perspective of negotiation theory, techniques just described are commitment tactics nailing down proposals. They strike me as very promising means of preventing recourse to trial, for the latter to be justified would have to yield at least the amount of the no-release or walk-away offer plus the additional processing costs. The expected fruits of trial would also have to be reduced by the degree of uncertainty apparent in the facts of the situation. It would thus be difficult for a conscientious attorney to take to trial a claim on which there was a reasonable offer, and the strong commitment implied by the claims man's departure from the scene effectively insulates the company from further negotiation short of trial.

From the organizational perspective the no-release settlement also promises to be useful. It offers an alternative to the release-or-denial dilemma. The adjuster can close the file more easily. Significantly, he need pay no premium to the claimant for the release alone. The claimant's signature does not have to be bought; he has merely to be induced to take no further action on the claim. I would be very surprised if substantial savings did not result from these techniques.

In a no-release or walk-away settlement, the file may be closed and the claim extinguished from an organizational viewpoint, but it remains open from the viewpoint of formal law until the time allowed by the statute of limitations for the filing of suit has passed. This is usually several years, though as a practical matter with passage of time the probability of the claim's reappearing diminishes to virtually zero. Should a suit develop on a claim closed without a release, the payments are generally deductible from any judgment that might be entered.

The lessening of organizational problems, the possibility of diminished litigation, the provision of benefits to some claimants who might otherwise be totally denied, and very likely lower costs to the insurance system all support the conclusion that no-release and walk-away settlements are important improvements in claims handling.

ADVANCE PAYMENTS

Another innovation that seems beneficent from a variety of perspectives is advance payments. It is fairly widely available to claims men today.[35] The Cooperative Claim Program of the Continental National American Group represents a typical advance payments program, which is wrapped in a package that includes no-release settlements and certain additional innovations. The Program is explained as follows:

> Basically, it is not a new way to handle claims. It is merely a change in timing. We have always tried to voluntarily settle proper claims for a fair amount and resist improper or exaggerated claims. There is no change in this policy. All we are saying is that on proper and fair claims we will pay the injured person for his expenses as he incurs them and not make him wait until some future time when he has completely recovered. [36]

The Program overcomes the limitation of benefits under the formal law to a one-time, once-and-for-all settlement.

The advance payments technique is applicable only to those claims on which payment would ordinarily be made, and benefits are limited to the amount that the claim would ordinarily be expected to obtain. Some companies will use it only in cases of clear liability, but the CNA rule is more liberal and adds to the usefulness of the technique:

> The Cooperative Claim Program may be applied on any claim where the facts of the accident (or perhaps the se-

35. Companies writing approximately 80 per cent of American liability insurance are using some form of advance payments. See Gordon H. Snow, "Advance Payments Under Liability Policies," address to the American Bar Association Convention, Honolulu, August 7, 1967.

36. "Continental's Cooperative Claim Program," leaflet of the Continental National American Group.

riousness of the injury combined with a questionable liability picture) reasonably dictate that a settlement would
be made under traditional handling. We cannot establish a
firm rule other than to exercise sound claim judgment.[37]

The technique is simply described. As direct expenses are met
by the claimant, they are paid by the company without a
release, but with an agreement that payments will be credited
against final settlement. Typical expenses reimbursed are automobile repairs, medical bills, and lost wages, but other pressing
needs can also justify payment, despite the fact that they are
not legally recoverable as special damages. CNA reports an
anecdote in which the adjuster paid the cost of plumbing fix-
tures for the claimant's girlfriend's bathroom. On the other hand,
no payment is made for items covered by collateral benefits—
sick pay, Blue Cross, etc.—though these are recoverable according to formal law.

On completion of investigation and evaluation, a settlement
including a release is envisaged, from which payments under
the advance payment plan are deducted. However, under the
CNA rules, the settlement may be without a release if necessary.

The principle of a one-time settlement is further eroded by
some supplementary techniques for handling post-release expenses. Claimants are sometimes unwilling to settle at a given
time for fear of possible future complications. One way of handling this problem is to include in the release a provision
promising to pay, for example, certain stated sums or the cost of
certain specific types of medical treatments, the promise usually
being conditioned by maximum amounts and time periods. This
procedure is untidy from the organizational perspective, because
the file cannot be definitively closed, nor can the final cost of
the settlement be computed. A solution that avoids these problems is used by CNA. The claims department purchases from the
accident and health or life insurance departments of the company a health insurance or annuity policy that constitutes part
of the settlement. The premium for this policy represents the

37. *Ibid.*

entire cost for the claims department. The claims file may thus be closed, and the cost is known, though the amount of later payments may be uncertain.

In making advance payments, the company voluntarily relinquishes some of its bargaining superiority, but it obtains an opportunity to demonstrate its good faith. It cannot, of course, threaten denial of the claim. On the other hand, the payments made, like those given with no-release settlements, are committed offers that may discourage litigation if they bear some relationship to formal value. Perhaps the major negotiation advantage of this technique for the company is that it gives the adjuster an opportunity to learn about the claimant's expectations and therefore potentially obtains saving from the maximum the company would be willing to pay.

The organizational perspective on advance payments is less favorable. Periodic payments may be burdensome to adjusters, and in some cases the file may remain open longer than when the claimant is under financial pressure to settle quickly. I would expect that adjusters have to be persuaded more to use advance payments than to use no-release settlements, and that they use this technique less often than management might desire.

Advance payments, like no-release settlements, have successfully escaped being taken as admissions of liability in formal law, and are deductible from a judgment.[38] The technique would seem to be beneficial in protecting claimants from situational financial pressures. Evidence of the general effect on the cost of claims is now available from two studies by Continental National American of its Cooperative Claim Program, which focuses on advance payments but includes a variety of supplementary techniques. One study of 100 claims handled under the Program compared these with an equivalent sample handled in the traditional fashion. The special damages in the two groups

---

38. The annotation in American Law Reports says: "Although there is some authority to the contrary, the cases generally have held or recognized as inadmissible, evidence of payment, or offer or promise of payment, of medical, hospital, and similar expenses. . . . Such payment or offer is usually made from humane impulses and not from an admission of liability." *American Law Reports* 2nd 20:293, 1951. See also Edwards *v.* Passarelli Bros. Automotive Service, 8 Ohio St. 6, 221 N.E. 2d 708 (1961).

were almost identical, but general damages in the claims handled under the Program were almost two-thirds less. Over-all, the claims handled by the Program cost one-third less than those handled traditionally.[39] A later study found similar results and noted that savings were greater in the larger claims, and that average time to closing was less than half as long in the Program than among the traditionally handled claims.[40] The methodology of the studies is only sketchily reported, and the matching is probably doubtful because the criteria used to select claims for the Program are vague, but it is nonetheless reasonable to conclude that advance payments lower the cost of claims.

REHABILITATION

The involvement of the insurance company in handling the injured claimant has been radically changed where liability claims are treated by rehabilitation. Techniques of rehabilitation were largely developed in the handling of military inquiries. They were first introduced into insurance by workmen's compensation carriers. The obligation to continue salary payments to injured workers for a long or indefinite period of time was a prime cost to the compensation carriers where disabling injuries were incurred. This obligation could be mitigated by returning the claimant to gainful employment of some kind, and rehabilitation was found useful in achieving this goal.

Rehabilitation is a complex of techniques applicable to very serious injuries, including some that in ordinary circumstances are considered seriously or totally disabling. Representative of these injuries are spinal damage causing paralysis, amputations, serious loss of use of a limb, certain back conditions, and serious loss of vision or hearing. To these injuries are applied, first, medical treatment, including hospital treatment and physical therapy. Psychological or psychiatric treatment is provided to aid the patient in coping with traumatic losses. Second, occupational therapy trains the injured individual to engage in occupations compatible with his reduced capacities. Third, advance

39. These results are reported in *News and Views,* a CNA house bulletin, for December 16, 1966.

40. CNA memorandum, September 25, 1967.

payments fill the financial hiatus between incapacitation for a previous occupation and entry into a new occupation.

The medical and occupational therapies may be offered by outside contractors, in which case rehabilitation becomes a special case of advance payments. However, some companies writing larger amounts of workmen's compensation insurance, for instance Liberty Mutual, maintain rehabilitation centers where services other than hospital treatment are provided.[41]

The use of rehabilitation in workmen's compensation cases is routine, dependent only on the appropriateness of the techniques to the injury in question. In automobile liability cases the degree of the company's exposure to loss is also relevant; rehabilitation is not inexpensive, and most companies restrict its use to cases of apparent liability and higher than minimum policy limits.

In favorable cases, rehabilitation can actually change the damages experienced by the claimant and thus affect the basic structure of negotiation. It can directly reduce economic loss, and thus indirectly reduce general damages:

> It costs at least $80,000 to care for a paraplegic for life. This is an average figure for custodial care alone. In many serious cases, however, overall costs to the insurer can be in excess of $250,000. Rehabilitating the same individual costs perhaps $10,000 to $20,000.[42]

Rather than wait passively for an injury to develop and damages to accumulate, the company can minimize the consequences of the accident at a cost over which it has some control. Furthermore, rehabilitation produces good will; it may discourage representation of claims, and in the event of suit allusions to the rehabilitation program may gain jury sympathy.

Rehabilitation claims, like advance payments generally, are not simple to handle, but large claims are seldom expected to be handled and closed expeditiously. Insofar as the bulk of nonroutine responsibilities can be passed on to a special coordinator

41. See "Liberty Mutual Rehabilitation Center Marks Quarter Century," *National Underwriter*, June 28, 1968.

42. "Rehabilitation Savings to Insured, Insurers, Injured," *Insurance Management Review*, April 15, 1966.

of rehabilitation services, this program may be regarded as a boon by the typical adjuster.

Toward Compensation

It has already been noted that the tort law in action departs from formal prescriptions in the direction of a compensation system. In addition to protecting negligent drivers from having to pay for the consequences of their wrongdoing, insurance is protecting victims of traffic accidents from the economic and other losses due to crashes. Judged by the standards of a well-designed compensation system, however, auto liability insurance operates in an arbitrary and inefficient manner, overpaying trivial injuries, underpaying severe ones, and rewarding factors of age and of representation and similar matters that ought to be irrelevant. For a half-century these facts have been recognized by some legal scolars, who have (in part erroneously) traced their origin to changes in the formal law and suggested further changes in order to bring the law applicable to injuries in auto accidents into line with generally accepted standards for compensation. The model of workers' compensation in the field of industrial accidents has served many of these scholars. For example, in 1913 Jeremiah Smith wrote in the Harvard Law Review:

> The ultimate result brought about by the workmen's compensation legislation is utterly incongruous with the result which would be reached under the modern common law of torts; and ... hence the enactment of this legislation, assuming it to be both constitutional and just, will give rise to agitation for further changes in the law so as to put certain other persons upon an equality with workmen.[43]

Was it not prophetic that in the years of the automobile's childhood, if not infancy, Smith used traffic-accident illustrations to elaborate this point!

Another notable commentator was the young lawyer, Richard M. Nixon, who wrote in 1936 that "it may be said that there has been a

---

43. Jeremiah Smith, "Sequal to Workmens Compensation Acts," *Harvard Law Review* 27:235 and 27:344, 1913 and 1914, p. 348.

steady erosion of fault as the ground of shifting the plaintiff's loss to the defendant."[44]

Among the manifestations of this trend noted by Mr. Nixon were, first, increasingly strict standards applied by the courts and especially by juries to the behavior of defendants, if not to that of plaintiffs. Second, the contributory negligence doctrine was under constant assault. Third, courts were trying to provide an insured defendant in most accidents by holding the car owner liable for virtually all uses of an automobile under master-servant, family purpose, and similar doctrines.

The trend noted by these commentators accelerated during the maturation of an automobile-based society, through such innovations as financial responsibility legislation (requiring proof of financial responsibility in the event of an accident, thus strongly encouraging the purchase of liability insurance), compulsory liability insurance, and uninsured motorist coverage. The contributory negligence rule, vitiated in practice, was formally altered by statute in several states. All of these measures improved the ability of the tort law in automobile injury cases to support an insurance mechanism acting as a compensation system, but a fundamental difference in purpose remained, which compromised the rationality of this approach. The problem has been succinctly stated as follows:

> Tort law shifts accidental loss from one party to another only upon proof that defendant's negligence causes plaintiff's injuries, and then only if plaintiff withstands a defense of contributory or comparative negligence. Negligence law is thus based upon a fault principal: absent wrongdoing, losses should lie where they fall. Liability insurance, in contrast, attempts to distribute losses assessed to tortfeasors among as large a number of insured as possible, many of whom are not wrongdoers. Tort law and liability insurance are thus conceptually inconsistent, the former focusing on individual account ability and the latter on distribution of risk.[45]

Dissatisfaction with this situation grew in the scholarly community

44. Richard M. Nixon, "Changing Rules of Liability in Auto Accident Litigation," *Law and Contemporary Problems* 3:476, 1936.
45. Daniel D. Caldwell, "No-fault Automobile Insurance: An Evaluative Survey," *Rutgers Law Review* 30:909, 1977, pp. 914-915.

with increasing knowledge concerning the relationship between economic losses and insurance payments. The milestone in this cumulation of knowledge was the Michigan Study of Alfred F. Conard and his associates.[46] Although a considerable number of empirical studies preceded the Michigan Study and their findings were by and large confirmed by Conard, the previous studies had all been small-scale and limited in the range and quality of data. The Michigan Study was the first to apply to the problem the highly sophisticated methods of contemporary survey research and, although it was limited in scope to a single state, it encompassed a variety of different claims climates and seemed more likely than any previous study to be representative of the problem in its national dimensions.

The Michigan Study found, first, that the problem of personal injury in automobile accidents was fairly widespread. Approximately one in a hundred Michigan residents had experienced some economic loss due to injury in an accident in the survey year, 1958. Most losses were found to be trivial, but a small percentage were catastrophic: two to three percent of the victims experienced economic losses in excess of $10,000, and these incurred more than half the total losses.

The Michigan Study also found that tort liability payments were the most important source of reparation to the victims and that they accounted for more than half of all reparation received. The overwhelming bulk of such payments were received in the form of negotiated settlements rather than formal judgments.

Overall, the tort reparation returned only about one quarter of the economic losses experienced by the victims. The total of all sources of reparation repaid only about half the losses. More than a fifth of all victims received nothing from any source, and, more striking among those recovering anything, those with the smallest losses recovered proportionately the most, and those with the largest losses were most underpaid. This was even more true of payments under the tort system than of other types of payments.

Given these facts, it is not surprising to learn that among victims suffering serious injury, dissatisfaction with the tort system was common. Approximately half of them thought their settlements were inadequate, and a similar number believed that the liability company had treated them unfairly.

46. Conard *et al., op. cit.*

The findings of the Michigan Study provided important factual grounds on which two law professors, Robert E. Keeton and Jeffrey O'Connell, based their landmark proposal for reforming the law of negligence and liability insurance.[47] Although Keeton and O'Connell's Basic Protection Plan was not enacted into law in any state, it crystallized thinking about reform and set the stage for serious consideration of change. Keeton and O'Connell have a good claim to be known as the "fathers" of any reform measures adopted in this field.

Just as the Michigan Study was an effort of an entirely different magnitude from previous studies, so the Keeton and O'Connell plan brought a new scale of effort to proposals for reform. With meticulous care, the empirical facts were marshaled to support the case for abandoning the principal of liability. Previous reform proposals were reviewed, and their virtues and failures were analyzed in detail. The political forces for and against change were appraised, and the plan was modified in an attempt to maximize support and to minimize opposition. Finally, a model statute was prepared to foresee and cope with the problems of implementation.

The Keeton and O'Connell Basic Protection Plan is very complex, and no summary can be completely fair. Without pretending to summarize, I will sketch the main ideas, which lead to a partial replacement of the tort liability system. Basic Protection's changes apply only to claims where losses are less than $10,000 or where damages for pain and suffering could not be expected to exceed $5,000. With larger claims, the negligence law would operate as at present, the recovery being subject to reduction by the amount of Basic Protection benefits paid on the claim. In the routine claim, Basic Protection benefits alone would be payable for injury. These benefits would come from a compulsory first-party insurance policy which would pay net losses, subject to deductibles, on a periodic basis, up to a maximum of $10,000. Optional coverages would be available to add benefits and to modify the deductibles.

The Keeton-O'Connell Basic Protection plan was soon joined by a variety of other well considered proposals with similar goals, differing mainly in detail. All of these met with enormous hostility from the organized bar, which correctly saw that a shift of the automobile

47. Keeton and O'Connell, *op. cit.*

accident insurance system from a basis in tort liability to the alternatives proposed was a clear and present danger to a significant part of the income of lawyers. The proportion of lawyers' income related to automobile negligence work has been estimated as high as fifty percent (though most responsible estimators place the figure closer to fifteen percent).[48] Negligence work bulks particularly large in the income not only of tort specialists, but also of the masses of general practitioners serving working-class and middle-class people. (Significantly, it appears to be unimportant to the bulk of the most elite lawyers, whose practice consists mainly in serving the business pursuits of corporations and wealthy individuals.) Concerted opposition by the organized bar frustrated proposals to adopt Basic Protection and strongly influenced the kinds of related legislation that were eventually adopted.

The adoption of legislation replacing the fault-based tort law system in part by a compensation-based or no-fault system was made possible when the academic reformers were joined by powerful allies from the business world in the form of a significant segment of the insurance industry. Insurance people had traditionally favored the status quo in the automobile area, but this line of insurance become unprofitable for many companies during the 1950's and 1960's. Between 1956 and 1965, losses of insurance companies from automobile liability insurance exceeded premiums collected by about $1.25 billion.[49] The reasons for this lack of profitability were seen to be increasing costliness of the procedures and outcomes of a liability-based system, and a reluctance of regulators to permit the premium increases necessary to finance these costs. Paradoxically, most of the insurance companies to switch sides on this issue were the traditionally structured companies. These companies used brokers and agents to sell insurance and the commissions diminished resources available to pay rising claims cost. In 1968, a group of these companies, through their industry association, the American Insurance Association, presented and endorsed a thoroughgoing no-fault proposal entitled Complete Personal Protec-

48. See Jeffrey O'Connell, *The Injury Industry and the Remedy of No-fault Insurance* (University of Illinois Press, 1971) p. 50.

49. Reported by Bradford Smith, Chairman of the Board, Insurance Company of North America, in an address to the 77th Annual Convention, Pennsylvania Association of Insurance Agents, Pocono Manor, Pennsylvania, on October 10, 1966.

tion. Simpler than Basic Protection, the insurance companies' plan would have totally abolished the tort system in the area of automobile accident injuries, substituting a compulsory plan providing unlimited medical and rehabilitation expenses and limited reimbursement for other economic loss. No payments would be made for pain and suffering, but limited amounts were payable for permanent disability and disfigurement.[50]

With the rising tide of support for some kind of change in the area of automobile insurance, the U.S. Department of Transportation undertook a two-year, $2 million study of the situation. In general the results of this mammoth enterprise confirmed the findings of the Michigan Study concerning the economic consequences of auto- mobile accidents and supported the reasonableness of substituting some kind of no-fault plan for the tort law in this area.[51] Subsequently, there were many attempts on a federal level, to introduce no-fault automobile insurance, but none came to fruition. Opponents argued that the legislation raised serious issues concerning the roles of state and federal governments, and that a massive federal bureaucracy would be required to enforce the proposed statutes.

No-fault compensation for traffic accident victims became reality as legislation in individual states. In Massachusetts, Robert Keeton's state of residence the nation's first no-fault law took effect on January 1, 1971.[52] In the next few years legislation termed no-fault was adopted in a total of twenty-four states. However, no adoptions have occurred since 1975.

State no-fault laws have in common the fact that some economic losses experienced by accident victims are reimbursed by the victims' insurance companies without regard to fault. Beyond this, the laws vary considerably.[53] None of them completely abandon the tort

50. American Insurance Association, "Report of Special Committee to Study and Evaluate the Keeton-O'Connell Basic Protection Plan and Automobile Accident Reparations," (privately printed, 1968).

51. The summary report is John Volpe, *Motor Vehicle Crash Losses and their Compensation in the United States: A Report to Congress and the President* (United States Department of Transportation, Automobile Insurance and Compensation Study, 1971).

52. Mass. Acts 1970, ch. 670.

53. See Roger C. Henderson, "No-fault Insurance for Automobile Accidents: Status and Effect in the United States," *Oregon Law Review* 56:287, 1977.

system, although in Michigan, Florida, and New York recourse to the tort system is restricted to cases of death and permanent or serious injury. None provided unlimited coverage for all economic losses, though New Jersey, Pennsylvania, and Michigan provide for unlimited medical benefits, and the maximum total benefits in New York and Michigan are substantial enough to qualify them as "pure" no-fault states, according to some commentators. On the other hand, the "no-fault" laws of some other states maintain the tort system intact, merely adding compulsory or even optional first-party benefits to liability insurance policies issued in those states. A third group of states maintains the tort system for injuries in which economic losses exceed relatively low "threshold" limits. These have been labeled "modified" no-fault systems. The latter two categories of no-fault laws clearly represent political compromises with the organized bar.

No-fault laws, though quite recent, have been the subject of considerable research concerning their success in fulfilling the promise of adequate compensation in a reasonable time at a reasonable cost. Review of the many studies to date[54] indicates that all forms of no-fault insurance, even including the "add-on" plans, provide compensation for some victims who would not have received compensation under the formal tort law, even as modified by the insurance system in action, and that this compensation is made available with relatively less delay. Studies of the "pure" no-fault states demonstrate that economic losses are better compensated, particularly with serious injuries, and at no greater cost than the traditional system. However, the promise is not so clearly fulfilled in the other no-fault systems, especially where "add-on" legislation governs. Recourse to lawyers, and lawyers' income, are considerably diminished by no-fault, indicating that bar opposition to the legislation is appropriate from a self-interested viewpoint.

Opposition to no-fault compensation has been active not only in the legislatures, where it has obtained defeat and modification of no-fault bills, but also in the courts, where constitutional challenges have occasionally been successful in promoting changes and even repeals of

54. Several survey reviews have been published. See Caldwell, *op. cit.*; Jeffrey O'Connell, "Operation of No-fault Auto Laws: A Survey of Surveys," *Nebraska Law Review* 56:23, 1977; and Jeffrey O'Connell and Janet Beck, "An Update of the Surveys on the Operation of No-fault Auto Laws," *Insurance Law Journal* 674:129, 1979.

strong no-fault laws. The Illinois no-fault law foundered on a finding
of unconstitutionality. Compulsory aspects of Michigan's "pure" law
have failed a court test and the law will require substantial revision.
Generally, however, the courts have upheld the consitutionality of no-
fault.

The present study of the law in action under a traditional tort system
provides support for characterizing the latter as inappropriate to
compensation-type goals. Although the law in action functions better
than might be expected, it is still a wasteful and arbitrary system for
compensating accident victims, overpaying those with small losses
and undercompensating those with large losses. The system is
cumbersome, expensive and unduly responsive to practical matters
that are formally irrelevant even to the tort law. Studies of the law in
action under no-fault statutes indicate that the motoring public is
getting much more compensation value per premium dollar spent for
insurance. It appears that the compromises and setbacks experienced
by the no-fault movement are the result of largely self-interested
political opposition by the legal profession.

Is the no-fault movement stopped? O'Connell thinks not, and offers
as a model workers' compensation, which was first enacted in the
United States in New York, in 1910, but which became universal only
in 1948, almost forty years later. Workers' compensation is a no-fault
compensation system applied to industrial accidents. It also generated
opposition on the part of negligence lawyers, slowing its adoption.
"But," notes O'Connell, "no one really doubted, at least after the first
few years, that workers' compensation would become the norm for
compensating industrial accidents to replace the fault-based system. It
is significant that after, more than fifty years of experience with no-
fault workers' compensation, none of the fifty states that have adopted
it has ever seriously considered voluntarily abandoning it."[55] O'Connell
concludes that the pause following 1975 in adoption of no-fault
automobile insurance is temporary, and that no-fault compensation's
fundamental advantages in meeting social needs ordain its eventual
adoption everywhere. As a driver who fears the consequences of
accidents, as a premium-paying insurance buyer, and as a scholar with
a strong personal commitment to the value of reason and logic, I hope
he is correct.

55. O'Connell, *op. cit.*, 1977, p. 48.

7. Epilogue

SETTLED OUT OF COURT was published in 1970; the files that supported its statistical analysis were closed in 1962; and this revision was prepared in 1980. In this Epilogue I would like to address the questions of how relevant are the data and conclusions of more than a decade ago for the problems and issues of today, and how the book is related to current social science. My answers, in brief, are that the picture of the insurance system administering the tort law and creating a law in action remains valid in detail in most jurisdictions, and in large part even where no-fault reform has most strongly affected the formal law; and furthermore, that *Settled Out of Court* forms part of a viable and growing literature on the application of law by bureaucratic administration.

A Nationwide Claims Study

As part of its landmark survey of the automobile insurance question in 1970, the United States Department of Transportation (DOT) organized a study of the claims files of the fifteen largest automobile insurance companies in the country, along with one smaller one.[1] The companies collaborated on the design and analysis of the study, and the results were published by the Government. The care with which this work was undertaken is symbolized by the fact that its methods and results were audited by the accounting firm of Ernst & Ernst. The participating companies together write more than half the automobile bodily injury insurance in the United States, and the survey of their files—which involved all bodily injury liability and uninsured motorist claims closed in nineteen representative states during ten days in the late 1969—involved nearly 36,000 cases. By and large the results of this survey confirmed the typicality of the data reported for Acme in Chapter Six above and elsewhere through this book.

As with Acme, the DOT study reported that most bodily injury claims were paid: only twenty-eight percent were closed without payment (compared with thirty-four percent at Acme). Overall, small claims predominated: fifty-six percent of paid claims had economic losses equal to or less than $500. The comparable figure for Acme was sixty-seven percent, but this difference seems largely accounted for by seven years of inflation between the dates of the respective surveys. Claims with economic loss over $5000 accounted for five percent of the DOT study files, compared with three percent for Acme seven years earlier. Importantly, 66 percent of the economic loss was experienced in the eleven percent of claims in which the loss amounted to over $1000. Moreover, the proportion of the loss that was uncompensated increased with the amount of loss experienced.

Formally irrelevant factors were shown to be effective in determining payment in the DOT files. The ratio of paid claims to those closed without payment was greatest for adults in the middle years and lowest for the young, as was found at Acme. White-collar people in general did better than blue-collar people, and city people better than rural people. Again, as with Acme, the represented

1. *Automobile Personal Injury Claims* (United States Department of Transportation, Automobile Insurance and Compensation Study, 1970).

recovered better than the unrepresented, though the advantage of the represented (in terms of payment as a proportion of economic loss) was found to decline as the size of loss increased. Adding various assumptions concerning the nature of represented cases and the costs of legal representation and of litigation, the insurance companies in the DOT study concluded that the net return to represented claimants was not greater than to the unrepresented, a conclusion that rests strongly on the validity of the assumptions and which I personally am inclined to doubt.

The DOT study also utilized accident configuration as an index of "presumptive negligence," in paid claims. The claims with stronger evidence of the insured's liability were paid more, controlling for size of loss, except in the case of represented claims in which the economic loss was $1000 or less, where "the apparent facts of presumptive negligence do not seem to affect the payment prospects."[2]

The representativeness of Acme figures on delay was confirmed: fifty-eight percent of paid claims nationwide were closed within 180 days, and seventy-six percent within a year. Small claims closed more quickly; represented and sued cases took longer.

Perhaps most important to support the generalizability of the Acme findings, the nationwide study reaffirmed that claims are settled out of court. Among claimants paid by insurance companies, forty-six percent were represented, one-third brought suit, three percent started trial, and a mere one percent obtained a verdict.

The Effect of Comparative Negligence and of No-Fault Insurance

To the extent that changes have occurred in the mandate of the adjuster, and especially to the extent that the changes affect the organizational pressures to which he must respond, the findings of the Acme study must be qualified. Two shifts occurring in the formal law during the 1970's must be noted in the light of possible effects: the growth of comparative negligence and the adoption of no-fault insurance.

The Acme data, as far as they go, suggested that the change from contributory to comparative negligence would have limited effect,

2. *Ibid.*, p. 66.

but the relevant data were restricted to cases with minor damages. The DOT study's finding of a limited role for presumptive negligence, especially in the case of small represented claims, is supportive. Although the shift in doctrine probably has some consequences—it surely could be used as a tactic in negotiation—I believe that the debate on the formal law overestimates the negative effect of the contributory negligence rule and the corresponding positive effect of comparative negligence in compensating victims in cases of questionable liability.

No-fault insurance is a more fundamental change. Consideration of the meaning of no-fault for the system described in this book leads to an examination of the extent of actual change achieved by statutes adopted up to the present time.[3] In my opinion, unfortunately the situation in the majority of states has not fundamentally changed. It should be noted at first that most states have failed to adopt any form of no-fault insurance. In these states there is no reason to believe that the system as described in this book functions much differently after more than a decade. Furthermore, eight of the twenty-four states that adopted some form of no-fault chose the "add-on" model, whereby no-fault coverage is grafted onto an unchanged tort law system. This model was believed to provide protection to victims not covered by negligence law at little or no additional cost by deterring tort claims on the part of those victims whose interest is merely in avoiding out-of-pocket loss. To the extent that they could have their losses repaid in multiples by merely filing a negligence claim, the claimants failing to pursue tort rights in "add-on" states might be called "suckers." Lincoln seems to have been right: the research literature suggests that victims in "add-on" states often do claim twice—once for no-fault compensation benefits and a second time in the system described here.

In a second group of eight states,[4] no-fault is modified by the right of victims to present tort claims in the event that medical bills exceed $500, or even less. In these states the most trivial negligence claims are probably eliminated. However, the low threshold in the light of contemporary medical costs suggests that many routine cases and all

3. See Daniel D. Caldwell, "No-fault Automobile Insurance: An Evaluative Survey," *Rutgers Law Review* 30:909, 1977.

4. In 1979 Nevada repealed its no-fault statute, reducing this number to seven and the total number of no-fault states to 23.

serious cases, as these terms are used in this book, remain in a basically unchanged system. Rampant inflation has reduced the effective level of most of these thresholds by half, at the present time, and no negligence attorney would have trouble in getting a routine injury to qualify for tort-law treatment with these thresholds.

There remain eight states where thresholds for the tort system exceed $500 or are described qualitatively, and where routine injuries are probably handled under a different system than the one described here. However, even the "purest" no-fault states leave the most serious injuries in the tort system, and most of this last group limit no-fault payments to a figure low enough that compensation for full economic loss is dependent on the resolution of a negligence claim. It is precisely in cases with the most serious injuries that the system described in this book is most lacking—where the ratio of payment to both tangible and intangible losses is lowest, and where the inequities introduced by bureaucratic pressures produce the great absurdities. To the extent that the system described here for large cases remains in operation, and I believe that it does, the policy implications of the previous chapter hold *a fortiori*.

The Study of the Law in Action

When the first edition of this book was written, social-scientific concern with the application of law was almost entirely restricted to studies of the police. The discovery of "police discretion," at first in noticing procedural irregularities and illegalities and later in the perception of police ability to shape and mold the law in application, was exciting but of narrow import. Policing was seen as an unusual occupation, fraught with danger, impossibly undermanned, and unusually isolated from the eyes of the world. In the ensuing decade more has become known about the police, enriching the theoretical content of the newer studies, and the police are now seen as less different from other law-applying officials, suggesting a broader utility for theory originally developed in police studies.[5]

5. See, for instance, James Q. Wilson, *Varieties of Police Behavior: The Management of Law and Order in Eight Communities* (Harvard University Press, 1968); John Gardiner, *Traffic and the Police: Variations in Law Enforcement* (Harvard University Press, 1969); and Kenneth Culp Davis, *Police Discretion* (West Publishing Co., 1975).

In addition to proliferating research on the police, the past decade has produced the recognition by social scientists that the legal system goes beyond the criminal law, that enforcement or application of law occurs in a wide variety of non-criminal settings, and that administrative procedure has profound implications for the structure and content of legal rights and duties. Studies of the police have now been supplemented by studies of housing inspection, income tax auditing, and the administration of occupational health and safety standards, among others.[6] Furthermore, the role of non-governmental organizations in the application of law has also begun to be acknowledged in research: in addition to the current study of insurance company officials, studies have been made of the role of real-estate brokers in the application of housing law and of store complaint personnel in handling consumer (contract) matters.[7]

Although many of these new studies have been stimulated by policy concerns rather than theoretical issues, they are beginning to develop their own distinctive concepts. An example is Michael Lipsky's concept of "street-level bureaucrats."[8] From such considerations as inadequacy of resources, the presence of challenge to authority, and the ambiguity of performance expectations, Lipsky has hypothesized effects on the style of application of the formal law by actors in such roles. He finds that street-level bureaucrats seek refuge from role strains through simplifications, the establishment of routines, and the development of coping mechanisms.

Another set of concepts developed in this literature is summarized in Robert Kagan's work on regulatory justice.[9] Kagan focuses on the dilemma presented to all regulatory agencies of legalism vs.

6. Pietro S. Nivola, "Distributing a Municipal Service: A Case Study of Housing Inspection," *Journal of Politics* 40:59, 1978; Susan B. Long, "The Internal Revenue Service: Examining the Exercise of Discretion in Tax Enforcement," paper presented before the Annual Meeting of the Law & Society Association, 1979; Steven Kelman, "Compliance and Public Policy," unpublished manuscript, 1979.

7. Rose Helper, *Racial Policies and Practices of Real Estate Brokers* (University of Illinois Press, 1969); H. Laurence Ross and Neil O. Littlefield, "Complaint as a Problem-Solving Mechanism," *Law and Society Review* 12:199 (1978).

8. Michael Lipsky, "Toward a Theory of Street-Level Bureaucracy," in *Theoretical Perspectives on Urban Politics* (Prentice-Hall, 1976), pp. 196-213.

9. Robert S. Kagan, *Regulatory Justice* (Russell Sage Foundation, 1978).

expediency, stringency vs. accommodation, or "police mission" vs. utilitarian goals of efficiency. In general, the pressures of the work situation produce strains toward the second member of these sets but, as Kagan notes, "...the legitimacy and continued viability of the agency are also dependent on building potentially and legally defensible degrees of stringency into its decision."

Settled Out of Court is a contribution to this enterprise. To Lipsky's perception concerning the effects of street-level bureaucracy on the application of law, this book adds the thought that the content of legal rights and duties is also affected. To the simplifications, routines and coping mechanisms noted by Lipsky should be added the simplicity, generosity, and arbitrariness of the resultant legal outcomes. The origins and resolutions of Kagan's dilemmas become clearer when the sources of pressure on the law administrator are dissected and analyzed. Case overload and institutionalized sensitivity to complaints will lead to expediency; giving free rein to adjusters' attitudes, insulated from these pressures, will result in legalism.

Interest in this line of social science research is building, with the usual delay, in legal education. If employment as a "street-level bureaucrat" is not yet regarded as a desirable or possible career contingency by law students, in some law schools they are being taught to realize that a large part of most legal practices involves interaction with people playing those roles. More of the attorney's time is spent practicing before insurance adjusters, tax auditors, safety and pollution inspectors, and similar officials than before any kind of judges—appellate or trial. More importantly, the outcome of the client's claim is much more likely to be decided by the former than by the latter, and the performance of the attorney as a successful representative hinges more on negotiation than on pleading skills. The stirrings of attention on the part of legal education to law-in-action research begin to acknowledge the enormous practical importance of the description and analysis contained in studies like this one.

Index